29 Ian Stone: *Canal Irrigation in British India: Perspectives on Technological Change in a Peasant Society*
30 Rosalind O'Hanlon: *Caste, Conflict and Ideology: Mahatma Jotirao Phule and Low Caste Protest in Nineteenth Century Western India*
31 Ayesha Jalal: *The Sole Spokesman: Jinnah, The Muslim League and the Demand for Pakistan*
32 N. R. F. Charlesworth: *Peasants and Imperial Rule: Agriculture and Agrarian Society in the Bombay Presidency, 1850–1935*
33 Claude Markovits: *Indian Business and Nationalist Politics 1931–39: The Indigenous Capitalist Class and the Rise of the Congress Party*
34 Mick Moore: *The State and Peasant Politics in Sri Lanka*
35 Gregory C. Kozlowski: *Muslim Endowments and Society in British India*

CAMBRIDGE SOUTH ASIAN STUDIES

These monographs are published by the Syndics of Cambridge University Press in association with the Cambridge University Centre for South Asian Studies. The following books have been published in this series:

1 S. Gopal: *British Policy in India, 1858–1905*
2 J. A. B. Palmer: *The Mutiny Outbreak at Meerut in 1857*
3 A. Das Gupta: *Malabar in Asian Trade, 1740–1800*
4 G. Obeyesekere: *Land Tenure in Village Ceylon*
5 H. L. Erdman: *The Swatantra Party and Indian Conservatism*
6 S. N. Mukherjee: *Sir William Jones: A Study in Eighteenth-Century British Attitudes to India*
7 Abdul Majed Khan: *The Transition in Bengal, 1756–1775: A Study of Saiyid Muhammad Reza Khan*
8 Radhe Shyam Rungta: *The Rise of Business Corporations in India, 1851–1900*
9 Pamela Nightingale: *Trade and Empire in Western India, 1784–1806*
10 Amiya Kumar Bagchi: *Private Investment in India, 1900–1939*
11 Judith M. Brown: *Gandhi's Rise to Power: Indian Politics, 1915–1922*
12 Mary C. Carras: *The Dynamics of Indian Political Factions*
13 P. Hardy: *The Muslims of British India*
14 Gordon Johnson: *Provincial Politics and Indian Nationalism*
15 Marguerite S. Robinson: *Political Structure in a Changing Sinhalese Village*
16 Francis Robinson: *Separation among Indian Muslims: The Politics of the United Provinces' Muslims, 1860–1923*
17 Christopher John Baker: *The Politics of South India, 1920–1936*
18 David Washbrook: *The Emergence of Provincial Politics: The Madras Presidency, 1870–1920*
19 Deepak Nayyar: *India's Exports and Export Policies in the 1960s*
20 Mark Holmström: *South Indian Factory Workers: Their Life and Their World*
21 S. Ambirajan: *Classical Political Economy and British Policy in India*
22 M. M. Islam: *Bengal Agriculture 1920–1946: A Quantitative Study*
23 Eric Stokes: *The Peasant and the Raj: Studies in Agrarian Society and Peasant Rebellion in Colonial India*
24 Michael Roberts: *Caste Conflict and Elite Formation: The Rise of a Karāva Elite in Sri Lanka 1500–1931*
25 J. F. J. Toye: *Public Expenditure and Indian Development Policy 1960–70*
26 Rashid Amjad: *Private Industrial Development in Pakistan 1960–70*
27 Arjun Appadurai: *Worship and Conflict under Colonial Rule: A South Indian Case*
28 C. A. Bayly: *Rulers, Townsmen and Bazaars: North Indian Society in the Age of British Expansion, 1770–1870*

Index

Nadwah al-'ulamā' 170–171, 181, 184–185
Najiban (courtesan of Bareilly) 51, 63
Nanotawi, Muhammad Qasim (Deobandi scholar) 52, 141
National Muhammadan Association 165–166
Nehru, Jawaharlal 8, 119
Nehru, Moti Lal 119, 122
Numani, Mawlana Shibli 117, 169–173, 181–182

Ottomans 2, 16–17, 20

Panjab 34–36, 42, 151
"paper book" 89, 111
Patna 93, 107
Paul, Sir Charles (Advocate General of Bengal) 145–146, 150
Permanent Settlement 33–34, 39, 127–128
perpetuities 148–149, 163–165, 182, 184
Persian language 64–65, 125–126
Pinhey, R. H. (Justice) 134, 135
Pirbhai, Jairajbhai 71–73, 151, 182
Pirbhai, Qasim Ali 72, 151–152, 179
Privy Council 5, 89, 96, 110, 116, 118, 122, 138–139, 146–151, 153, 167–168, 179, 183, 187–189

Qamr ud-din 43, 57–58, 134–137
qāzī 21, 49, 97, 102–107, 126, 132–133, 143, 157
Qur'ān 2, 3, 7, 10–11, 40, 55–57, 60–62, 64, 66–67, 70, 73, 74, 76, 92, 97, 100, 102, 140, 147, 175, 184, 189, 192

Rahim, Abd ur- 116, 130, 184
ra'īs (title used by local leaders) 4, 34, 47–49, 51, 59, 67–68, 73, 75, 79, 190, 193
ra'īyat see ryot
Rajputs 21, 82
Ramazān 4, 30, 48, 70, 75
Ramlah (10th cent. *waqf* at) 14–15
Rankin, G. C. (Justice) 115–116
Rashid ud-din (Mongol *wazir*) 15–16
rent 80–81
Revolt of 1857 3, 78, 83
riāsat (dominion/state/estate) 47, 54, 79, 193
ryot 33, 34, 48

Sadat, Muhammad Abu l Anwar us- (Egyptian scholar) 18–19
Sadi, Shaikh of Shiraz 38, 64
Sadr Diwani Adalat 107, 109, 131–133, 140, 142

Sadr Nizamat Adalat 107, 109
Salim Chishti, Shaikh 23–24
Salim-ullah (Nawab of Dacca) 167, 182
Sawad (province of Iraq) 11, 15
Sawda, Mir (poet) 31–32, 79
Seljuk Turks 16, 17, 26
Shafii, Imam and his "school" 43, 100, 137, 151
sharīf (genteel classes) 6, 48, 70
Shī'ī 4, 15, 17, 27–30, 63, 71, 74, 76, 100–101, 105, 116–118
Siqilli, Fa'iq al-Hadim ibn-Abd-allah al- (founder of a *waqf* at Ramlah) 14–15
Smith, Adam 148–149
sons and endowments 55–75
Stanley, Lord, of Alderly 168–169
sufis 11, 19, 22–23, 37, 69–70, 74, 76–77, 104–105, 132
Sunnī 6, 17, 29, 63, 72, 74, 76, 100–101, 105, 117–118
Supreme Courts 107, 109, 112
Sylhet 89, 96, 144–145

ta'alluqdārs 32, 34, 36, 84, 141, 159, 163
Tagore, Maharaja Sir Jotendra Nath 163–164
takyahs 23, 94
Taqi, Mir (poet) 31–32
Tazhīb al-Akhlāq 158–160
ta'zīyahs 28–30
Trevelyan, E. J. (Justice) 145–146
trusts 149–150, 164
Tyabji, Badr ud-din (Justice) 116, 143–144
Tyabji, Faiz Badr ud-din (Justice-textbook author) 116, 131, 152, 154

'ulamā' 18–19, 20, 43, 66, 68–69, 76, 101, 105, 112, 117, 131, 153–154, 161, 166, 169–173, 181
Umar al-Khatib (Caliph) 10, 12, 15
United Provinces of Agra and Avadh 3, 43, 113
'urs (death anniversary) 4, 75–76
Utilitarians 33–34, 128–129

wakil (legal practitioners) 87–88, 121
Walli-ullah, Shah 7, 69, 76–77
West, R. (Justice) 134–136, 168
Whigs and Whiggery 33, 127–128
women and endowments 55–58
Woodroffe, J. T. (Advocate General of Bengal) 139–143, 146

Yusuf, Abu 13, 125

zamindars 33–35, 47–49, 51, 84, 86, 144, 164

Index

Governor General's Legislative Council 5, 73, 129, 159, 175–176, 178–190
The Guidance see Hidayah
Gujarat (province)/Gujarati language 22, 71–72
"Gup" (mythical correspondent of Muhammad Ali's *Comrade*) 180, 181, 183

Ḥadīs̱ 7, 10–11, 66, 147, 186
Hafiz (Persian poet) 10, 21, 38, 76
Hamilton, Charles 126–127, 130, 135–136, 142, 153
Hanifah, Imam Abu and his "school" 13, 100, 102–103, 105, 118, 125, 130, 137, 151–152, 170–171
Hasan, Imam (grandson of the Prophet) 28, 76
Hasan Ali, Sayyid 45–46
Hastings, Warren 106, 125, 140
Hedaya see Hidayah
hibah (gift) 147–153
Hidayah, Al- 125–126, 130, 135, 136, 141, 142, 147, 153
Hindus 25, 64–65, 71, 75–76
Hobhouse, Lord Arthur 122–123, 138–139, 140–141, 146–150, 152, 186, 191
Hughli (Hooghly) Imambarah/College 38–39, 133, 174
Husain, Imam (grandson of the Prophet) 28–29, 76, 133
Husain, Karamat (Justice) 118, 144, 184
Husainabad Imambarah (Lucknow) 28–29

Ibrahim, Sir Karimbhai 151–152
imambarah(s), in the homes of individuals 62–63, 68, 73, 85–86
in'ām 24, 25, 132
Indian National Congress 5, 167–168
iqtah 16, 26
Iran 16, 20

Janpur 22, 43, 51, 69
Jinnah, Muhammad Ali 119, 152, 154, 178, 191
joint family/household 55–56

Kanizak Fatima, Begam 52, 57
Karbala 28–29, 30, 31, 38
Kayseri (Anatolia) 17–18
khānqah(s) 23, 25
Khojahs 71–72, 151–152
Kotwal 104, 105

Kundu, Amarchand and Krishnadas 137–138

Lahore 23, 109, 166
lakhiraj 39–40
Lincoln's Inn 122, 191
Lucknow 27, 28, 49, 74, 161, 170

Macaulay, T. B. 128, 133
MacDonald, D. B. 124, 125
MacNaghtan, W. 130, 136
madad-i ma'āsh 24, 25, 103, 105, 132
Madras (province) 3, 36
Madras High Court 109, 110, 116
madrasah 63, 65, 170, 175
Mahmud, Sayyid (Justice) 118–119, 139
Mahommedan Law (textbook by Amir Ali) 130, 139, 146, 153
Maine, H. S. 121, 129–130, 150, 164
majālis see majlis
Majjid, Khwajah Abd al- 168, 172
majlis 28–29, 30, 74, 77
maktab 63–64, 174
malik (title employed by local leaders) 4, 47, 49
Marathi 43, 72
Marghinani, Burhan al-din al- *see Hidayah*
marsīyah 29–30
Mecca 10, 38, 52–53, 172–173
Medina 10, 38, 172–173
mehr (bridal gift) 51, 113
Mehrban Ali, Sayyid 50, 52, 57–58, 67–68, 71, 82
milād-i sharīf 4, 19, 74, 76
milk 24, 47
Mill, James 33–34, 128
Mill, John Stuart 149
Mughals 22, 26, 27, 70, 72, 86, 105, 107, 111, 124–125, 128, 132
muhallah 62, 75
Muhammad, Imam Ibn- 13, 125
Muhammad Ali Shah (Nawab of Avadh) 28–29
Muharram 28–30, 61, 63, 74–76
Muin ud-din Chishti, Khwajah 23, 25–26, 38
Muslim Brotherhood of Progress 168, 172
Muslim League 5, 72, 167–168, 175–176, 181
Mussalman Wakf Validating Act 5, 6, 179–190
mutawallī 1, 3, 39, 54, 56, 69, 132, 135, 144, 159, 176–177
Mymensingh 67, 68

INDEX

Abbasid caliphs 15, 72, 102
Abd ul-Fatah 90, 97, 144–150, 155, 162–163, 166–167, 186
Aḥadīs see Ḥadīs
Ahl-i Ḥadīs 6, 76, 77, 172
Ahmad Khan, Sir Sayyid 65, 76, 77, 111–112, 118, 157–163, 169–170, 173, 175, 177, 186
Ahsan-ullah, Nawab of Dacca 158, 161–165, 167
Ahsan-ullah Chaudhri, Shaikh Muhammad (and his son and namesake) 56, 62, 67, 74, 91–92, 137–138, 146
Akbar (Mughal Emperor) 24, 26
Ali, Basharat (of Gorakhpur) 47, 56
Ali, Imam (son-in-law of the Prophet) 27, 28, 71, 101
Ali, Muhammad (Indian journalist) 180, 181, 183, 189
Ali, Muhammad (of Kanpur) 52, 68–69
Ali, Muhammad (Khedive of Egypt) 19–20
Ali, Qaim 51, 53, 60–61
Ali, Sayyid Amir (jurist) 116–117, 122, 130, 139–143, 145–147, 150, 153–155, 161–163, 165, 167–168, 172–173, 186–187
Ali Chaudhri, Nawab (of Mymensingh) 67–68, 164–165
Aligarh University (M.A.O. College) 65–66, 111, 119, 169, 175, 184–185
Allahabad High Court 85, 88, 109–110, 118–119, 122, 139, 144, 168
Anjuman-i Islam (of Bombay) 72, 156
ashrāf see sharīf
'Ashūrā see Muharram
Avadh, Nawabs of 28–31, 34, 49, 84, 116, 176

Baillie, N. B. E. 130, 136
Barelwī (group of religious scholars) 6, 77
Beaman, Frank (Justice) 115, 152
Bengal (province) 3, 33, 35, 36, 39, 106, 116, 127, 164–165

Bengal Settled Estates Act 163–165
Bikani Mian, Hajji Shaikh 52–54, 56, 85, 139–140, 146
Blackstone, William 97, 120, 127
Bombay (city and province) 3, 50, 70–72, 81, 134
Bombay High Court 109–110, 115, 117, 134, 143, 151–152, 158
Bundelkhand Encumbered Estates Act 84

Cairo 18, 69
Calcutta 48, 62–63, 70, 72, 81, 116, 130, 145, 165
Calcutta High Court 89, 93, 109–110, 115, 139, 143, 145, 162–163, 168
Chittagong 62, 67, 137
Comer-Pretheram, Sir William (Justice) 115, 143, 168
custom and customary law 151, 152

Dacca, Nawabs of 49–52, 68, 73, 91, 144–145, 158, 161–165, 182, 189
Deoband (school of theology) 6, 66, 67–69, 76, 131, 173, 181
dharmaśastra 123, 163

Edge, Sir John (Justice) 115, 119, 139
Egypt 17, 18–20, 172
entail/entailment 1, 149–150

Farhat un-nissah, Begam 63–65, 66, 74–75
Fatah Sahib Bibi (Phate Saheb) 134–137, 158
Fatāwa-i 'Ālāmgīrī 105, 130, 136, 141–142, 147, 158
fatihah 73–74, 76–77
Fatima Bibi 50, 137–138
fatwā 13, 101–102, 133, 169–173
fiqh 12–14, 100–101, 105
Firangi Mahal 69, 161, 181
Fitzpatrick, Dennis 160, 162

Ghani, Khwajah Abd al- (Nawab of Dacca) 145, 163

Udovitch, A. L. *Partnership and Profit in Medieval Islam*, Princeton University Press, 1970
Vachha, P. B. *Famous Judges, Lawyers and Cases of Bombay during the British Period*, Bombay, Tripathi, 1962
Verdon, Michel. "The Stem Family: Toward a General Theory", *Journal of Interdisciplinary History*, X, 1 (1979), 87–105
Vesey-Fitzgerald, S. *Muhammadan Law*, Oxford University Press, 1931
Von Grunebaum, Gustave E. *Classical Islam*, Chicago, Aldine, 1970
Medieval Islam, University of Chicago Press, 1946
Modern Islam, New York, Random House, 1964
Washbrook, D. A. "Law, State and Agrarian Society in Colonial India", *Modern Asian Studies*, XV, 3 (1981), 649–721
Weber, Max. *The Theory of Social and Economic Organization*, ed. Talcott Parsons, New York, Free Press, 1964
Whitcombe, Elizabeth. *Agrarian Conditions in Northern India*, Berkeley, University of California Press, 1971
Wolpert, Stanley A. *Morley and India, 1906–1910*, Berkeley, University of California Press, 1967
Yaduvash, Uma. "The Decline of the Role of the Qāḍīs in India, 1793–1876", *Studies in Islam*, VI (1969), 155–171
Yusuf, K. M. "The Judiciary in India under the Sultans of Delhi and the Mughal Emperors", *Indo-Iranica*, XVIII, 4 (1965), 1–12
Zakariah, K. *History of Hooghly College*, Alipore, Bengal Government Press, 1936
Zaki, M. "Organization of Islamic Learning under the Saiyids and Lodis", *Medieval India*, IV (1977), 1–9

Dictionaries and encyclopedia

Dozy, R. *Supplément aux Dictionnaires Arabes*, Beyrouth, Libraire Du Liban, 1968
The Encyclopedia of Islam, 1st edn, Leiden, Brill, 1913–1942; 2nd edn, London and Leiden, Brill, 1960–(in progress)
Farhang-i Asifiyyah, Khan Sahib Mawlwi Sayyid Ahmad Dihlavi, reprint edn, 4 vols.; Delhi, Taraqqi-yi Urdu Bord, 1974
Lane, Edward W. *An Arabic–English Lexicon*, reprint edn, Beirut, Libraire Du Liban, 1968
Lughātnāmah, Ali Akbar Dehkhudah *et al.*, Tehran University, in progress
Platts, J. T. *A Dictionary of Urdū, Classical Hindī and English*, Oxford University Press, 1970
Steingass, F. *A Comprehensive Persian–English Dictionary*, reprint edn, New Delhi, Manoharlal, 1973
Wehr, Hans. *A Dictionary of Modern Written Arabic*, ed. J. Milton Cowan, 3rd revised edn, Ithaca, Spoken Language Services, 1971

Ray, Ratna and Ray, Rajat. "Zamindars and Jotedars: A Study of Rural Politics in Bengal", *Modern Asian Studies*, IX, 1 (1975), 81–102

Reeves, P. D. "The Landlords' Response to Political Change in the United Provinces of Agra and Oudh, India, 1921–1937", unpublished Ph.D. dissertation, Australian National University, 1963

Religious Organization and Religious Experience, ed. J. Davis, Association of Social Anthropologists Monograph 21, London, Academic Press, 1982

Robinson, F. "Consultation and Control, The United Provinces' Government and its Allies, 1860–1906", *Modern Asian Studies*, V, 4 (1971), 313–336

Separatism among Indian Muslims, Cambridge University Press, 1974

Rothermund, Dietmar. "Freedom of Contract and the Problem of Land Alienation in British India", *South Asia*, 3 (1973), 57–78

Russell, R. and Islam, K. *Three Mughal Poets: Mir, Mir Sauda, Hasan*, London, Allen and Unwin, 1969

Rypka, Jan et al. *History of Iranian Literature*, Dordrecht, D. Reidel, 1968

Saiyd, Matlubul Hasan. *Muhammad Ali Jinnah*, Lahore, Ashraf, 1945

Saksena, K. P. *Muslim Law as Administered in India and Pakistan*, Lucknow, Eastern Book House, 1973

Schacht, Joseph. *An Introduction to Islamic Law*, Oxford University Press, 1964

"On the Title of the *Fatāwā al-ʿĀlamgiriyya*", in *Iran and Islam*, ed. C. Bosworth, Edinburgh University Press, 1971, 475–478

The Origins of Muhammadan Jurisprudence, Oxford, Clarendon Press, 1950

Seal, Anil. *The Emergence of Indian Nationalism*, Cambridge University Press, 1968

Shackle, Christopher. "The Multānī *Marsīya*", *Der Islam*, LV, 2 (1978), 281–311

Shah, A. M. *The Household Dimension of the Family in India*, Berkeley, University of California Press, 1974

Shaked, Haim. "The Biographies of *'Ulamā'* in Mubarak's *Khiṭṭāt* as a Source for the History of the *'Ulamā'* in Nineteenth Century Egypt", *Asian and African Studies*, 7 (1971), 41–76

Sharon, M. "A *Waqf* Inscription from Ramlah", *Arabica*, XII (1966), 77–84

Siddiqi, Noman Ahmad. "The Classification of Villages under the Mughals", *The Indian Economic and Social History Review*, I, 3 (1964), 73–83

Skhlar, Judith N. *Legalism*, Cambridge, Mass., Harvard University Press, 1964

Smith, Wilfred Cantwell. "The Concept of *Sharīʿa* among some *Mutakallimun*", *Arabic and Islamic Studies in Honor of Hamilton A. R. Gibb*, Leiden, Brill, 1965, 582–602

Islam in Modern History, New York, New American Library, 1957

Modern Islam in India, reprint edn, Lahore, 1969

Sources of Indian Tradition, ed W. T. DeBary, 2 vols., New York, Columbia University Press, 1958

Spear, P. *The Twilight of the Mughals*, Cambridge University Press, 1951

Stokes, E. *The English Utilitarians and India*, Oxford, Clarendon Press, 1959

The Peasant and the Raj, Cambridge University Press, 1978

The Story of Our Inns of Court, D. Plunkett Barton et al., London, Foulis, n.d.

Taxation in Islam, ed. and trans. A. Benshemesh, London, Luzac, 1969

Taʿziyeh: Ritual and Drama in Iran, ed. Peter J. Chelkowski, New York University Press, 1979

Misra, B. B. *The Central Administration of the East India Company, 1773–1834*, Manchester University Press, 1959
The Indian Middle Classes, Delhi, Oxford University Press, 1978
Moosvi, Shireen. "Sūyūrghāl Statistics in the *Ā'īn-i Akbārī*: An Analysis", *Indian Historical Review*, II, 2 (1976), 282–298
Muhammad, Khair ud-din. *Tazkirat al-'ulamā', A Memoir of the Learned Men of Jaunpur*, trans. Muhammad Sanaullah, Calcutta, Abul Faiz, 1934
Mujeeb, M. *The Indian Muslims*, London, Allen and Unwin, 1967
Mukherjee, S. M. *Sir William Jones*, Cambridge University Press, 1968
Musgrave, P. J. "Landlords and Lords of the Land: Estate Management and Social Control in Uttar Pradesh, 1860–1920", *Modern Asian Studies*, VI, 3 (1972), 257–275
Muslim Self-Statement in India and Pakistan, 1857–1968, ed. Aziz Ahmad and G. E. Von Grunebaum, Wiesenbaden, Harrasowitz, 1970
Neale, W. C. *Economic Change in Rural India*, New Haven, Yale University Press, 1962
Nehru, J. *The Discovery of India*, ed. R. I. Crane, Garden City, Doubleday, 1960
Nielsen, Jørgen S. "*Mazālim* and *Dār'al-'adl* under the Early Mamluks", *Muslim World*, LXVI, 2 (1976), 114–132
Nizami, K. A. "Early Indo-Muslim Mystics and their Attitude Towards the State", *Islamic Culture*, 22 (1948), 387–398; 23 (1949), 13–21, 162–170, 312–21; 24 (1950), 60–71
"Socio-Religious Movements in Indian Islam, 1763–1898", *Islamic Culture*, 44 (1970), 131–146
Palit, Chittabrata. *Tensions in Bengal Rural Society*, Calcutta, Progressive Publishers, 1975
Pandey, B. N. *The Introduction of English Law into India*, Bombay, Asia Publishing House, 1967
Pearson, M. N. "Political Participation in Mughal India", *Indian Economic and Social History Review*, IX, 2 (June 1972), 113–121
Petry, Carl F. *The Civilian Elite of Cairo in the Later Middle Ages*, Princeton University Press, 1981
Poliak, A. N. *Feudalism in Egypt, Syria, Palestine and Lebanon, 1250–1900*, London, Royal Asiatic Society, 1939
Potter, H. *Potter's Historical Introduction to English Law*, 4th edn, ed. A. K. R. Kiralfy, London, Sweet and Maxwell, 1962
Pradhan, M. C. *The Political System of the Jats of Northern India*, Bombay, Asia Publishing House, 1966
Qureshi, Ishtiaq Husain. *Ulema in Politics*, Karachi, Maaref, 1972
Rabitoy, Neil. "System vs. Expediency: The Reality of Land Revenue Administration in Bombay Presidency, 1812–1820", *Modern Asian Studies*, IX, 4 (1975), 529–546
Rahman, Matiur. *From Consultation to Confrontation*, London, Luzac, 1970
Rashid, Sheikh Abdur. "*Madad-i Ma'ash* Grants under the Mughals", *Journal of the Pakistan Historical Society*, 9 (1961), 98–108
Rashid, S. Khalid. *Wakf Administration in India*, New Delhi, Vikas Publishing House, 1979
Ray, Ratna. "Land Transfer and Social Change under the Permanent Settlement: A Study of Two Localities", *Indian Economic and Social History Review*, XI, 1 (1974), 1–45

Land Control and Social Structure in Indian History, ed. R. E. Frykenburg, Madison, University of Wisconsin Press, 1969
Land Tenure and Peasant in South Asia, ed. R. E. Frykenburg, New Delhi, Orient Longman, 1977
Laslett, Peter. *The World We Have Lost*, New York, Scribner's, 1965
Law in Culture and Society, ed. Laura Nader, Chicago, Aldine, 1969
Law in the Middle East, ed. M. Khadduri and H. J. Liebesny, Washington, D. C., Middle East Institute, 1955
Lelyveld, David. *Aligarh's First Generation*, Princeton University Press, 1978
"Three Aligarh Students: Aftab Ahmad Khan, Ziauddin Ahmad and Muhammad Ali", *Modern Asian Studies*, IX, (1975), 103–116
Lingat, Robert. *The Classical Law of India*, ed. and trans. J. D. M. Derrett, Berkeley, University of California Press, 1973
Locality, Province and Nation, ed. J. Gallagher et al., Cambridge University Press, 1973
Lyon, Bryce. *A Constitutional and Legal History of Medieval England*, New York, Harper, 1960
McCormack, William C. "Caste and the British Administration of Hindu Law", *Journal of Asian and African Studies*, I, 1 (1966), 27–34
"Mahmood Number", *Aligarh Law Journal*, V (1973)
Mahmood, Tahir. *Muslim Personal Law*, New Delhi, Vikas Publishing House, 1977
Makdisi, George. *The Rise of Colleges*, Edinburgh University Press, 1981
Marsot, Affaf Lutfi al-Sayyid. "The Political and Economic Functions of the 'ulamā' in the Eighteenth Century", *Journal of the Economic and Social History of the Orient*, XVI, 2 (1973), 130–154
Mason, Philip (under pseud. Philip Woodruff). *Call the Next Witness*, New York, Harcourt, 1946
A Shaft of Sunlight, New Delhi, Vikas Publishing House, 1978
Masud, Muhammad Khalid. *Islamic Legal Philosophy*, Islamabad, Islamic Research Institute, 1977
Medieval India, 4 vols., Bombay, Asia Publishing House, 1972
Megarry, Robert. *Inns Ancient and Modern*, London, Selden Society, 1972
Mendelsohn, Oliver. "The Pathology of the Indian Legal System", *Modern Asian Studies*, XV, 4 (1981), 823–863
Metcalf, Barbara D. *Islamic Revival in British India: Deoband, 1860–1900*, Princeton University Press, 1982
"The *Madrasa* at Deoband: A Model for Religious Education in Modern India", *Modern Asian Studies*, XII, 1 (1978), 111–134
Metcalf, Thomas R. *Land, Landlords and the British Raj*, Berkeley, University of California Press, 1979
"Landlords without Land: The U.P. Zamindars Today", *Pacific Affairs*, XL, 1 and 2 (1967), 5–18
Minault, Gail. "Islam and Mass Politics: The Indian '*Ulamā*' and the *Khilāfat* Movement", in *Religion and Political Modernization*, ed. D. E. Smith, New Haven, Yale University Press, 1974, 168–182
Minault, Gail and Lelyveld, David. "The Campaign for a Muslim University", *Modern Asian Studies*, VIII (1974), 168–182
Minturn, Leigh. *The Rajputs of Khalapur, India*, New York, Wiley, 1966

Hodgson, Marshall G. S. *The Venture of Islam*, 3 vols., University of Chicago Press, 1974
Holdsworth, W. S. *A History of English Law*, 9 vols., London, Methuen, 1925
Hollister, John N. *The Shī'a of India*, reprint edn, New Delhi, Oriental Reprints, 1979
Hooghly College Register, 1836–1936, Alipore, Bengal Government Press, 1936
Hosain, Atia. *Sunlight on a Broken Column*, New Delhi, Heinemann, 1979
Household and Family in Past Time, ed. Peter Laslett and R. Wall, Cambridge University Press, 1972
Husain, Fida. *The Musalman Law of Wakf*, Nagpur, by the author, 1939
Husain, Imtiaz. *Land Revenue Policy in North India*, Calcutta, New Age, 1967
Husain, Wahed. *Administration of Justice during the Muslim Rule of India*, reprint edn, Delhi, Idarah-i Adabiyat-i Delli, 1977
Ibn-i Sarbuland-i Jang, Mahomed Ullah. *A Dissertation on the Development of Muslim Law in British India*, Allahabad, Juvenile Press, 1932
The Imperial Impact, ed. C. Dewey and A. Hopkins, London, Athlone Press, 1978
Inalcik, Halil. "Capital Formation in the Ottoman Empire", *Journal of Economic History*, XXXIX, 1 (1969), 97–140
"Land Problems in Turkish History", *Muslim World*, XLV, 3 (1955), 221–228
Indian Economy in the Nineteenth Century, Delhi, Delhi School of Economics, 1969
Iyer, Raghavan. "Utilitarianism and All That – The Political Theory of British Imperialism in India", in *St Anthony's Papers*, 8, Carbondale, Southern Illinois University Press, 1960, 9–71
Jennings, Ronald G. "Loans and Credit in Early Seventeenth Century Ottoman Judicial Records: The *Sharia* Court of Anatolian Kayseri", *Journal of the Economic and Social History of the Orient*, XVI, 2 and 3 (1973), 168–216
Kerr, I. J. "The British and the Administration of the Golden Temple in 1859", *Panjab Past and Present*, X, 2 (October 1976), 306–321
Kerr, Malcolm H. *Islamic Reform*, Berkeley, University of California Press, 1966
Kessinger, Tom G. *Vilyatpur*, New Delhi, Young Asia, 1979
Khan, Paunchkouree (pseud.). *Revelations of an Orderly*, Benares, E. J. Lazarus, 1866
Khare, R. S. "Indigenous Culture and Lawyers' Law in India", *Comparative Studies in Society and History*, XIV, 1 (1972), 71–96
Kopf, David. *British Orientalism and the Bengal Renaissance*, Berkeley, University of California Press, 1969
Kozlowski, Gregory C. "Indian Secularity and the Islamic Law: A Liberal Muslim's Response", *The Islamic Quarterly*, XVIII, 3 and 4 (1974), 33–47
Kumar, Dharma. *Land and Caste in South India*, Cambridge University Press, 1965
Labib, Subhi Y. "Capitalism in Medieval Islam", *Journal of Economic History*, XXXIX, 1 (1969), 79–96
Ladd, John. "The Concept of Community: A Logical Analysis", in *Community*, ed. C. J. Friedrich, *Nomos II* (*Yearbook of the American Society of Political and Legal Philosophy*), New York, Liberal Arts Press, 1959, 269–293
Lambton, Ann K. S. *Landlord and Peasant in Persia*, Oxford University Press, 1953

Compendium of Fatamid Law, Simla, Indian Institute of Advanced Studies, 1969
"The Impact of English Law on *Sharī'āt*", *The Egyptian Revue of International Law*, 18 (1962), 1–27
"The Muhammadan Law in India", *Comparative Studies in Society and History*, 5 (1963), 401–415
Outlines of Muhammadan Law, 4th edn, Delhi, Oxford University Press, 1974
Galantar, Marc. "Changing Legal Conceptions of Caste", in *Structure and Change in Indian Society*, ed. M. Singer and B. Cohn, Chicago, Aldine, 1968, 299–336
"Modernization of Law", in *Modernization*, ed. M. Weiner, New York, Basic Books, 1966, 153–165
"The Uses of Law in Indian Studies", in *Languages and Areas*, University of Chicago Press, 1967, 37–44
Geertz, Clifford. *The Interpretation of Cultures*, New York, Basic Books, 1973
Islam Observed, New Haven, Yale University Press, 1968
Geldart, William. *Elements of English Law*, 8th edn, ed. D. C. M. Yardley, London, Oxford University Press, 1965
Gibb, H. A. R. *Modern Trends in Islam*, University of Chicago Press, 1947
Studies on the Civilization of Islam, Boston, Beacon Press, 1962
Gibb, H. A. R. and Bowen, H. *Islamic Society and the West*, 1, Part 2, London, Oxford University Press, 1957
Gledhill, A. *The Republic of India: The Development of its Laws and Constitution*, London, Stevens, 1964
Goitein, S. D. *Studies in Islamic History and Institutions*, Leiden, Brill, 1966
Goody, J. *Production and Reproduction*, Cambridge University Press, 1976
Graham, G. F. I. *The Life and Work of Syed Ahmed Khan*, reprint edn, Delhi, Idarah-i Adabiyat-i Delli, 1974
Griffin, Lepel H. *The Punjab Chiefs*, 2 vols., Lahore, Civil and Military Gazette Press, 1890
Guha, Ranajit. *A Rule of Property for Bengal*, Paris, Mouton, 1963
Habakkuk, H. J. "Family Structure and Economic Change in Nineteenth Century Europe", *Journal of Economic History* xv, 1 (1955), 1–12
Habib, Irfan. *The Agrarian System of Mughal India*, Bombay, Asia House, 1963
"The Political Role of Shaikh Ahmad Sirhindi and Shah Waliullah", *Inquiry*, v (1961), 36–55
"Potentialities of Capitalistic Development in the Economy of Mughal India", *Journal of Economic History*, xxxix, 1 (1969), 32–78
"The Social Distribution of Landed Property in Pre-British India", *Enquiry*, new series, II (1965), 21–75
ul-Haque, Zia. *Landlord and Peasant in Early Islam*, Islamabad, Islamic Research Institute, 1977
Hardy, P. "Modern European and Muslim Explanations of Conversion to Islam in South Asia", *Journal of the Royal Asiatic Society*, 2 (1977), 177–208
Muslims of British India, Cambridge University Press, 1972
Hasan, A. *The Early Development of Islamic Jurisprudence*, Islamabad, Islamic Research Institute, 1970
Historians of India, Pakistan and Ceylon, ed. C. H. Philips, London, Oxford University Press, 1961
Hitti, P. K. *History of the Arabs*, 10th edn, New York, Macmillan, 1970

during the Seventeenth Century", *Indian Economic and Social History Review*, III, 4 (1966), 321–331

Chaudhuri, Binay Bhushan. "The Agrarian Question in Bengal and the Government, 1850–1900", *The Calcutta Historical Journal*, I, 1 (1976), 33–43

Cohen, Hayyim J. "The Economic Background and Secular Occupation of Muslim Jurisprudents and Traditionalists in the Classical Period of Islam (until the middle of the 11th century)", *Journal of the Economic and Social History of the Orient*, XIII, 1 (1970), 16–61

Cohn, Bernard. "Comments on Papers on Land Tenure", *The Indian Economic and Social History Review*, I, 2 (1973), 177–183

"From Indian Status to British Contract", *Journal of Economic History*, XVI, 4 (1961), 613–628

"The Initial British Impact on India: A Case Study of the Benares Region", *Journal of Asian Studies*, XIX, 4 (1959), 418–431

"Some Notes on Law and Change in North India", *Economic Development and Cultural Change*, VIII (1959), 79–93

Conrad, Joseph. *Lord Jim*, ed. and notes by Thomas Moser, New York, Norton, 1968

Coulson, N. J. *A History of Islamic Law*, Edinburgh University Press, 1964

Succession in the Muslim Family, Cambridge University Press, 1971

Daniel, Norman. *Islam, Europe and Empire*, Edinburgh University Press, 1966

Dennett, Daniel C. *Conversion and the Poll Tax in Early Islam*, Cambridge, Mass., Harvard University Press, 1950

Derrett, J. D. M. *Religion, Law and the State in India*, New York, Free Press, 1968

The Developmental Cycle in Domestic Groups, ed. J. Goody, Cambridge University Press, 1967

Dobbin, C. *Urban Leadership in Western India*, Oxford University Press, 1972

Dumont, Louis. *Homo Hierarchicus*, University of Chicago Press, 1970

Religion, Politics and History in India, The Hague, Mouton, 1970

Eaton, R. M. *Sufis of Bijapur, 1300–1700*, Princeton University Press, 1978

Ewing, K. "The Politics of Sufism: Redefining the Saints of Pakistan", *Journal of Asian Studies*, XLII, 2 (1982), 251–268

The Extended Family, ed. Gail Minault, Columbia (Missouri), South Asia Books, 1981

Family and Inheritance: Rural Society in Western Europe, 1200–1800, ed. J. Goody, J. Thirsk and E. P. Thompson, Cambridge University Press, 1976

Family, Kinship and Marriage among Muslims in India, ed. Imtiaz Ahmad, New Delhi, Manoharlal, 1976

Feaver, G. *From Status to Contract*, London, Longman, 1969

Foran, Paul G. "The Status of the Land and Inhabitants of the Sawad during the First Two Centuries of Islam", *Journal of the Economic and Social History of the Orient*, XIV, 1 (1971), 25–37

Fox, Richard G. *Kin, Clan, Raja and Rule*, Berkeley, University of California Press, 1971

Frykenburg, R. E. *Guntur District, 1788–1848*, Oxford University Press, 1965

The Function of Documents in Islamic Law, trans. and ed. J. A. Wakin, Albany, University of New York Press, 1972

Fyzee, A. A. A. *Cases in the Muhammadan Law of India and Pakistan*, Oxford University Press, 1965

The Mughal Nobility under Aurangzeb, Bombay, Asia Publishing House, 1966
Allahabad High Court Bar Association, Centenary Volume, 1873–1973, Allahabad, Bar Association, 1975
Anderson, J. N. D. "The Nature and Sources of Islamic Law" and "Islamic Law and its Administration in India", in *Contributions to the Study of Indian Law and Society*, Philadelphia, University of Pennsylvania South Asia Seminar, 1966–1967
  "Recent Developments in Sharī 'a Law IX: The *Waqf* System", *Muslim World*, XLII, 4 (1952), 257–276
  "The Religious Elements in *Waqf* Endowments", *Royal Central Asian Journal*, XXXVIII, 4 (1951), 292–299
Ansari, Muhammad Azeer. "Court Ceremonies of the Great Mughals", *Islamic Culture*, 36 (1962), 182–195
Anthropology of Folk Region, ed. Charles Leslie, New York, Random House, 1970
Ashraf, K. M. *Life and Conditions of the People of Hindustan*, New Delhi, Manoharlal, 1970
Aziz, K. K. *Ameer Ali*, Lahore, Publishers United, 1968
  Britain and Muslim India, 1857–1947, London, Heinemann, 1963
Baden-Powell, B. H. *The Land-Systems of British India*, 3 vols., reprint edn, New Delhi, Oriental Publishers, 1974
Baer, Gabriel. *A History of Land Ownership in Modern Egypt, 1800–1950*, London, Oxford University Press, 1962
Bailey, Clinton. "A Note on the Bedouin Image of '*adl* as Justice", *Muslim World*, LXVI, 2 (1976), 133–135
Barriar, N. G. *The Punjab Alienation of Land Bill of 1900*, Duke University, Occasional Papers 2, 1966
" 'The Beard' by Abu Tālib al-Makkī", trans. E. H. Douglas, *Muslim World*, LXVIII, 2 (1978), 100–110
Blake, Stephen P. "The Patrimonial–Bureaucratic Empire of the Mughals", *Journal of Asian Studies*, XXXIX, 1 (1979), 77–94
Bolitho, Hector. *Jinnah*, London, Murray, 1954
Brass, Paul R. *Language, Religion and Politics in North India*, Cambridge University Press, 1974
Brewer, John. "An Ungovernable People? Law and Disorder in Stuart and Hanoverian England", *History Today*, 30 (1980), 18–27
Broomfield, J. H. *Elite Conflict in a Plural Society*, Berkeley, University of California Press, 1968
  "The Regional Elites: A Theory of Modern Indian History", *Indian Economic and Social History Review*, III, 3 (1966), 279–291
Browne, Edward G. *A Literary History of Persia*, 4 vols., Cambridge University Press, 1964
Bryce, James. *The Roman and British Empires*, London, Oxford University Press, 1913
Burrow, J. W. *Evolution and Society*, Cambridge University Press, 1966
Butterfield, H. *The Whig Interpretation of History*, New York, Norton, 1961
Cahen, C. "Réflexions sur le *waqf* ancien", *Studia Islamica*, 14 (1961), 37–56
Cambridge History of Islam, ed. P. M. Holt, A. K. S. Lambton and B. Lewis, 4 vols., Cambridge University Press, 1970
Chandra, Satish. "Some Aspects of the Growth of a Money Economy in India

Shri Guru Adi Granth, With a Life of Guru Nanak, trans. E. Trumpp, London, Tuebner, 1877

Al-Sirajiyyah or the Mahommedan Law of Inheritance, trans. William Jones, ed. A. Rumsey, reprint edn, Lahore, Premier Book House, 1959

Sircar, S. C. *The Muhammadan Law*, 2 vols., Calcutta, Thacker and Spink, 1875

Smith, Adam. *Lectures on Jurisprudence*, ed. R. Meek *et al.*, Oxford University Press, 1978

Tupper, C. L. *Punjab Customary Law*, 4 vols., Calcutta, Government Printing Office, 1881

Tyabji, Faiz Badruddin. *Principles of Muhammadan Law*, Bombay, Taraporvala, 1913

Who was Who, 1916–1928, London, 1929

Wilson, H. H. *A Glossary of Judicial and Revenue Terms*, London, Allen, 1855

Wilson, R. K. *A Digest of Anglo-Muhammadan Law*, London, W. Thacker, 1895

Wright, F. N. *Report on the Settlement of Cawnpore District*, Allahabad, Government Press, 1878

Newspapers

Al-Ḥilāl (Calcutta), 1912–1913
Amrita Bazar Patrika (Calcutta), 1905–1912
Comrade (Calcutta and Delhi), 1911–1913
Oudh Punch (Lucknow), 1908–1909

Works used as secondary sources

Ahmad, Aziz. *An Intellectual History of Islam in India*, Edinburgh University Press, 1969

  Islamic Modernism in India and Pakistan, 1857–1964, London, Oxford University Press, 1867

  "Muslim Kinship Terminology in Urdu", *Journal of the Economic and Social History of the Orient*, XX, 3 (1977), 344–350

  "Political and Religious Ideas of Shah Waliyullah of Delli", *Muslim World*, LII (1962), 22–30

  "The Role of Ulema in Indo-Muslim History", *Studia Islamica*, 31 (1970), 1–13

  Studies in Islamic Culture in the Indian Environment, Oxford, Clarendon Press, 1964

Ahmad, Imtiaz. "The *Ashrāf-Ajlāf* Dichotomy in Muslim Social Structure in India", *Indian Economic and Social History Review*, III, 3 (1966), 268–278

  "Social Stratification among Muslims", *The Economic Weekly*, 10 July 1965, 1093–1096

Ahmad, M. B. *The Administration of Justice in Medieval India*, Aligarh, Aligarh Historical Research Institute, 1941

Akbar, M. *The Administration of Justice by the Mughals*, Lahore, Ashraf, 1948

Ali, Ahmed. *Twilight in Delhi*, New Delhi, Sterling Publishers, 1973

Ali, M. Athar. "*Mansab* and Imperial Policy under Shah Jahan", *Indian Historical Review*, III, 1 (1976), 94–104

Hobhouse, Arthur. *The Dead Hand*, London, Chatto and Windus, 1880
Hobhouse, Leonard T. *Lord Hobhouse*, London, Arnold, 1905
Hunter, W. W. *The Indian Musalmans*, reprint edn, Lahore, Premier Book House, 1974
Indian Biographical Dictionary, ed. C. Hayavadana Rao, Madras, Pillar, 1915
Indian Judges, Madras, G. A. Natesan, 1932 (?)
Irvine, W. *Report on the Revision of Records and Settlement Operations in Ghazipur District, 1880–1885*, Allahabad, Government Press, 1886
Khair ud-din, Muhammad. *Takzirat ul Ulama, A Memoir of the Learned of Janpur*, trans. Muhammad Sana, Ullah, Calcutta, Abul Faiz, 1934
MacDonald, D. B. *The Development of Muslim Theology, Jurisprudence and Constitutional Theory*, reprint edn, Lahore, Premier Book House, 1972
MacNaghtan, William Hay. *Principles of Hindu and Mohammadan Law*, ed. H. H. Wilson, London, Williams and Norgate, 1860
Maine, Henry Sumner. *Ancient Law*, New York, Holt, 1888
Village Communities in the East and West, New York, Holt, 1889
al-Marghinani. *Hedaya*, trans. Charles Hamilton, reprint edn, Lahore, Premier Book House, 1975
Markby, William. *An Introduction to Hindu and Mahomedan Law for the Use of Students*, Oxford, Clarendon Press, 1906
The Meaning of the Glorious Koran, trans. M. M. Pickthall, New York, Mentor, n.d.
Mill, James. *Essays on Government, Jurisprudence, Liberty of the Press, and Law of Nations*, reprint edn, New York, A. M. Kelley, 1967
Moens, S. M. *Report on the Settlement of Bareilly District*, Allahabad, Government Press, 1874
Morley, William H. *The Administration of Justice in British India*, London, Williams and Norgate, 1859
Porter, F. W. *Final Report of the Settlement of the Allahabad District*, Allahabad, Government Press, 1878
Rahim, Abdur. *The Principles of Muhammadan Jurisprudence*, reprint edn, Lahore, All Pakistan Legal Decisions, 1974
Rahman, A. F. M. Abdur. *Institutes of Mussalman Law*, Calcutta, Thacker and Spink, 1907
Rankin, George C. *Background to Indian Law*, Cambridge University Press, 1946
Russell, Alexander D. and Suhrawardy, Abdullah al-Mamun. *Muslim Law: A Historical Introduction to the Law of Inheritance*, London, Kegan and Paul, 1923(?)
Ruswa, Mirza Mohammad Hadi. *The Courtesan of Lucknow (Umrao Jān Ādā)*, trans. Khuswant Singh, Delhi, Hind Pocket Books, 1970
Saḥīḥ Muslim, trans. Abdul Hamid Siddiqi, 4 vols., Lahore, Ashraf, 1973
Sayings of Muhammad, A Selection of Traditions, trans. Ghazi Ahmad, Lahore, Ashraf, 1968
Sharar, Abdul Halim. *Lucknow: The Last Phase of an Oriental Culture (Guzashtah Luknaw)*, trans. E. S. Harcourt and Fakhir Hussain, London, Paul Elek, 1975
Sharif, Jaafar. *Qānūn-i Islām, Islam in India*, trans. G. Herklots, rev. and ed. W. Crooke, reprint edn, New Delhi, Oriental Reprints, 1972

ur-Rahman Barker *et al.*, 3 vols., vol. I, Ithaca, Spoken Language Services, 1977
Qāmūs al-Kutub Urdū, ed. Daktar Mawlwi Abd al-Haqi, 1 vol., vol. I (*Maẓhabīyat*), Karachi, Anjuman-i Taraqqī-yi Urdū Pakistān, 1961
Razaqi, Shahid Husain. *Sayyid Amīr 'Alī*, Lahore, Idarah-yi Saqafat-i Islamiyah, 1970
Saḥīḥ al-Bukhārī, *Urdū*, trans. Shabbia Ahmad Uthmani, Karachi, Idarah-yi'ulūm-i Shariah, A.H. 1393
Shibli Numani, Muhammad. *Maqālāt-i Shiblī*, 8 vols., vol. I, Azamgarh, Maarif, 1954
Tārīkh-i Adabīyat-i Mussalmānān-i Pakistān-o Hind, 8 vols. IV and VII, Lahore, Panjab University Press, 1971
Thanvi, Ashraf Ali. *Fatāwa-yi Ashrafīyyah*, Karachi, H. M. Sayyid, 1977

Works in English and translations used as primary sources

Abdul Majid, Syed H. R. *England and the Moslem World*, York, Yorkshire Printing Company, 1912
Ahmad Khan, Sir Sayyid. *Review of Dr Hunter's Indian Musalmans*, reprint edn, Lahore, Premier Book House, n.d.
Ali, Mrs Meer Hasan. *Observations on the Mussulmauns of India*, 2 vols., reprint edn, Delhi, Idarah-yi Adabiyat-Delli, 1973
Ali, Mohamed. *My Life: A Fragment*, Lahore, Ashraf, 1942
  Selections from Mawlana Mohammad Ali's Comrade, ed. Syed Rais Ahmad Jafri, Lahore, Mohammad Ali Academy, 1965
Ali, Sayyid Amir. *Mahommedan Law*, 2 vols., Calcutta, Thacker and Spink, 1892
  Memoirs and Other Writings of Syed Ameer Ali, ed.
    Syed Razi Wasti, Lahore, People's Publishing House, 1968
  The Spirit of Islam, reprint edn, Karachi, Pakistan Publishing House, 1976
Allen, B. C. *Dacca, East Bengal District Gazetteers*, Allahabad, Pioneer Press, 1912
Austin, John. *Lectures on Jurisprudence*, ed. Robert Campbell, 5th edn, 2 vols., London, John Murray, 1911
Baillie, Neil B. E. *A Digest of Muhammadan Law*, reprint edn, Lahore, Premier Book House, 1974
Buckland, C. E. *Dictionary of Indian Biography*, reprint edn, Delhi, Indological Book House, 1971
Cases Illustrative of Oriental Manners, London, Rayner and Hodges, n.d.
Congress Presidential Addresses, First Series (1885-1910), Madras, G. A. Natesan, 1935
Duff, M. E. Grant and Stokes, Whitley. *Sir Henry Maine*, London, John Murray, 1892
Eminent Mussalmans, Madras, G. A. Natesan, n.d.
Foundations of Pakistan, ed. S. S. Pirzada, 2 vols., vol. I, Karachi, National Publishing House, n.d.
Gracey, H. K. *Final Report of the Settlement of Cawnpore District*, Allahabad, Government Press, 1907
Harrington, J. H. "Remarks upon the Authorities of Mosulman Law", *Asiatik Researches*, Asiatic Society of Bengal, X (1811), 475–512

BIBLIOGRAPHY

Works in Urdu, Persian and Arabic

Abd al-Hai, Mawlana. *Fatāwa-yi 'Abd al-Hai, Urdu,* Deoband, Malik Publisherz, 1969
Abd al-Qadar, Mufti Muhammad. *Fatāwa-yi Firangī Maḥal,* Lucknow, Mufti Muhammad Reza Ansari, 1968
Ahmad Khan, Sir Sayyid. *Khuṭbāt-i Sar Sayyid,* ed. Muhammad Ismail Panipati, 2 vols., Lahore, Majlis-i Taraqqī-yi Adab, 1972
Maqālāt-i Sar Sayyid, ed. Muhammad Ismail Panipati, 5 vols., Lahore, Majlis-i Taraqqī-yi Adab, 1962–1965
Bakhtawar Khan, Muhammad. *Mir 'at 'al-'Ālam,* ed. S. Alvi, 2 vols., Lahore, Research Society of Pakistan, 1979
Bukhari, Ahmad. *Waqf alā 'al-Awlād ki Maẓartain,* Calcutta, Sayyid Zahur al-Haq, 1915
Din, Shaikh Ghulab. *Qānūn-i Waqf alā 'al-Awlād,* Lahore, Hamidiyyah Press, 1916(?)
Diwān-i Ḥāfiẓ, ed. Mawlana Qazi Sajjad Husain, Delhi, Sabrang Kitab Ghar, 1972
Fatāwa-i Ahl-i Ḥadīs̱, Sargodha, Idarah-yi Ihya 'al-Sunnah 'al-Nabuwiyyah, 1973
Fatāwa-yi 'Ālamgīrī, Urdū Jadīd, ed. Mawlwi Mufti Kafil al-Rahman Nashat, 25 vols., vols. XX–XXI, Deoband, Wasim Buk Dypo, 1968
Fatāwa-i Deoband, 10 vols., Deoband, Dar'al-'Ulūm, 1968
Fatāwa-yi 'Ulamā'-yi Hindūstān, Muta'liq Masa'lah-i Waqf alā' al-Awlād, Lucknow, Nadwah al-Ulama, 1910
Gangohi, Rashid Ahmad. *Fatāwa-yi Rashīdiyyah,* Moradabad, 1906
Ghafut-allah, Mustaq Ahmad. *Waqfnāmah,* Moradabad, Mirza Ishak Beg, 1919(?)
Gulzar Ali. *Tardīd Masawwadah Qānūn-i Waqf-i Khāndānī-yi Ahl-i Islām,* Patna, Muhammadi Press, n.d.
Husain, Mawlana Nazir. *Fatāwa-yi Naẓirīyah,* Delhi, Dilli Printing Press, 1914
Malihabadi, Josh. *Yādōn ki Barāt,* Karachi, Kutub Printerz-o Publisherz, n.d.
al-Marghinani, Burhan al-din. *Al-Hidayah* (Arabic), 4 vols., Cairo, 1975
Al-Hidāyah, Fārsī Tarjumah Kardā, Kalkatta, A.H. 1221/A.D. 1806
Mohani, Sayyid Muhammad Jawwad. *Risalah-i Waqf alā 'al-Awlād-o Naql-i Dastawīz Waqfnāmah Murattabah-i ...,* Lucknow, Sayyid Akbar Husain, 1919
Muzaffar Husain, Muhammad. *Nāmah-i Muẓaffarī,* Lucknow, 1917
Nadvi, Sayyid Sulayman. *Ḥayāt-i Shiblī,* Azamgarh, Maarif, 1943
Naqsh-i Dilpaẕīr, An Anthology of Classical Urdu Poetry, ed. Muhammad Abd

history connect. They bring together "Islam" as a universal faith and "Islam" as it is practised in numberless congregations. The first view of Islam is the more common. Recent events, like the Iranian Revolution, only reinforced the emphasis on the seeming unity of Islam. Looking at the history of *awqaf* in India reminded us, however, of the second, particularist style in Islam. The controversy over endowments also pointed to the possibility that politics sometimes shaped "Islam" quite as much as "Islam" shaped politics.

by the standards they set forth. Muslim history provided few examples of the actualizing of those aspirations. Religious beliefs and practices were, as befits a living faith, diverse, sometimes contrary to scripturalist norms. Ironically, a state run by non-Muslims did much to spread and implement that vision of Islam, to confirm and encourage the work of generations of religious reformers.

The politicians who became official spokesmen for Islam in South Asia were men closely connected to the imperial government. Their close association with the raj meant that they were constantly exposed to the categorizations it employed. Most of them did not come from families which maintained a tradition of religious learning. They were the sons of local gentry and government servants. Most of them attended schools in which the curriculum followed British models. Indeed, many were lawyers trained in Britain. Their understanding of their own faith developed in the context of imperial institutions and their acceptance of scripturalist rhetoric seemed as much inspired by a sense of political strategy as it was by a genuine concern for Islam.

In the legal and political controversy over endowments, judges and administrators defended their view that a *waqf* must be "charitable" and "religious" by referring to the standards of Islamic orthodoxy. In defence of their position, Muslim politicians adopted similar logic. In the course of the debate, opponents exercised a subtle influence on each other so that, in the end, both employed similar presuppositions and concepts. Muslim scholars did not supply those arguments. After all, a significant number of them disagreed with the politicians. Even those who agreed had to be guided by the politicians so that they expressed themselves in effective legislative fashion.

Court decisions and political debates did not wholly displace the perspective which had originally determined the character of endowments in India. The pious still regarded the state with some apprehension. Local chiefs still tried to maintain their place in the social microcosms they lived in. The faith remained something practised in countless small town and neighbourhood mosques. The rituals endowments supported – *milads*, Muharram *majalis*, saints' death days and *fatihahs* for the souls of *waqifs*, continued as the most common expressions of devotion for ordinary Muslims. Muslim communities remained internally divided by class and culture. Even personal ill will between Muslims could still be found. These aspects of the reality of being a Muslim in South Asia did not disappear. But the politicians, religious reformers and imperial administrators developed and broadcast a discourse which lacked all of the nuances noted above.

Endowments stand at a point where two dimensions of Muslim

When disputed endowments were brought before the Anglo-Indian courts, they came under the purview of institutions which had few links to the local societies for which those *awqaf* were originally created. The courts, even at the district level, were part of a hierarchically organized system controlled by the imperial government. They considered the question of the nature of *awqaf* with two sets of law in mind. The first was formulated by the British for use in India. It paid particular attention to private property rights, rights whose definition was influenced by the growing importance of a market in which those same rights were bought, sold, inherited, mortgaged, gained and lost. The second set of laws derived from the court's understanding of *shariah* and the place it supposedly had in Muslim life. Though in practice Muslims did not always follow strictly the letter of *Quran* or the precepts of classical religious thinkers, Anglo-Indian judges assumed that Muslims should comply. Therefore, the judges usually insisted on the application of any clear rule they found. Where no such rule existed, as in the case of *awqaf*, they created one. In that way, the Anglo-Indian courts made judgments supposedly based on "Islamic law", but which actually bore little relation to the ways Muslims lived. For example, they posited a distinction between "public" and "private" endowments.

The raj also introduced a number of political innovations. The most prominent of these was a centralized, bureaucratic form of government which, like the courts, had clear lines of authority. The presence of this form of state was almost unprecedented in Muslim history. For example, *awqaf* in Muslim history often shielded individual property or religious institutions from the state's interference. Endowments pointed to the suspicion, even contempt, with which many pious Muslims looked at their rulers. But Muslim kings seldom managed to dominate completely either local elites or local religious establishments. The British empire, by contrast, commanded greater power than most sultans ever had. It was able to manipulate both petty leaders and religious institutions more effectively. The political controversy over endowments showed how the imperial government gained influence over the form which Muslim institutions took.

Although the Anglo-Indian government proclaimed itself religiously neutral, officials used "religion" as a key interpretive concept. Perhaps they over-applied it, used it in situations in which it was really irrelevant. Administrators seemed to favour an understanding of the religion of Islam derived from a scripturalist vision of that faith. Part of that religious ideal was the notion that Muslims constituted a world-wide community guided by the same rules derived from *Quran* and *shariah*. Every aspect of behaviour, including political life, was supposed to be directed plots of land, those alien laws and attitudes established a new foundation for the social, economic and political order.

Courts founded by the British empire enforced these new rules. They also operated with a highly abstract, textbook version of "Islamic law". Anglo-Indian judges rigorously invoked the rules on inheritance. Many Muslim notables apparently felt that they faced the prospect of having their lands divided among numerous heirs, some of whom were not part of their immediate families. Since the land provided their livelihood and their claim to authority in the communities in which they lived, most of these individuals feared that a loss of dominion (*riasat*) would follow a division of property. The men and women who created *awqaf* in the nineteenth and early twentieth centuries were caught between values generated in a tribute-based society and those of one moving towards capitalism. Though not necessarily the descendants of Mughal aristocrats, most founders of endowments defined their status in categories derived from the age of Muslim dominance. Their deeds of endowment tried to blend Mughal images of the "leader" (*rais*) with the demands the new laws made of "landlords". As in other times and places, *awqaf* seemed to promise continuity, the chance to smooth the adjustment from one regime to another.

Providing support for religious institutions and activities marked a leader. The chief who provided the money, food or other gifts distributed at ritual gatherings received popular recognition and respect. Whether those holy places or activities were inspired by the scripture and early history of Islam or by local traditions or by the desire to commemorate members of the founders' own families, an offer of food and a display of piety were part of an assertion of superiority. Likewise, the acceptance of food or use of facilities a patron provided expressed a bond of deference and dependence. For that reason, no easy distinction existed between the "private" concerns of a would-be chief and the "public" patronage he or she gave religion.

On both the material and spiritual levels, endowments benefited the people and places most familiar to their founders. Proximity to them established the priorities in distributing a *waqf*'s income. The donor's family came first, then kindred, dependants, members of the same sect or status group and the inhabitants of the donor's neighbourhood or town. A few very rich *waqifs* gave support to one or another translocal organization. Most often, each endowment involved complex sets of personal relationships between the founder and those a *waqf* sustained. Not surprisingly, the disputes which eventually led to legal challenges to endowments were rooted in the *waqifs*' own families or in the circle of their acquaintances and neighbours.

CONCLUSION

Conflicts were nothing new in the history of *awqaf*. Two kinds of disagreement seemed perennial. The first of those was purely personal, the result of inequalities, real and imagined, in the distribution of endowments' proceeds. The second sort of conflict involved the relationship of endowments to the institutions of religion and the state. While the sources of discord remained remarkably consistent, the context in which it occurred changed considerably. Because *awqaf*, in their many forms, proved effective in preserving the property and supplying the spiritual needs of Muslims, their importance tended to increase at those moments which marked a transition from one social or political system to another.

Kings, warrior–nobles, merchants and religious scholars in Egypt, Iran and Anatolia founded endowments to settle their property and support mosques, schools and shrines. While endowments for mosques and shrines were common in India before the arrival of the British, their use as a method of settling estates appeared to follow the imposition of British rule. Before that time, the character of property relations made them unnecessary. Most Muslims were too poor to establish *awqaf*. Where Muslim cultivators enjoyed some wealth, for example in Panjab, they usually followed customs of inheritance which prevented the division of land. Merchants, local chiefs and the states' warrior–nobles possessed sufficient wealth to create endowments, but it was generated by trade or control of the crops and cash which land produced, not by land ownership. A division of estates based mostly on moveables would have been easier than the carving up of land. Also, a number of sources pointed to the possibility that Muslims ignored the rules of inheritance found in the *Quran* or texts of *shariah*. No need arose for endowments which settled property in a way less egalitarian than the one the Holy Book commended.

The establishment of British rule gradually shifted the character of wealth and the social status connected with it. The possession of land became for many the measure of power and influence in society. The British introduced new rules governing the acquisition, control and loss of property. Though intended to safeguard individual claims to specific ticipants several lessons which they carried with them. It taught those who had seen the "new light" that they could work with traditional and not-so-traditional religious scholars. Aspiring leaders learned that they could bring different regional and ethnic groups together under the banner of religion. They learned too that political discourse based on an appeal to one faith, one community, one law camouflaged internal religious and social discord. They learned these lessons first in the courts and councils, but applied them effectively in the political forums which led to the establishment of the independent states of South Asia.

If the controversy over endowments in India seems insignificant today, it is only by contrast to weightier political events. The fall of empires, the movements of peoples, the divisions of territory and the creation of new states are by far more gripping history. Few in the here and now can relish a small irony in the placement of Lord Hobhouse's and Muhammad Ali Jinnah's portraits at Lincoln's Inn. Since both men went to the Bar from Lincoln's, their likenesses have a semi-prominent place in a corridor leading to the Inn's library. The Privy Councillor who made Muslim law and the barrister who founded a Muslim state face each other across six or seven feet of hallway. That their portraits' eyes are averted seems fitting. Yet the proximity of their images in that solidly British institution says as much about them and Muslim endowments as does their painted sideward gaze.

In August of 1913, the "Kanpur Mosque Incident" marked the beginning of an extended confrontation between government and more radical Muslim leaders. The incident, sparked by local government's encroachment on the precincts of a mosque, encouraged the radicals in their belief that the British had no respect for Muslims or their faith. Though a compromise was pieced together, the declaration of war against Turkey in 1914 brought a new round of government repression.

Because Muslim soldiers of the Indian army fought their Turkish brother Muslims in Palestine and Mesopotamia, the government feared that leaders in India would encourage Muslim soldiers to refuse to fight. Though its fears proved groundless, the government exiled or interned religious scholars, journalists and politicians. After the war, the Khilafat movement when joined to the Congress party's non-cooperation agitation presented the raj with a formidable challenge. By contrast, endowments seemed a minor issue.

The changing political status of wealthy magnates also contributed to the lack of action on family endowments. The Wakf Validating Act was designed to protect a fairly small body of landholders or merchant princes. Before 1913, political associations depended on the money and prestige of such men. During the Khilafat and non-cooperation movements, however, politicians discovered that mass contributions could support their activities as well as provide leverage by mobilizing thousands of individuals. They also realized that their better off patrons tended to be conservative. Since the landlords feared that political protest led to social protest, they were usually unwilling to challenge the British government. Before 1913, a close relationship to the government was an asset, but after 1919 it became a liability. Politicians were no longer interested in protecting the old-fashioned *rais*. Finally, in 1930, politicians got around to passing another law which extended the privileges of Jinnah's Act to *awqaf* created by 1913.

The Wakf Validating Act was the first, and probably the last, piece of "liberal" legislation passed during the raj. Soon after 1913, most politicians lost interest in moderate measures meant to encourage steady, but slow, economic and social progress. Creating a nation-state seemed the only way to bring real change. No one was sure what that state would look like, but the prospect of independence absorbed the energies of most politicians. As it turned out, several states emerged in South Asia, each connected with a particular creed.

Indeed, the emphasis on faith and the solidarity of confessional communities, so obvious during the legal and political debate over endowments, remained central during the struggles which led to the division of the subcontinent. Political success on the matter of *awqaf* taught the par-

Wakf Validating Act was not retrospective. For the majority of *waqf*-holders the Act's passage did not make their endowments more secure.

After 1913, the courts kept overturning *awqaf* on the ground that they benefited their donors' families. Since the terms of a *waqf* were supposed to be permanent, the courts did not permit the abrogation of old deeds and the drafting of new ones which would be covered by the Act. For example, in 1922, the Privy Council refused to uphold the Dacca Nawabs' *awqaf*, originally composed in the 1880s. Despite attempts to reach a compromise, members of the family continued to bicker about their shares. Those most distant from the family's main branch received comparatively small cash allowances. They realized that a division of the estate according to Quranic rules of inheritance would bring them more wealth. The courts, including the Privy Council, agreed with the disgruntled relatives and ordered that the property be divided among the Quranic heirs.[80] The Nawabs were among the most vocal supporters of Jinnah's bill. In the end it did not provide them with the protection they sought. Many other wealthy Muslims experienced a similar disappointment.

All the work involved in passing Jinnah's bill was not completely in vain. Politicians and British administrators gained some temporary advantages. The bill's passage allowed Muslim politicians to lay claim to a legislative victory. It put men like Jinnah in the limelight and provided them with the beginnings of a record of success on which to base further appeals for support.

The administration, surveying the political climate in the years 1911–13, dropped its opposition to the measure. The government had, after all, disappointed many Muslims when it revoked the partition of the Bengal province in 1911. When the province was divided in 1905, officials defended the separation of its eastern and western sections as a move designed to improve the lot of East Bengal's Muslims. Muslim politicians generally supported the partition, while non-Muslim Bengali nationalists opposed it. The nationalists resorted to boycotts and even violence against the British. When the province was reunited, many Muslim politicians, for example Muhammad Ali, felt betrayed. They argued that the government was not the best guardian of Muslim interests. They also noted that radical opposition succeeded while loyalists got a slap in the face. Perhaps the government believed that a legislative success would soothe Muslim feelings. If the passing of Jinnah's bill made a few politicians and landlords happy, events soon after it became law forced officials and Muslim leaders to consider weightier matters.

[80] Khajeh Solehman Qadir's case, *IA*, XLIX, 152ff.

Only one Muslim member, Malik Umar Hayat Khan, expressed some misgivings. He voiced the fear that *awqaf* would be used to avoid the ordinary rules which governed inheritance. The possibility that *awqaf* would be used to favour one family member over another also bothered him. He was, however, persuaded that the Validating Act was based on opinions found in the "sacred books" and therefore necessarily approved by every good Muslim. His approval was conditional. So long as a *waqf* did not encompass more than the one-third of an individual's property which the *shariah* allowed her or him to distribute according to their own wishes, he was prepared to give his support.[78]

The Khan Sahib must have been cat-napping during the proceedings or left the Act unread. Nothing in Jinnah's bill limited a *waqf* to one-third of an estate. Moreover, the documents submitted in the court cases showed that *awqaf* generally did limit or exclude regular heirs. In the end, the Khan Sahib swallowed his qualms and voted for the bill.

In the Council only one member spoke contemptuously about the Act and the motives which inspired it. C. Vijiaraghavachariar, a member from Madras, expressed the view that the Privy Council really had upheld Muhammadan law. Jinnah's bill was not the correction of a judicial error, but the creation of a new law. He did not object to the creation of new law, but he did protest the self-deception involved in this one. For one thing, he said that assertions of the unity of Muslim opinion were "poetic licence". (He must have been reading the newspapers.) Making an appeal for honesty, he urged that Muslims admit the Wakf Validating Act was intended to establish the right of primogeniture by the back door. He claimed that, in private, Muslims confessed that their aim was to establish the principle that the eldest son inherited an undivided estate. He implied that all the talk about sacred law was a smokescreen concealing the Muslims' real aim. He also warned that the Muslims might end up frustrated when they discovered that the "youngest wife" rather than the "eldest son" became the chief beneficiary of an endowment. Having said his piece, he noted that "it is a great thing to be in harmony", took his seat and voted in favour of Jinnah's bill.

Jinnah's bill passed into law unanimously on 17 February 1913. It was the first major victory of Jinnah's political career. Those who had *awqaf* were pleased. The associations were pleased. Their satisfaction was short-lived. Even before the Act's passage, a few people detected a serious flaw in the draft: it never specified that it applied to endowments founded before 1913.[79] This lacuna allowed the courts to rule that the

[78] *Ibid.*, 51, 36.
[79] (IO) L/J+P/1079.

lims. In works like *The Spirit of Islam*, Amir Ali presented an image of Islam as a progressive force in history. His book tried to prove that Islam was not a static creed and its adherents capable of initiating social or economic development. An admission that Muslims in British India adapted one of their institutions to suit contemporary conditions would have been more consistent with those views. Perhaps the reason for selecting the conservative line was political. The "modernist" argument might not have worked. Thus, Jinnah and his backers continued to operate within the conceptual universe created by the raj.

One argument advanced in the council was not based on a defence of the "orthodoxy" of family endowments. It was that the Privy Council's decisions against the institution spelled ruin for the Muslim landed classes. The assertion that endowments of this sort were of ancient origin implied that the institution was in large part responsible for the very existence of this class. For Jinnah and his supporters, the Privy Council's rulings amounted to "a revolution in the law of property under Muhammadan Law". Family endowments were presented as the only shelter available.

If a man cannot make a *wakf alalawlaud*, as it is laid down in our law, then it comes to this, that he cannot make any provision for his family and children at all and the consequences are that it has been breaking up Mussalman families.[76]

Jinnah put the blame entirely on the British, implying that family *awqaf* had existed undisturbed for centuries. Sir Sayyid was willing to place part of the blame on the families themselves. Also, we have seen that many *awqaf* ended up in the courts because of discontent within the family. But Jinnah blamed only the British courts or perhaps moneylenders interested in "hunting down" ancient *awqaf*.

Though his arguments were simplistic and consisted mostly of assertions about the law or the community or the ancient landlord families, the council let them pass, almost without challenge. Perhaps because his proposal came at the earliest stage of representative government in India, little opposition expressed itself. Perhaps non-Muslim members thought that their support on Jinnah's bill would be repaid at some later date with Muslim support for a measure dear to their hearts. Rai Sita Nath Roy and several other members did not oppose the measure, but wished to be sure that such endowments were not used to defraud creditors.[77] Even without the registration clause, Jinnah tried to reassure them by saying that according to Muhammadan law a debt encumbered estate could not be turned into a *waqf*.

[76] *PGGC*, vol. 49, 481, 483.
[77] *Ibid.*, vol. 51, 340–343.

As the bill's sponsor, Jinnah took the lead in arguing for its acceptance by the council. Amir Ali's textbook on Muhammadan law provided almost his only source of information on *shariah* and the history of endowments. Indeed, Jinnah's remarks often paraphrased passages of Amir Ali.[75] Neither of them argued with much reference to actual historical or social conditions. Like good advocates, they tried to establish the correct point of law. So Jinnah, like Amir Ali, appealed to the example of the Prophet whose sanction of the use of *awqaf* for the donors' families was reported in *hadis* literature. He repeated that authoritative texts approved and stressed that Muslims in Egypt and other countries used those endowments.

Like the British jurists whose rulings the Wakf Validating Act scotched, Jinnah focused on holy law and the unity of the Muslim/Muhammadan community. He emphasized that the practice of using endowments to benefit their founders' families was "ancient". Thus, he did nothing to contradict the common judicial and administrative perception of Muslims as traditionalists bound to follow a law unchanged for centuries. Because his approach confirmed the suppositions of Anglo-Indian judges and administrators, it was politically effective. Muslim leaders could not be blamed for choosing the line of argument most likely to obtain their goal.

In hindsight, however, Jinnah and the others might have chosen another way of presenting their case, one which did not depend on so abstract a reading of Islam or the people who professed it. Sir Sayyid, for example, tried to place the institution in the context of changing economic conditions in the Muslim world and India in particular. Sir Sayyid readily admitted that the use of endowments as family settlements suited the conditions created by British rule.

One problem in Jinnah's approach was that it did not address the seeming contradiction between the laws of inheritance and the ease with which a *waqf* allowed Muslims to ignore them. Hobhouse pointed to that difficulty in his judgment in Abd al-Fatah's case. Jinnah's stress on Muslim orthodoxy appeared to confirm Hobhouse's view that Muslims ought to obey their law. Sir Sayyid acknowledged the difficulty in his writings, but claimed that Muslims never followed the inheritance regulations rigorously. He also tried to give a historical explanation for that behaviour. Moreover, he argued that the British courts applied the law more strictly, which forced Muslims to fix upon endowments as a way of avoiding the excessive division of their estates. Jinnah simply ignored the difficulty.

Amir Ali and Jinnah considered themselves "forward thinking" Mus-

[75] Compare *PGGC*, vol. 49, 483, and S. A. Ali, *Mohammadan Law*, I, p. 2.

pamphlet on "Charitable Public Endowments by Muslims". In it, he argued that Jinnah and the others were encouraging a lie. While a *waqf* could be used for members of one's family, it was limited to "poor relations". He also mentioned his own experience in the courts which proved that *awqaf* were constant trouble. They were usually mismanaged and did no one any good.[71]

In addition to those who thought the principle bad, a few Muslims objected to the government getting involved with *shariah*. Only Muslims were competent to deal with it. If the law was passed, they feared that it would lead to further government encroachment.[72]

Throughout the period the bill was under consideration and local opinion being sought, the vernacular and English press displayed keen interest in the debate. Though most "Muslim" papers favoured the bill, a few did not. The arguments put forward in the press were similar to those noted above. Some objected to the government interfering with *shariah*.[73] Others pointed out that endowments were usually so badly managed that it was amazing anyone wanted to have one. Editors made frequent attacks on Shibli Numani. Some objected to his involvement, saying that he had no authority in matters of religion. Some complained that the Nadwah had taken to beating the drum for Aligarh by supporting this measure. They accused Jinnah of being "unrepresentative" and "unorthodox". Finally, some writers worried that women, whose property rights were already ignored, would be further victimized by permitting people to create this type of *waqf*.[74] In sum, many, not a "majority" perhaps but a significant number, found reasons for attacking Jinnah's *waqf* bill. Their criticisms were both theological and personal. They showed that religious principle and private animosity divided Muslims in India. Those dissenting opinions, however, seldom got a hearing in the Legislative Council. In that chamber, assertions of dogmatic and legal unity dominated the discussion.

The council formally discussed Jinnah's bill on three separate occasions. During the debate, supporters of the measure employed three arguments in its favour. The first was that a family *waqf* was religiously orthodox, an "ancient and universal practice" approved by the faith. The second was that the "Muhammadan community" was united in favouring passage of the bill. The third argument implied that without the power to use endowments to settle their estates, Muslim aristocratic families faced financial ruin.

---

[71] (NAI) *HJP B* (June 1911), 124.
[72] (IO) L/J+P/1079.
[73] *VPN* (1911), 885–886, 627.
[74] *Ibid.* (1912), 375, 451, 462, 470.

the measure. The Governor of the U.P. wrote that the Privy Council's decision should not be dismissed as it was "the highest judicial authority in the empire". "Is the Legislative Council a better authority on Muhammadan Law than the Privy Council?" asked one U.P. commissioner. Others claimed that the politicians never proved their point. The Privy Council was not in error because a few Muslim lawyers said it was.[70]

Justice Karamat Husain of the Allahabad High Court argued that Jinnah's bill bore no resemblance to Muslim law. If the Privy Council's objection was to perpetuities, then someone should pass a law allowing Muslims to violate that principle. Justice Piggott of the same court said he was in sympathy with Muslims, but had to uphold the wisdom of banning perpetuities. Justice Abd ur-Rahim of the Madras High Court had to admit that *awqaf* for one's progeny was permitted by *shariah*, but his personal opinion was that they were a bad device and should be avoided.

A few officials did support the measure. Otto Rothfeld, the collector of Broach, observed that Jinnah's bill was an example of the "lucidity and symmetry of Islamic Law". It was wonderful when contrasted to "the curious mass of illogical and contradictory elements by which the civil law of England still continues to be proped". (Small wonder he was in Broach.) A. G. Younghusband gave the most common official reason for supporting the measure. He noted that throughout the history of the raj, the impoverishment of Muslim families, not their aggrandizement, caused trouble.

Some local officials did take the trouble to consult a prominent Muslim or two. A few asked subordinates who happened to be Muslim. All their responses, often of essay length, were forwarded to the central government. In addition to personal statements, local organizations like the Anjuman-i Islam of Hoshiarpur or local branches of the Muslim League sent along memorials. Meetings were held in several towns to voice support for the measure. Most individual Muslims and most organizations favoured passage. But some notable exceptions appeared.

A *mawlwi* named Zahir ud-din wrote that the whole idea violated "the clear sense of the *Quran*". He argued that all "orthodox" Muslims were against the bill. The proposal itself was put forward by those who had received the "new light" of political ambition. He claimed that "an unholy alliance between Aligarh and the Nadwat" created the controversy.

Several High Court lawyers wrote to object. Muhammad Nizam uddin Hasan, a *vakil* of Calcutta, wrote and published at his own expense a

[70] (IO) L/J+P/1079.

As that administrative debate showed, the Government of India did not have a policy on Muslim endowments. Unlike the courts, the administration was not bound to follow the precedent of the Privy Council. Some officials agreed with it, others did not. Their disagreements meant that government made a series of *ad hoc* decisions on handling the political dimensions of the endowment controversy. The lack of a unified response enabled Muslim politicians to proceed with the attempt to push through Jinnah's bill.

Lord Harding, the Viceroy, and some of his senior advisers were more concerned about the mechanics of proposing legislation than the question of Muslim endowments. Other, more radical, proposals followed Jinnah's into the Legislative Council. For example, Gokhale drafted a law providing for the establishment of free, compulsory primary education in India. Harding thought that both measures pointed to the weaknesses of the Morley–Minto reforms. Giving non-official members too much legislative freedom provided them with the opportunity to embarrass the government. It would have to oppose both measures, thereby increasing its unpopularity. To prevent future incidents, Harding wanted amendments in the Morley–Minto regulations. He wanted a longer interval between a member's announcement of his intention to submit a bill and the formal consideration of it by the council. Also, he thought that members should be forced to provide a complete draft of a proposed law when they first gave notice.[68]

Administrative doubts and grumblings delayed immediate consideration of the Wakf Validating Act. The council turned it over to a special committee for study. Also, the secretariat circulated a draft of the measure through all levels of government, ordering local officers to return their own opinion as well as obtaining native views on it. As Gup described it, "Having minted the new coin of Moslem representation, the administration was reluctant to accept it as legal tender."[69]

An informal polling of officials and a few Indians hardly constituted a plebiscite, though it did give the government an excuse for putting off consideration of Jinnah's bill. Also, some officials who opposed the Act probably hoped to obtain more general support for their position. Many of the officials returned not a careful response, but a "The commissioner has the honour to state that he has no opinion." Higher officials and High Court judges showed a tendency to express a negative view. The Lieutenant Governors of Bengal, Bombay and the United Provinces, areas in which large numbers of endowments were located, all opposed

---

[68] *Ibid.*
[69] *Comrade*, 15 April 1911, 274.

ment agreed to consider a law "if generally approved by the Muhammadan community", Shibli and the others tried hard to fulfil its expectations.

A number of big landlords, whose interests were directly affected, lined up to give their support. The Nawab Salim-ullah of Dacca, whose father encouraged the introduction of this bill, was understandably eager to see it made law.[64] The merchant-*rais* Sir Karimbhai Ibrahim (Bart.) put his name behind the measure.

As a trustee of the Pirbhai *waqf* (see p. 151), Karimbhai witnessed the dismantling of an estate much like his own. He wanted to avoid the same wrangle over his wealth. Because the Wakf Validating Act was still pending, he was forced to resort to another approach. In February 1912, members of the Legislative Council introduced a special bill on Sir Karimbhai's behalf. The Sir Churimbhoy Ibrahim Baronetcy Bill allowed the baronet to preserve his property intact by granting immunity from the *shariah*'s regulations on inheritance.[65]

Karimbhai counted on the support of Jinnah, whom Karimbhai employed as an attorney in the Pirbhai suit. By happy chance, Fazlbhai Karimbhai, the baronet's son, had a seat on the Legislative Council. The Karimbhai Bill passed unopposed. A. K. Ghaznavi reminded the council, lest anyone missed the point, that were the Wakf Validating Act law, private legislation would be unnecessary.[66]

Though Jinnah's bill mustered a lot of vocal support, some administrators opposed it. In the Governor General's secretariat, officials held a debate similar to the one carried on when Sir Sayyid presented his *waqf*-bill over thirty years before. Opponents expressed the view that most Muslims did not favour Jinnah's Act. The opposition conceded that many Muslims approved of the principle of family endowments, but argued that Muslims did not like government meddling in matters connected with *shariah*. Just as in Sir Sayyid's day, officials thought it necessary to uphold the ban on perpetuities, while others believed that India's backward economic state and the politicial importance of the Muslim community outweighed legalistic scruples. Neither side showed any sign of yielding the point. One official memorandum outlined a compromise. It noted that government would eventually have to oppose Jinnah's bill. The government could not afford to contradict its own judiciary. But, in the short run, officials could safely give the appearance of neutrality.[67]

[64] (IO) L/J+P/1079.
[65] *PGGC*, vol. 51, 223.
[66] *Ibid.*
[67] (NAI) *HJP A* (March 1911), 182–183.

had to be for "charitable and religious" purposes. Jinnah's bill contained a clause stating that after the bill's approval dedications to members of one's own family would be considered as "charitable and religious". It was a legal incarnation of the proverb "charity begins at home". The Urdu–Persian version "awwal khwīsh ba'd darwīsh" ("first me and then beggars") was a little more pungent, but the principle was the same in both England and India.

Only one clause of the Act excited any opposition. That was a provision requiring the official registration of all *waqf*-deeds. Jinnah intended this limitation to still the fear expressed by some members of the Council that a *waqf* might be used to defraud creditors.[60] But texts of *shariah* put no such restriction on the power of an individual to create a *waqf*. The inclusion of this provision caused Gup to comment that the Bombay Duck "had forgotten what little he knew of Muslim law".[61] Shibli Numani even made a special trip to Bombay to argue the point with Jinnah.[62] He dropped the offending clause from the final draft of the bill.

Whether they were happy or unhappy about the *waqf* Act's author, the bill gave those in favour of family endowments a common focus. Now, when associations like the Muslim League held their meetings, they were able to pass resolutions which had a specific rather than a general intent. Resolutions favouring the passage of the bill were placed before those bodies and the results forwarded to the government.

The *ulama* gathered by Shibli Numani also began lobbying in favour of the Act. After 1908, he was able to enlist the support of scholars who did not belong to the *Nadwah*'s organization. In September of 1911, Shibli sent a letter to the Viceroy asking him to receive a delegation of Muslims who favoured passage of Jinnah's bill. Besides Shibli, the delegation included the following individuals:

1 Mawlwi Abd ul-Bari of the Firangi Mahal
2 Mawlwi Muhammad Husain of Deoband
3 Mian Muhammad Shafi (barrister from Lahore)
4 Mister Hasan Imam (member of the Congress Party, Bihar)
5 Mawlwi Rafih ud-din
6 Sahibzadah Aftab Ahmad Khan (Aligarh).[63]

The delegation's composition was obviously designed to show that Muslims all over the subcontinent favoured the measure. The inclusion of a Congress member and of scholars from three of the most important theological schools was proof of communal solidarity. Since the govern-

[60] *PGGC*, vol. 51, 340–343.
[61] *Comrade*, 23 March 1912, 258.
[62] Nadvi, *Ḥayāt-i Shiblī*, 547.
[63] (NAI) *HJP B* (September 1911), 190–192.

government would consider a legislative proposal, provided that it was "generally approved by the Muhammadan Community".[56]

Jinnah took Sir Harvey at his word and on 17 March 1911 he introduced the Mussalman Wakf Validating Act. At the time, some complained that Jinnah rushed the matter in order to further his own career. His proposal stole a march on Shams al-Huda, who was in the process of drafting a similar law.[57]

Though fellow politicians moved to support Jinnah's initiative, a few grumbled about his haste. Some of the most biting criticism appeared in the newspaper *Comrade*, which was edited by Muhammad Ali, a student of Aligarh and graduate of Oxford who later became a leader of the Khilafat movement. Muhammad Ali satirized the activities of the Legislative Council in a column titled "Gup", a shortened form of the Urdu word for "gossip", *gup-shup*. Gup, his mythical correspondent, claimed, like Falstaff, "as great a license as the wind to blow on who I please". Gup blew especially hard on the Legislative Council, calling it a "variety stage" and providing each of its members with unflattering nicknames. Gup referred to Jinnah as the "Bombay Duck", a name derived from a small dried and salted fish. As for the "Bombay Duck's" performance on the variety stage, Gup's review was that he "loved not to hear the voice of others so much as his own".[58]

Perhaps Jinnah took some consolation in the knowledge that he was not the only victim of Gup's breezy lampooning. Ali Imam, whom Gup called the "Moslem Dowager", was another frequent target. Ali Imam had just received the appointment of legal adviser to the council, a post which Gup described as a "two-*anna* share in the government". Ridicule aside, Ali Imam's presence in the official camp helped move Jinnah's bill along.

Gup's satire sometimes contained a serious undertone. In referring to the submission of the bill, he criticized Jinnah for rushing ahead, implying that it made Jinnah inattentive to the religious dimension of the issue. "The Bombay Duck", wrote Gup, "had not only his whole community behind him, but had left his religion behind him as well."[59]

Gup accused Jinnah of being loquacious and self-important, but the draft of his bill was neither long nor pompous. It took up only a page of small print. It was in sharp contrast to Sir Sayyid's effort, which was over twenty pages long. Jinnah's bill had only one purpose and that was to eliminate the ground on which the High Courts and Privy Council refused to recognize family *awqaf*. The courts declared that a valid *waqf*

---

[56] *PGGC*, vol. 48, 185.
[57] *Comrade*, 16 March 1912, 226, and Rahman, *From Consultation*, 189.
[58] *Comrade*, 15 April 1912, 274.
[59] Ibid.

Ali Jinnah, a newly elected Muslim member for Bombay, rose to ask a question of the government.

Are the government aware that there is a strong feeling prevailing amongst the Muhammadans against the present state of the system of the *wakf* law as expounded by the recent decisions of the Privy Council affecting in particular the system of *wakf aala ad awlaud*?[54]

Jinnah's interest in the issue of family *waqf* was based partly on his experience as a lawyer and partly on his own political ambition. In the case of Qasim Ali Jairajbhai Pirbhai, Jinnah served as one of the battery of advocates hired in the unsuccessful attempt to preserve a Bombay magnate's *waqf* (see p. 152).

Politically, Jinnah was numbered among the bright young men. He was noted for his oratorical skill, tenacity and good looks. Photographs of the period depict him dressed in his barrister's regalia of wig, tab collar and gown, or in stylish Edwardian frock coats. His politics were as British as his dress. Like many other leaders of the day, Jinnah received his formal training in England. While at Lincoln's Inn, he received as well a practical political education. He was involved in various "Indian" and "Muhammadan" student associations and took part in Dadabhai Naoroji's campaign for a seat in parliament. On his return to India, he first devoted himself to establishing a legal practice: "making his pile", he called it. But when that was accomplished, he began to work for prominent Bombay politicians. In particular, he was attached to Gopal Krishna Gokhale and once spoke of his desire to be a "Muslim Gokhale".[55] While in England he developed an admiration for the Liberal Party and was determined to pursue its style of politics in India. In short, Mr Jinnah seemed an unlikely spokesman for "orthodox" Islam, but that was precisely the role which he claimed throughout the subsequent debate on the subject.

His intentions were made clear in his initial statement. He did not allow the matter to drop after a single query. He asked the government whether it had any plans to satisfy Muslim discontent on the subject of family *waqf*. What steps, he asked, had the government taken to "bring the law on the subject into conformity with the texts and wishes of the Muhammadans?"

Sir Harvey Adamson answered for the government, saying that though the government was aware of some agitation in the Muhammadan community, it was not prepared to take any action which overturned the Privy Council's decisions. However, he added, the

---

[54] *Ibid.*, vol. 48, 185.
[55] H. Bolitho, *Jinnah*, 17ff.

changed a great deal after 1879. The increasing importance of associations, both Hindu and Muslim, an ever more vocal press and a series of government reforms altered the institutional context in which legislation was proposed and considered.

For those agitating for changes in the law of family *awqaf*, the "Morley–Minto reforms" brought significant political gains. In 1908, John Morley, a Liberal Party politician and the Secretary of State for India, started to plan a series of modest alterations in the way in which India was governed. With the grudging consent of the Viceroy, the Earl of Minto, he proposed that the number of "non-official" (read "Native") members on the Governor General's and Provincial legislative councils be increased. The administration appointed some of the new members; others were elected. The franchise was narrowly defined by qualifications of wealth and membership in particular civic bodies. Also, Muslims received separate representation.

In his public statements, at least, Morley was quick to deny that these measures were intended to introduce truly representative government to India. The commonly accepted view was that India's racial, historical, social and economic situation made it impossible to transplant the Westminster system without remodelling it to suit imagined differences between England and India.[52]

The first meeting of the reorganized Governor General's Council was held on 25 January 1910. Despite official modifications of the parliamentary ideal, the speeches of the Indian members made it clear that they considered themselves the representatives of particular regions, classes or interests. Mir Asad Ali, for instance, referred to himself as the representative of the Muslims of Madras. Malik Umar Hayat Khan claimed to represent the Muslims of the Panjab and the Raja Dighapatia billed himself as the representative of "Hindu and Muhammadan Land Lords of East Bengal and Assam".[53] Yet the constituencies were not that definite and these statements were rhetorical bids for a particular slot. One position which was still up for grabs was the representative of the "Muhammadan community".

The "question" was one element of parliamentary procedure which British officials considered safely exportable to India. In the British parliament, the question was a way for members, especially opposition members, to challenge the government's policies and actions. This vehicle was used to raise the issue of family *awqaf*.

One month to the day after the council's initial meeting, Muhammad

---

[52] S. A. Wolpert, *Morley and India*, 3, 131, 153.
[53] *PGGC*, vol. 51, 336, 337, 387.

or extravagant. Even if they did occasionally misuse funds, would their critics do any better? They had no proof that their system was an improvement. "The men of the new light", the editor wrote, were not so much interested in improvement as they were in diverting the money to suit their own tastes. If the present system was not perfect, at least it was free from meddling by the British government.[50]

An ambivalence towards the government marked the discussion of both public and family endowments. On the one hand, some participants looked to the government to provide protection of their interests and support for their causes. They saw its authority as a way of binding all the subcontinent's Muslims into a cohesive political force. At the opposite extreme were individuals who were suspicious of their British overlords. Their apprehension was not simply sullen contempt for an alien regime. Distrust of kings, nobles and governors was almost as old as Islam. For centuries, the pious criticized and condemned even Muslim rulers. India's British rulers tended to see opposition to their empire as an expression of the inherent religious fanaticism of Muslims. Officials like W. W. Hunter seemed to believe that a murderous zealot lurked within the breast of the most pacific looking Muslim.[51] Officials did not consider the possibility that their opponents were affected by a more profound and persistent dissatisfaction with all less than ideal states.

Doubtless the opinions of most Muslims fell somewhere between the poles of absolute loyalty and complete contempt. However, in the circumstances of colonial rule, their voices were not the ones most easily heard. Those who had little contact with the government had no hope of influencing the affairs of state. Politicians with some link to the British government had undisputed possession of the field. When it came to the consideration of questions on *awqaf*, the initiative belonged to those most committed to working within the institutional framework established by British rule. As the twentieth century proceeded, the government extended, ever so slightly, their opportunities to help in the moulding of law and policy.

The Mussalman Wakf Validating Act of 1913

In Sir Sayyid's day, imperial politics occurred in a clublike atmosphere. Sir Sayyid withdrew his *waqf* proposal after a number of private conversations with his friends in the administration. But the political landscape

---
[50] *VPN* (1909), 117.
[51] Hunter, *The Indian Musalmans*, 105–107.

same general accounting. If the government would not take a hand in ensuring the good management of endowments, then it ought to supply interested parties with a list of all the *awqaf* in India, thereby making it possible for private citizens to investigate custodians.[45] Delay was the official response to those demands. The administration perfected several variations of the stall. One was to insist that the league or organization involved take the matter up with the local government. Rather than petitioning the central secretariat, they should try to get satisfaction from the district officers concerned.[46] Another evasion was to insist that memorialists provide concrete proof that funds were being misused.[47]

The bureaucrats found it impossible to put off the associations permanently. The controversy eventually spilled over into the provincial and central legislative councils. "Native" members of those bodies had the right to question officials. Muslim members were not reluctant to use the privilege.[48] In 1909, Nawab Sayyid Muhammad, a member of the Governor General's Legislative Council, put in a request for a list of *awqaf*. The administration eventually supplied a list of only those endowments in which officials participated as custodians. The thirty-eight endowments mentioned were of two types.[49] Many of them were founded in the last quarter of the nineteenth century. Most were scholarship or hospital funds established by wealthy Muslims. The terms of these endowments stipulated that a government official serve as one of the trustees. The second sort were *awqaf* established by India's former rulers. The tombs of the Nawab-Wazirs of Avadh or a hospital founded by one of the former kings were examples. The British acquired management of these by default when they deposed the Nawabs.

Clearly, Muslim leaders were looking for something more than this short list of tame endowments. They wanted a catalogue of all existing *awqaf*. The government's final argument was that it would take too much time and cost too much money to prepare a complete listing. Thus, those who wished to use the funds of public endowments to further their educational and social programme were frustrated once again. Not until the 1920s, when Muslims had a greater voice in India's legislatures, were the first halting steps taken towards the registration and government supervision of *awqaf*.

The unreformed system of Muslim endowments did have a few defenders. The *Union Gazette* of Bareilly, for instance, published an editorial in 1909 which claimed that *mutawallis* were not really self-seeking

[45] *Foundations of Pakistan*, I, 82, 133, 199.
[46] (NAI) *HJP A* (January 1910), 230–232.
[47] *Ibid.* (August 1910), 7–10.
[48] *VPN* (1910), 425.
[49] (NAI) *HJP B* (April 1909), 36–51.

hazard *madrasahs* was a waste of money. Along with some of the graduates of Aligarh, he began to demand that modern schools receive a share of funds previously dedicated to the older system.

Sir Sayyid had confronted this issue during his life. He was asked why the *awqaf* funds already used for education were not redirected to pay for Aligarh and similar schools. Sir Sayyid objected to the idea. *Awqaf*, he said, were founded to teach *Quran*, theology and Persian. The people who created them had a right to see their bequests carried out to the letter. Even after the donors died, no one had the power to alter the terms of their establishments. *Awqaf*, according to Sir Sayyid, should continue to be used for religious education. He believed that newer schools would have to pay their own way by cultivating new financial sources. Sir Sayyid also opposed invoking the power of the government to effect changes. The government should not try to pressure custodians. The reformers should not attempt to pass laws which forced educational change.[40] Sir Sayyid did not wish to alter patterns of patronage to squeeze out *madrasah*-style schools.

In spite of Sir Sayyid's opposition, the pressure for change grew. For similar reasons, both Muslim and Hindu reformers supported legislation to make possible the shift of resources to modern education. In 1897, Anand Charlu asked the Governor General's Legislative Council to pass a law which increased the government's power to intervene in the management of "public charities".[41] In 1908, Rash Bihari Ghose offered a bill which made it easier for the general public to sue the custodians of trusts.[42] The government generally refused to respond to such proposals. A comment of H. H. Risley summed up the official attitude. He wrote that the best policy was "to do nothing".[43] An attempt by the government to interfere on a regular basis with public religious institutions would be like "putting a hand in a hornet's nest".

Attempts to pass laws giving either the public or the government greater power in the management of endowments failed for lack of official support. Politicians developed another tactic. Associations or individuals began asking the government to prepare complete lists of endowed institutions.

In 1910, the *Aligarh Institute Gazette* reported with approval on the efforts of political leaders to secure the names of all endowments' custodians. It also expressed the hope that the government would cooperate.[44] The Muslim League was actively engaged in pressing for the

[40] Sayyid Ahmad Khan, "Mutawalīyān-i Awqāf ki Taʻlīm ke Muʻtaliq" *Khuṭbāt*, 1, 606ff.
[41] (NAI) *Public Deposit* (March 1901), 31.
[42] (NAI) *HJP B* (April 1908), 26.
[43] (NAI) *Home–Public A* (March 1903), 115–121, and *HJP A* (September 1909), 94–95.
[44] *VPN* (1910), 884, and (1908), 155, 1048.

about how to change it. Political associations usually lined up behind the programme of one of those leaders. The different approaches of leaders were partly the source of the proliferation of those groups. With reference to Muslims in India, almost all of them agreed that they were economically and educationally backward, but they differed in their notions of how to improve the situation. To implement their plans, the reformer–politicians needed money and a platform on which to air their views. The large public endowments had wealth and provided access to an audience. Therefore, leaders and their supporters were anxious to acquire control or influence over the big endowments. But their different estimates of what to do with the funds put them in competition with each other. While they tried to come together on the issue of family *awqaf*, they found themselves divided over the future of charitable and religious endowments.

New lights for old: the debate over public endowments

The British in India never had a consistent policy for dealing with religious endowments. Some regulations forbade official involvement in Hindu, Sikh or Muslim religious institutions. The government was never eager to meddle in their affairs for fear of negative fiscal or political consequences.[38] At the same time, administrators seemed unable to avoid taking a hand in the affairs of temples, schools and the like. Disputes among trustees or complaints of mismanagement inevitably drew local officers into the affairs of larger endowments. That happened in the 1830s with regard to the Hughli *Imambarah* (see pp. 138–9). In that instance, government involvement led to a major reorganization of the institution. Even when officials did not disturb the functions of an endowment, they sometimes replaced managers in order to ensure that accurate accounts were kept. The shrine of "Mian Sahib" experienced a forced replacement of custodians (see p. 94). By 1900, many political leaders agreed with those officials who criticized the programmes supported by public endowments or who censured the behaviour of those entrusted with their management.

Amir Ali had some definite ideas about how the funds of public *awqaf* should be used. Amir Ali was a graduate of Hughli College. He evidently approved of the changes in curriculum which the British made in the Hughli *maktab*. He wanted money taken from the old endowments and spent to encourage "modern learning": the English language and European sciences.[39] According to Amir Ali, supporting the old, hap-

---

[38] I. J. Kerr, "The British and the Administration of the Golden Temple", 306–321.
[39] Shahid Husain Razaqi, *Sayyid Amīr 'Alī*, 101–102.

create new ones. The decline of Muslim rule caused some to think that God was punishing believers for failing to practise the faith purely.[35] In another way, Britain incorporated India into an expanding world empire. Improved communications made contacts easier and made possible more concrete expressions of the perennial ideal of a single, international Muslim community. Britain's empire builders tended to think of Islam in global terms which provided some with an added impetus to bring in outside help to settle Indian squabbles.

Even when supplied by the scholars of Mecca, *fatawa* rarely provided definitive solutions to disputed points. Religious scholars thrived on debate. Their opinions usually inspired contradiction by other scholars. Moreover, *fatawa* sometimes turned personal antipathies into theological contests. Also, the individuals seeking the views of the *ulama* could manipulate the form a *fatwa* took. They could rig the question to make certain that they would obtain a particular response. No one was immune to the use of that weapon. Sir Sayyid's enemies procured a *fatwa* in the Hijaz condemning him and his ideas.[36] But opinions issued in the Holy Cities also condemned those seeming pillars of orthodoxy, the *ulama* of Deoband.[37] Far from settling disputes, the verdicts of religious scholars usually added more fuel to the fires of controversy. As they busily solicited opinions both in and outside India, none of the politicians seemed interested in facing up to the possibility that the *fatawa* they got were not conclusive. The attempt to present the image of a united Muslim community threw together men who in other circumstances had little to agree upon. Shibli found himself in the same camp as Amir Ali. He even had to quote with approval the latter's views. Though on previous occasions Shibli ridiculed Amir Ali, in this instance unity was a more pressing need.

Though leaders tried to hide it, Muslims did disagree on the question of using endowments as family settlements. Nor were they able to conceal serious conflicts over those *awqaf* which supported mosques, schools and shrines. The controversy over family endowments served only to encourage debate over the more public endowments. Their involvement in the first type sharpened and focused their interest in the second. The individuals and associations taking part in the discussion of public *awqaf* were the same, but the stakes were different.

In the early twentieth century, political leaders in India were also social reformers. Each of them had a pet theory to explain the condition of the society in which he lived. More importantly, each had an idea

[35] Ahmad, "Political and Religious Ideas of Shah Waliyullah of Delli", 22–30.
[36] Lelyveld, *Aligarh*, 132.
[37] B. D. Metcalf, *Islamic Revival*, 307–311.

were actually used in India or anywhere else in the Islamic world. Unlike Sir Sayyid, Shibli displayed no interest in the social and economic conditions which influenced the use of *waqf*. He dealt with the problem as an abstract religious issue and supplied the same material that Amir Ali introduced years before. His approach was similar to the courts. The only difference was that they ruled "Nay" while Shibli wrote "Aye." Ironically, both paid no heed to Sir Sayyid's efforts to explain endowments in a way that made sense to British judges.

The 1908 meeting proposed that the opinions it approved be circulated among all the *ulama* in India. They wanted all of them to sign one or another of those *fatawa*. Shibli's biographer claimed that thousands of scholars did signify their approval. Government records indicated that the number was inflated. However, during the entire process, no one mentioned those religious scholars who disapproved of *waqf-i awlad*. Some had refused to take part in the first place. Others did not consent to its declarations. Outside Shibli's circle, *ulama* (for example those connected with the Ahl-i Hadis movement) continued to argue that the *shariah* forbade such endowments.[33]

In a quest for a religious authority which would convince the British government, some politicians turned to *ulama* from outside India. In 1911, under the leadership of Khwajah Abd al-Majjid, the Muslim Brotherhood of Progress in London requested a *fatwa* from three Egyptian scholars: Mawlwi Muhammad Ashur Bukhari, the grand Mufti of Egypt, Muhammad Mujib, the Chief Qazi of Alexandria, and Muhammad Shakir, the Vice-Principal of the school of Al-Azhar mosque. The message, "What do the learned say... Zaid created a *waqf* of all his properties for generation after generation..." travelled from London to Egypt. The three scholars despatched favourable *fatawa* back to London and these were presented to the Government of India.[34]

During the long years of Muslim political dominance in India few Muslims solicited *fatawa* from other parts of the Muslim world. Distance made it unlikely that scholars in other areas would understand the conditions prevailing in India. Since the Mughal emperors declared themselves the refuge of the caliphate, Muslims in India had little reason to acknowledge their inferior status by consulting foreign scholars. Of course the pilgrimage and the comings and goings of religious scholars maintained links with the Holy Cities, but in matters of *shariah* Indian Muslims seemed to accept the authority of their own scholars.

The advent of British rule seemed to strengthen existing ties and

---

[33] *Fatāwa-yi Ahl-i Hadīs*, III, 94–98, and Rahim, *The Principles of Muhammadan Jurisprudence*, 177.
[34] (IO) L/J+P/1079.

type described in the question was proper. In addition to providing the expected moral verdict, the opinions supplied some political ammunition. One *alim* argued that the sources of the Hanafi school were clear on the subject of *waqf*. The Imam Abu Hanifah had not really condemned the institution, nor was there disagreement between Abu Hanifah and his disciples. Another major concern expressed at the meeting was that the correct form be used in establishing a *waqf*. Finally, a number of scholars expressed the view that it was completely wrong to allow Hindu and British judges to give decisions on points of *shariah*. That was a duty which only the *ulama* were properly able to fulfil.[31] The scholars ignored the potentially divisive issue of whether Muslim judges who had no training in *shariah* could speak on such matters. Perhaps the scholars would have denied their authority as well.

In addition to publishing *fatawa*, the meeting at the Nadwah came up with several proposals for continuing the agitation. Participants agreed to establish a national association for *waqf ala al-awlad* and named Shibli its president. They appealed for contributions to carry on its work. Finally, they suggested that an essay on the subject be prepared in Urdu, circulated among the *ulama* and published in newspapers. The essay should then be translated into English and presented to the government. Shibli assumed the burden of composing an "authoritative" essay which he published in 1910.

Shibli's essay on the problem of family *awqaf* was very different from the one Sir Sayyid composed thirty-three years before. Sir Sayyid's essay did not pay much attention to the *shariah*. He was content to quote a few passages from textbooks. His main interest was to describe a deed of *waqf* which would stand up in British courts. Shibli, on the other hand, concentrated wholly on the question of religious law. His essay contained none of the practical focus of his old friend's work. He began it by describing the High Courts' and Privy Council's decisions on endowments. He also quoted Urdu translations of long passages from the judges' opinions. Having laid out their views, he pointed out that the judges had always assumed that Muslim sources were unclear about the institution. The rest of Shibli's essay was an attempt to demonstrate that the sources were very clear. Shibli spent a few pages quoting from the *hadis* literature. He repeated all the stories, like that of Hazrat Umar (see pp. 10–11), which showed that *awqaf* in favour of the donor's own family were used in the time of the Prophet. Shibli quoted from a number of texts on the *shariah* to prove that the *ulama* of the past had permitted the institution.[32] Shibli's essay was an exercise in intellectual history, but made no attempt to describe the way in which such *awqaf*

[31] *Ibid.*, 5–7.
[32] Shibli Numani, "*Waqf-i Awlād*", *Maqālāt*, 1, 81–102.

to Sir Sayyid's interest. According to his biographer, Shibli did not turn his attention to the problem until 1908. At that time Shibli posed three questions to himself.

1. Was it really a religious problem or not?
2. How could the government be made aware of the truth?
3. Could the opinion of the Privy Council be overturned?

The second and third "questions" were really points of strategy – only the first was a genuine question. Once Shibli answered it in the affirmative, he set about working on the tactics to accomplish the aims mentioned in his second and third statements. His first letters were not addressed to members of the *ulama*, but to old Aligarh associates such as Ali Imam, Wiqar ul-Mulk and Sayyid Husain Bilgrami. With their encouragement Shibli began to organize the *ulama* with whom he was in contact. The vehicle he used to gather them was the Nadwah al-ulama.[29] The Nadwah was founded in 1894 as an association of *Sunni* scholars. The group established its own *madrasah* at Lucknow.

In November of 1908, Shibli organized a meeting of *ulama* at Lucknow. The meeting itself showed how easily the traditional methods used by religious scholars mingled with the political protocol of the period. The *ulama* who attended the meeting were asked to give a *fatwa* on the question of *waqf ala al-awlad*. They were presented with a question similar to that usually posed to a single scholar. The religious sanction attached to a formal opinion jostled with the need for the instant consensus of a political caucus. The traditional *fatwa* was a moral judgment on a particular action. In this instance, it was not so much a moral opinion that Shibli sought but a political statement on the "law" involved. An opinion on which a large number of scholars agreed would impress the administration.

A question was presented to the assembly in the same form used for centuries in requesting a *fatwa*.

What do the *ulama* of the faith and the *muftis* of *shariah* say, if someone makes a *waqf* of his own property which benefits him [and] the profits [of the property] will always be given to his progeny and the progeny of his progeny, then is this *waqf* good or not? The answer should be according to the Hanafi *fiqh*.[30]

Scholars did not easily abandon their old habits. Several of the prominent ones insisted on formulating individual opinions. The less well known signalled their assent to one or another of the leaders. Shibli himself, whose claim to recognition as an *alim* was tenuous, did not submit an opinion. The *fatawa* read at the meeting concluded that a *waqf* of the

---

[29] Nadvi, *Ḥayāt-i Shiblī*, 541–543.
[30] *Fatāwa-yi 'Ulamā'-yi Hindūstān*, 1–4.

question of family endowments. He charged that it really knew that Muslim law approved of them as a method of settling estates, but preferred perpetuating a falsehood to telling the truth. Lord Stanley's verbal assault was so harsh that the Lord Chancellor ordered him to moderate his tone or sit down.[27]

The British public generally had little interest in Muslim or Indian affairs, except when they involved war or peace. On a subject so esoteric as family endowments, even the ranting of an eccentric peer probably did not generate much enthusiasm. The publicity which the issue got in England was important, not so much because it moved the British, but because it encouraged Muslim politicians. Favourable attention seemed to confirm the validity of their approach. It encouraged a further appeal to the faith of Islam, its religious law and religious history, for it was that style of argument which excited the most positive response. It also carried the most political weight in India.

By the end of the first decade of the twentieth century, the judges and the lawyer–politicians had limited the issue of family *awqaf* to a question of religious authority. The courts gave one estimate of Muslim orthodoxy. When it became a political issue, politicians introduced another. But their view was simply an antithetical statement on the nature of orthodoxy. Some authoritative voice had to confirm one or the other.

Most of the lawyers, judges and politicians who contributed their views on Muslim orthodoxy were not trained in the traditional fashion. They had little, if any, claim to authority in matters connected with the *shariah*. For that reason, in the early years of the twentieth century an effort was made to involve the *ulama* on the question. In Sir Sayyid's day, a few *ulama* supported his *waqf* proposal, some opposed it. A comparatively small number took a stand either way, indicating that most scholars completely ignored the issue, Collections of the *fatawa* of religious scholars in India contained both favourable and unfavourable statements on the institution.[28] The problem which the politicians faced was not only how to get the *ulama* to speak, but how to get them to say the right thing.

On the *waqf* question, Shibli Numani provided the crucial link between English educated politicians and traditionally educated *ulama*. Shibli had been a teacher at Aligarh. Despite his early association with Sir Sayyid, his involvement in the *waqf* controversy was not connected

---

[27] (IO) L/J+P/1079. This thick volume contains most of the papers on Muslim endowments sent from India to London.
[28] Compare Abd al-Hai, *Fatāwa*, 264–267, and Mawlana Nazir Husain (an *alim* connected to the *Ahl-i Hadīs*), *Fatāwa-yi Nazirīyah*, 126–127.

awqaf figured prominently in his inaugural address to the London branch of the League.[25]

In addition to the Congress and League, Indian students founded smaller, more informal associations like the Muslim Brotherhood of Progress. Such groups gave young men a chance to serve a political noviatiate. As newcomers to politics, they usually adopted positions similar to those of senior leaders. On the question of family *awqaf*, they had the same opinions. The "Muhammadan law", especially as preached by Amir Ali, provided them with a convincing brief. Claims of doctrinal certainty and communal solidarity made it a very good issue to pursue within the context of colonial politics. So petitions and resolutions from smaller organizations in England joined those forwarded from India.

Muslim politicians received some assistance from Englishmen, including a number of retired judges who once served in India. Sir William Comer-Pretheram, for instance, served as Chief Justice of both the Allahabad and Calcutta High Courts. During his time on the bench, he heard cases involving family *awqaf* (see p. 143). He always took the view endorsed by the Privy Council. After his return to England, however, he changed his mind on the issue. In articles like one published in the *Law Quarterly* of 1897, he expressed the view that family endowments really were permitted by the *shariah*. He repudiated his earlier decisions against them and added his voice to those calling for a revalidation of the Muslim right to make such endowments.

Sir Raymond West, who sat on the Bombay High Court, was another former justice who provided help in publicizing Muslim demands. West invited Khwajah Abd al-Majjid, then a law student, to deliver a paper on the subject of "*Wakf* as Family Settlement" at a meeting of the Society of Comparative Legislation. Abd al-Majjid's paper was mostly a repetition of the arguments which Amir Ali had been making for fifteen years. Abd al-Majjid described the institution as an old Arab method of settling property, one which preceded the coming of the Prophet. Though other scholars disputed his views on *waqf*'s origins, Abd al-Majjid was correct when he used *awqaf* as proof that the *shariah* was capable of development and change.[26] Also, delivering his paper to a public meeting of a learned society provided a chance to make the case before an audience which included Britons.

The issue of family endowments even acquired a sympathizer in the House of Lords. Lord Stanley of Alderly, who described himself as a convert to Islam, took the Indian government to task for lying on the

[25] Rahman, *From Consultation*, 95, 164–165.
[26] Syed H. R. Abdul Majid, *England and the Moslem World*, 122–146.

necessarily striking at the basic character of Anglo-Indian law or the courts. Delegates at the seventeenth meeting of the Indian National Congress in 1901 raised the matter of Abd al-Fatah's case. They used it to demonstrate that British jurists erred because they did not understand or sympathize with Indian laws. But the resolution the Congress passed called for the appointment of more Indian judges, not an overhaul of the legal system.[22] No one noted the possibility that Indian judges trained in British law schools might be as ignorant of Indian legal systems.

From the time of its foundation, the Congress claimed to represent all Indians, Muslims included. However, it always had some difficulty in drawing Muslim members. The founding of the Muslim League in 1906 made it even harder for the Congress to attract Muslims. The Congress leadership realized that their organization would have to give more attention to the issue of Muslim endowments in order to make a credible appeal to Muslims. At its 1906 session, the fifth resolution passed by the Congress called upon the government to correct the legal error committed by the Privy Council in 1894. Speaking in favour of the resolution, Mawlwi Abd al-Qasim called the resolution proof that Muslim interests were best furthered by the Congress, not the League. The Mawlwi's speech on endowments attacked the League. He said that it was likely that the League's meeting would not address the issue. The League, he said, was too loyal to the British to adopt a position which criticized a government institution. Abd al-Qasim was so eager to impugn the League that he claimed it would oppose any change in the decisions on Muslim endowments simply because the Congress favoured one.[23]

Abd al-Qasim was probably trying too hard to impress Muslims with the Congress's concern for them. The League did take up the matter of family endowments. Like the Congress, the League was thick with lawyers as founding members and leaders. Some of the League's members were involved in lawsuits on the matter. The Nawab Salim-ullah, Ahsan-ullah's son, was one of the founders of the League. He served as its president. It was hardly surprising that every year the League passed another resolution about family *awqaf*.[24]

Indian students, many of them aspiring barristers, brought the programme of association politics to England. The Muslim League established its London branch in 1908, the same year that Amir Ali arrived in the capital to take a seat on the Privy Council. The question of family

---

[22] *Report of the Seventeenth Indian National Congress* (Calcutta, 1901), 106.
[23] *Report of the Twenty-Second Meeting of the Indian National Congress* (Calcutta, 1907), 68–70.
[24] *Foundations of Pakistan*, I, 24, 231ff, and Rahman, *From Consultation*, 82.

The style of those memorials and petitions was usually the same. They were firm, but polite. They constantly spoke in the soft, indirect voice of moderation. The repetition of the words "humbly" or "respectfully" implied only quiet, law-abiding criticism. By nature, petitions were not the tools of revolution. They did not question the basic premises of colonial rule in India. They did not dispute the legitimacy of Britain's authority. They did not even attempt to challenge the government's right to enforce the "Muhammadan law" in a system of courts which operated without the sanction of the *ulama*. The petitions concentrated on the single point of family endowments. They did not criticize the structure of the courts. In the case of *waqf*, they respectfully pointed out that the courts were in error on the question. The petitions did not employ subtle arguments designed to prove the point, but employed broad assertions about the "Muhammadan community" and the validity of *waqf ala al-awlad* according to the law which that community faithfully followed.

For many years these petitions had no noticeable effect on the way in which the government treated the issue. The administration seemed at least as slow as the judiciary. Perhaps officials had an even keener interest in delay. While a judge might claim that lengthy deliberation served the ends of justice, an administrator might hope that memorialists exhausted themselves in waiting. Officials always dawdled before replying to the petitions. The National Muhammadan Association sent its first memorial in 1894. It sent another in 1900.[20] After a suitable period of delay, the government returned a statement expressing its unwillingness to question a decision taken by the empire's highest judicial authorities. Officials also added that the "community" as a whole did not appear interested in obtaining a change.

The press began to comment on the *waqf* issue soon after the Privy Council's decision in Abd al-Fatah's case. In its criticism the press was often more direct than the associations. For instance, in 1897, the *Paisa Akhbār* (*Penny News*) of Lahore referred to the case. It did not make assertions about whether or not the *shariah* approved of the institution. It did not mention the community's unanimity. The issue which the *Paisa Akhbar* focused on was the right of an individual to dispose of his property as he pleased. The British courts were unfairly trying to limit that right.[21]

The *Paisa Akhbar* found another reason to attack the decision. It was made by judges who were completely ignorant of Indian customs and conditions. In questioning the competence of judges, critics were not

[20] (NAI) *HJP A* (July 1900), 104–105.
[21] *VPP*, x, 737.

singh (see pp. 67–8), drafted a deed under the terms of the Settled Estates Act.

In a letter to the government dated 11 June 1893, the Nawab Ahsanullah presented his opinion of the Act. It might have been a fine idea for all he knew, but it did not solve his problem. He did not need a new law, he wrote, but a way of maintaining the endowments already in existence. How was it possible to keep them from being challenged and invalidated in the courts of law?[17]

The government had not satisfied the Nawab Ahsan-ullah by passing the Estates Act. But it had inadvertently supplied him with an argument. The Settled Estates Act proved that the rule against perpetuities was not inviolable. It could be set aside when political circumstances required. Nawab Ahsan-ullah, Amir Ali and their supporters had to find a way of making Muslim endowments a political issue. India's political associations became the vehicle to accomplish that aim.

Associations, endowments and the Indian government, 1893–1910

As the wealthiest Muslim landlord in the Bengal province, the Nawab Ahsan-ullah commanded much influence. His contributions to fledgling social reform and political organizations guaranteed him a hearing and support. In Calcutta in the 1890s the two most important associations were the Muhammadan Literary and Scientific Society, founded by Abd al-Latif, a former government servant, in 1863 and the National Muhammadan Association, founded by Amir Ali in 1878. Each of them attracted a different class of member and emphasized somewhat different social agendas. Also, their respective founders disliked each other.[18]

The Nawab's eminence transcended petty rivalries. His connection with Amir Ali was established. He also maintained a cordial relationship with Abd al-Latif. The Nawab managed to get the two groups, which rarely agreed on anything, to despatch almost identical memorials protesting the terms of the Bengal Settled Estates Act. Both of them claimed that the Act violated basic provisions of the *shariah*. It was not a substitute for family *awqaf*. "Muhammadans" had their own law and a solution had to be found within that system.[19] They asked that government turn its attention to solving the problem created by the High Courts' decisions.

They were only the first of many petitions sent to the government by associations which claimed to speak for India's Muslim community.

[17] (NAI) *HJP A* (January 1894), 340–345.
[18] A. Seal, *The Emergence of Indian Nationalism*, 309–313.
[19] (IO) L/J+P/367.

argued that the rule against perpetuities had precedence. The free flow of property was essential for economic progress and most "modern" societies rejected permanent limitations on the transfer of land ownership. Some made the additional point that the measure would destroy the credit of landholding families. What moneylender having a moiety of his wits would extend credit without collateral?

Since the Settled Estates Act originated in government circles, arguments against it did not prevent its passage into law. Those who supported the measure refuted the opposition. Following the evolutionary arguments of H. S. Maine, some of the proponents argued that India was not a modern society. "The social condition of the native population of India does not differ greatly from that of the people of England under the Plantagenets... [when] the use of perpetual and unbreakable entails was the rule in England," wrote one officer eager to see law enacted.[16] A concern for the continued prosperity of a select number of influential men probably carried greater weight than any theoretical argument. Within the administration a strong lobby always existed for any measure designed to protect India's "natural aristocracy". Critics of such favouritism made themselves heard, but as the swift passage of the Settled Estates Act indicated, officials who supported the big landholders were usually more powerful.

The powers granted a settlor by the Act of 1894 were similar to those implicit in a *waqf*. A landlord turned his estate into a perpetual trust. His immoveable property remained undivided. The settlor gave all of his children and dependants only cash stipends while reserving for himself full control and the right to name an heir, usually his eldest son. From the landlords' point of view, those advantages were offset by several drawbacks. To be protected by the Act the landholder had to submit a detailed list of his property. He had to specify in writing the terms for succession and the cash allotments. Once made, those provisions were difficult to change. Most of Bengal's landlords apparently thought that the Act gave the government a licence to meddle in their affairs. In spite of the close ties which many magnates had with the government, they seemed unwilling to let it have any control over their property and family affairs. Also, they had no wish to surrender flexibility. Bengali landlords did not, therefore, flood the provincial authorities with applications to have their holdings placed under the Act. Between 1894 and 1900, only four landlords asked to be included. The Tagores were the first, but the Nawab Ahsan-ullah of Dacca refused to join them. Only one Muslim *zamindar*, Nawab Ali Chaudhri of Mymen-

[16] *Ibid.*, also (NAI) *HJP A* (January 1894), 340–345; (July 1907), 157–159, 177–178.

ficials and important lawyers like Amir Ali. The Nawab's willingness to help was magnanimous, since Abd al-Fatah was suing him. Clearly, the Nawab's interest was not in his nephew's endowment, but in his own family's *awqaf*. When the court refused to allow Abd al-Fatah's plea, the Nawab's voice was among the first heard in protest. The Nawab began writing letters to the government which pointed out that the High Court's judgment seriously affected the estates of a number of leading Muslim families.[13] Though the letters did not stress the decision's impact on his own family endowments, they drew official attention to the question.

Government intervention had saved the *awqaf* of the Dacca Nawabs once before. In 1879, some of the family claimed that the funds allowed them under the terms of the original deeds of *waqf* were insufficient. They brought suit and the legal arguments were heard in 1881. Before a decision was given, friends of the Nawab's family, including Sir Ashley Eden, the Lieutenant Governor of Bengal and the Dacca district magistrate, intervened. They managed to persuade the aggrieved parties to agree to a negotiated, out of court settlement.[14] A new set of deeds was drawn up, but this did not eliminate discontent. The Nawab Ahsanullah (Khwajah Abd al-Ghani's successor) feared that these delicate arrangements were endangered by a decision against the principle of family *waqf*. Nawab Ahsan-ullah had the ear of Bengal's officials. His protests soon set the wheels of the state's machinery in motion. What the administration proposed first was a special Act which would meet the Nawab's requirements.

Arrangements with the *taalluqdars* and laws such as the Bundelkhand Encumbered Estates Act demonstrated the government's willingness to grant legal immunity to politically important groups. In this instance, the Bengal government knew that other prominent landholders had troubles similar to those of Nawab Ahsan-ullah. For instance, the inheritance of Maharaja Sir Jotendra Nath Tagore's estate was contested in the courts. Some members of the provincial government wanted to pass a law to prevent the fragmentation of the estates of the richest landholders. The Bengal Settled Estates Act of 1894 was the result of their concern.[15] Any estate placed under the protection of that law was immune from partition by the rules of inheritance of *shariah* or *dharmasastra*. The Act also restrained creditors' rights to seize assets for debt.

As with Sir Sayyid's *waqf*-law, once the Settled Estates Act was proposed, it drew criticism from a few members of the government. They

---

[13] (NAI) *HJP A* (May 1893), 47–55.
[14] *Khajeh Solehman Qadir* v. *Nawab Sir Salimullah Khan Bahadur, IA*, XLIX, 152–160.
[15] (IO) L/J+P/345, papers related to *Bengal Settled Estates Act*.

"perpetuities of the worst sort".[10] Sometime during the years that followed, Amir Ali changed his mind about the wisdom of family endowments and lost his fear of perpetuities.

British officials were not agreed on the value of the idea. Fitzpatrick, the secretary of the Council, seemed to be leaning in favour of it, but several others took the opposite view. They thought the prohibition on perpetuities traditional in British law a sufficient reason for refusing to consider the measure. An official of the Revenue Department expressed the fear that such a law would allow landlords to escape the land tax. Without the fear of confiscation and sale how was it possible to ensure the prompt payment of revenue? As for Sir Sayyid's argument that noble families were being ruined, some officials felt that this was the unfortunate consequence of the operation of the law of property, but not a sufficient reason to change the laws. One officer pointed out that were such a law in operation, the "junior members" of rich families would be at a tremendous disadvantage. Passing Sir Sayyid's proposal seemed to balance one evil by fostering another.[11]

Though the officials did not agree on the merits or demerits of Sir Sayyid's proposal, they did share several assumptions. The most important of these concerned the existence of a "Muhammadan community". Another was that this community possessed a divinely revealed law which included certain prescriptions about inheritance. As for Sir Sayyid's place in this picture, he was an individual far in advance of the rest of the community. The pamphlets and arguments against Sir Sayyid seemed to confirm that the majority of the community opposed his ideas on religious grounds.

The opposition of critics and the advice of his British friends in the administration led Sir Sayyid to withdraw his proposal.[12] His attempt was not completely forgotten. Later, when the idea of putting a law of family *waqf* on the books was revived, his effort was remembered. However, very little of the form of his draft bill was employed. More importantly, later proposals had little of his pragmatic focus.

Politically, the problem of family endowments remained in the background between 1879 and 1893, when the Calcutta High Court ruled against Abd al-Fatah. The revival of interest in the issue had much to do with that case. Abd al-Fatah was the maternal grand-nephew of the Nawab of Dacca. Before instituting the suit, Abd al-Fatah sought the counsel and financial support of his great-uncle. The Nawab's prominence also meant that Abd al-Fatah was able to consult government of-

---

[10] Letter of Amir Ali in (NAI) *HJP B* (April 1880), 73.
[11] (NAI) *HJP B* (October 1879), 44–45.
[12] Sayyid Sulaiman Nadvi, Ḥayāt-i Shiblī, 538–539.

sition would arise to Sir Sayyid's plan. He pointed out that most of the *ulama* of India were poor. They would therefore have little personal interest in the measure. However, the *ulama* were also "extremely bigoted" and likely to oppose it just because it was Sir Sayyid's idea.

Expectations of opposition proved correct. Pamphlets attacking Sir Sayyid's proposal appeared as soon as it was publicized. Especially prominent among his critics were members of the group sometimes called "Wahabis" but who called themselves "Muhammadis". This group was generally opposed to British rule. They sometimes supported armed resistance to it. Sir Sayyid's close personal and political connection to the British government earned their anathema upon all his words and deeds.[7] Others also attacked his plan. At least one member of the Firangi Mahal school in Lucknow wrote against the bill.[8] Apart from a general abhorrence of Sir Sayyid, criticism focused on the "evil intent" which the critics detected in the proposed law. They argued that for *shariah* the intention behind any action was the basis for considering it good, bad or neutral. The proper intention for creating a *waqf* was the wish to attain spiritual merit. When that was the aim, a *waqf* was approved. But the kind of *waqf* which Sir Sayyid advocated had the intention of escaping the duty of following the rules of inheritance. Such *awqaf* were therefore "bad", not legally, but morally. This sort of criticism had little practical value, since it was difficult to tell one sort of endowment from another. The government's anticipation of conflict perhaps gave greater weight to the criticisms than they deserved. Nobody seemed interested in discovering whether any religious scholars supported Sir Sayyid.

Amir Ali raised a number of milder objections. At that time Amir Ali was still a Calcutta advocate. He wrote to recommend that Sir Sayyid's plan be rejected. Amir Ali's views in 1880 were in sharp contrast to those he later expressed. At the time he wrote, he was involved in defending the *awqaf* of the Dacca Nawabs. Some dissatisfied members of the family were about to challenge the endowment. Amir Ali was instrumental in arranging an out of court settlement which temporarily saved the Nawabi endowments.[9] He wrote to say that he thought Sir Sayyid's motive in proposing the bill was a "good one". His objection was that Sir Sayyid's bill went far beyond the letter of the *shariah*. In 1880, Amir Ali had a further objection based on his attachment to the categories of British law. He argued that, if passed, Sir Sayyid's bill would permit

[7] Gulzar Ali, *Tardīd Masawwadah Qānūn-i Waqf-i Khāndānī-yi* . . . , 5ff.
[8] S. K. Rashid, *Wakf Administration*, 133 n. 20.
[9] S. A. Ali, *Memoirs and Other Writings*, p. 51.

published in *Tazhib al-Akhlaq*. Along with the draft he turned in a statement of his reasons for asking the government's consideration of a special law of family *waqf*.⁶ His statement contained an appraisal of how the system of inheritance currently applied in the British courts was detrimental to families of wealth and power. It also contained a short description of Sir Sayyid's views on the history of the *shariah*'s regulations demanding the division of property among several different heirs. He wrote that these rules were developed while the Prophet was still alive. The community of faith was at that time a kind of "republic" in which there were no distinctions of rank. In that context, the egalitarian intent of a mandatory partition made sense. It was designed to prevent the rise of inequalities based on wealth. But this republican organization did not long survive the death of the Prophet. Within thirty years the community shifted to a monarchical form of government. In such a system the king alone controlled access to all wealth. A king's servants did not actually own property. They held it temporarily at the king's pleasure. Such circumstances required no change in the rules formulated in the earliest period. Because no one really possessed a proprietary right, inheritance did not affect the foundations of wealth and power. By enforcing the letter of the *shariah*, the British were imposing a strict interpretation of laws which had not been scrupulously adhered to since the earliest period of Muslim history. That rigour combined with the nobility's internal weaknesses to create the dismal condition which characterized the Muslim aristocracy and disturbed Sir Sayyid.

Sir Sayyid's concern for the decline of prominent families was evidently inspired by his belief that they should remain the leaders of society. Also, he saw them as intermediaries between British rulers and Indian subjects. Such a group was essential to a smooth adaptation to the new circumstances of alien rule. On the practical side, the financial support of the wealthiest families would be required to make progress possible. Sir Sayyid's own ambitious educational and social programme had need of such aristocratic patronage.

The government's initial response to Sir Sayyid's proposal was cautious. They were anxious to determine how the "Muhammadan community" viewed the measure. That concern for popular opinion was founded partly on the officials' view of Sir Sayyid and what he represented. "As all of us who know him best and admire him most are aware", wrote Dennis Fitzpatrick, the secretary to the Legislative Council, "he is so far in advance of his coreligionists that he cannot be said to altogether represent [sic] their views." Fitzpatrick was sure that oppo-

⁶ (NAI) *HJP B* (October 1979), 44–45. The following paragraphs summarize this document.

trate. The shares of the *waqf*'s income had to be precisely laid out. Also, the succession to the office of *mutawalli* had to be clearly established. This kind of specificity was necessary to preclude the kind of familial disagreement which had disturbed the *awqaf* established by the Nawab Ahsan-ullah.

In constructing the provisions of a *waqf*-bill, Sir Sayyid took as a model the special laws which governed inheritance for the *taalluqdars* of Avadh. He aimed at achieving the stability which characterized their privileged position. One highly restrictive clause was probably inspired by his admiration of the *taalluqdari* system. He limited the protection which his Act provided to estates which produced an annual income of at least Rs. 10,000. Therefore, most of the forty *awqaf* discussed in preceding chapters would not have qualified for the legal protection Sir Sayyid proposed. That exclusivity was probably not the result of his belief that only the richest landholders were worth protecting. Sir Sayyid knew from long association with the British government that it was cautious, even stingy, in granting social and economic privileges. It offered a special accommodation to the *taalluqdars* only because some of them were involved in the Revolt of 1857. Sir Sayyid's realistic appraisal must have been that his proposal had a better chance of getting a hearing if it were modest in its scope.

If Sir Sayyid had been an ordinary journalist or social reformer, his article would have attracted no more than a short paragraph in the *Vernacular Press Reports*. He was, however, a very prominent man. Though a voluminous writer on subjects ranging from historical archaeology to scriptural commentary, his reputation with the government rested on the steady devotion he gave the British during the troubles of 1857. This first brought him to the attention of administrators and gave him access to the centres of imperial government. At the time he published the draft of a family *waqf* law, he was serving as a member of the Viceroy's Legislative Council. Before 1857, this body was made up solely of British officials. In the wake of the Mutiny, "native" representatives joined this group to keep the government abreast of the thoughts and feelings of their Indian subjects. Government officials selected the men who served on the Council. They were usually the rulers of princely states or men, like Sir Sayyid, who were closely associated with the administration. Their position in the imperial order cast some doubt upon their ability to represent truly the views of the great mass of Indians. Yet they were accorded some of the legislative powers held by elected members of the British parliament. This included the right to propose legislative Acts.

In 1879, Sir Sayyid submitted a translation of the Act he had first

When that proved impossible, they borrowed, trying to maintain extravagant tastes. The result was family ruin. Strict division of property ensured that only two or three generations were required to accomplish a fall from nobility to beggary.

In 1877, Sir Sayyid published an article in his journal, *Tazhīb al-Akhlāq*, titled "A Plan for Saving Muslim Families from Destruction and Extinction".[5] The article included a first draft of "A Law of Family *Waqf* for Muslims". As the title suggested, Sir Sayyid's scheme aimed at eliminating the ill effects of the laws of inheritance that the British courts so assiduously enforced. When he drafted the article, Sir Sayyid was aware that there was a suit under adjudication in Bombay which would probably result in the overturning of a particular *waqf* (Fatah Sahib Bibi's case). He also mentioned the endowments created by several other individuals: Ali Muzaffar Khan of Moradabad, Hajji Imam Bakhsh of Janpur, Niaz Ali of Agra and the Nawab Ahsan-ullah of Dacca. Sir Sayyid knew that family discord threatened all of those *awqaf*. He laid the blame for these difficulties on the settlors themselves. Their deeds of endowment were stupidly drawn. They had not clearly outlined provisions for managing their estates. Sir Sayyid wanted to prevent this sort of difficulty in the future by giving a detailed guide to writing an iron-clad *waqfnamah*. He did not, apparently, contemplate the possibility that the British courts would do more than quash a few badly constructed endowments, that they would entirely ban the institution of family *waqf*.

The essay he published concentrated on the nuts and bolts of constructing a solid *waqf*. Its only reference to *shariah* was in the beginning of the article. It noted that a *waqf* was "allowed", or "permitted" (*mujāz*). To support his point he quoted a few short paragraphs in Arabic from standard *shariah*-texts such as the *Fatawa-i Alamgiri*. He also translated the passages into Urdu. Having made this nod in the direction of the *shariah*, he proceeded to lay out in meticulous detail the various articles of what he considered a model piece of legislation on the subject. The topics covered and the way in which they were presented bore greater similarity to British law than they did to *shariah*. Sir Sayyid was familiar with the Anglo-Indian legal system through his long experience as a subordinate judge. He knew first hand what the courts looked for in a deed.

His first concern was that the property placed in a *waqf* be accurately and fully described. Next, his proposal insisted that, once drawn up, a *waqfnamah* be registered with the district officer or the district magis-

[5] S. A. Khan, "Ek Tadbīr: Mussalmānon ke Khāndānon ko Tabāhī awr Barbādī se Bicāne ki", *Maqālāt*, I, 97ff. The next few paragraphs summarize this article.

Sir Sayyid Ahmad Khan first raised the issue of Muslim family endowments in a political context in 1879 which was, in political terms, a different epoch. Much time, trouble and money might have been saved if a law he proposed had been passed. His interest in the subject of family endowments stemmed from a general concern for the welfare of socially prominent and wealthy Muslim families. He believed that such families were in grave danger, partly through their own fault and partly through external pressures created by British rule. He thought that the internal troubles of leading families stemmed from self-indulgence. The ancestors of such families gained wealth and prominence through self-discipline and hard work. By contrast, their descendants were content to live on the memory of past glories. They did not imitate their forebears' energy and ingenuity. They added nothing to what they inherited. In the past, titles like "*Khwajah*" or "*Nawab*" had to be earned. The nobles of his own day, Sir Sayyid argued, used the same high-sounding honorifics, expected to be deferred to, but did nothing to earn either the title or the respect due it.[1]

British rule only encouraged internal weakness. According to Sir Sayyid, British control of India was a mixed blessing. It brought peace to a troubled and insecure land. But, for a nobility which held its prominence through service to warrior kings, peace meant idleness. In the days of Muslim rule, an individual's fame rested on his accomplishments on the field of battle or in the sovereign's hall of audience (*razm-o bazm*).[2] The British stopped the battles and broke up the old kingdoms, leaving the aristocracy without a focus. The courts of law came with peace. Sir Sayyid thought it praiseworthy that these courts permitted the use of *shariah*, but considered certain aspects of the way in which they employed it harmful. For instance, in applying the *shariah*'s regulations on inheritance, the British courts were much stricter than Muslim kings or their *qazis* had ever been.[3]

The certainty that an estate would be partitioned into the shares prescribed by *shariah* was responsible for much evil. A father, who had no hope that his wealth or reputation would survive intact, had little reason for frugality.[4] Sons, assured that some portion of their fathers' wealth would be theirs, did not try to make a career for themselves. They waited for their fathers to die. When sons did get a share, it was invariably small. Yet they expected to live in their fathers' grand style.

---

[1] S. A. Khan, "Hindūstān ke Mu'azzaz Khāndān", *Maqālāt*, I, 87ff.
[2] *Ibid.*
[3] Note by Sir Sayyid in (NAI) *HJP B* (October 1879), 44–45.
[4] *Ibid.*

6

Muslim endowments and the politics of religious law

> But it goes without saying that spiritual leaders and those learned in religion can not be concerned with politics, neither can they be counsellors to the state or statesman.   Abd al-Halim Sharar

The last decades of the nineteenth century saw an expansion of several political forums open to Indian participation. The press, in terms of newspapers, books and pamphlets, was one. In this period, the number of publications in English and the vernacular languages greatly increased. As the public controversy on endowments grew, more ink flowed.

Political and social associations also took up the debate. Such organizations were founded on several different constituencies. Some, for example the Oudh Landholder's Association, drew on particular regional or class interests. Others, like the Anjuman-i Islam of Bombay, added a religious dimension to the mix. Most of them did not have solid political platforms. Their membership was often factionalized and the personal rivalries of leaders often expressed themselves in the founding of competing groups.

India's British rulers provided a third new forum when they slowly extended their subjects' involvement in legislative bodies. Viceroys and provincial governors accepted, sometimes reluctantly, larger numbers of Indians on their councils. Princes, merchants, landowners and lawyers became fledgling legislators.

Indeed, lawyers took a leading role in all these forms of political activity. Drawing on their experience in the courts, they used legal categories to define the issue of Muslim endowments. They shaped political discourse on that and other matters with an eye to the way the courts defined and resolved problems. As in the courtroom, religious law and the community which supposedly lived by it became the focus of discussion. But, as the previous chapter showed, judicial discourse excluded serious consideration of particular social, economic or historical contexts. Rather than elaborating on legal abstractions, the lawyer–politicians increased their circulation.

Councillors or High Court judges. Moreover, they introduced them into a political context.

By 1900, Amir Ali, and those who agreed with him, realized that the courts would never overturn the precedent created in Abd al-Fatah's case. Slowly a coalition of landholders, lawyers and journalists formed around the issue. They began to agitate in public forums for a change in the law. As they brought their agenda into a new arena, they carried with them the categories shaped by the practice of the imperial courts.

mean that the juridical perception of Islam was broader or more correct. Indeed, it seemed much narrower. Legal theory and reform in Britain acted to limit the importance of local customs and tribunals. Those Muslims trained in the history and philosophy of British law began looking at their own social, religious and political realities in similar metropolitan, abstract terms.

Those Muslims who so readily accepted perceptions developed in an alien legal system were, as noted, themselves not well trained in *shariah*. Like Amir Ali, F. B. Tyabji or Muhammad Ali Jinnah, they often came from minority sects of the *Shiah* persuasion. They were usually the scions of comparatively wealthy landholding families with traditions of government service under Muslim and British rule. With so little grounding in the traditions of Islam, they were more open to the ideas presented to them during their legal apprenticeship and practice. After all, the judicial perspective had the advantage of being clearer than more diffuse local perceptions of the day to day realities of Muslim life. When centralizing states, like that of British India, employed the more succinct, sharply constructed ideas, they became hard currency in the economy of ideas.

In practical terms, the mass of Muslims also contributed to the dominance of the British legal system. While they consulted the *ulama* about prayer or ritual, they invariably took property disputes to the Anglo-Indian courts. Because the basic rules governing the ownership of real property were established by colonial legal fiat, they had little choice. Only the imperial courts provided definitive judgments on rights to property. Those Muslims who won their suits were probably satisfied with the Anglo-Indian courts' understanding of "Muhammadan law". But the acceptance of these rulings also contributed to a bifurcation of ideas and values. The official ones were employed in the courts and other public contexts, but the other, more complicated, indigenous categories did not disappear. They continued to be used to manage the relationships of daily life, but ceased to be employed when Muslims used government institutions.

The courts, as we have seen, did not consider the issue of endowments from the perspective of the men and women who actually created them. Their concern for establishing a point of law pushed the ordinary concerns of people into the background. Thus, the courts contributed to a more abstract perception of Muslims and the way they lived their lives. Those who argued against the ruling on endowments used the same set of premises. They disagreed with a particular interpretation of Muslim law, but they still employed the same terms and concepts as the Privy

described in this chapter showed, the imperial courts did not so much resolve a sticky point as create a law where none existed. The courts, not the *shariah*, drew a line between "public" and "private" interests. They provided the standard which distinguished between a "substantial" dedication to religion or charity and a "customary" philanthropy. They separated a *waqf* from an ordinary gift (*hibah*). In the process of deciding such matters, the courts worked to shape *shariah* in a more general fashion, in a way which went beyond the specific problem of endowments. By persistently referring to a small number of texts, the *Hedaya* of Hamilton or the *Mahommedan Law* of Amir Ali, the courts established them as "authoritative sources". By constantly, if somewhat inaccurately, reiterating the point that *shariah* was ancient, changeless, religious law, they influenced the views of the lawyers who became official spokesmen for Muslims. By introducing the principle of precedent, the courts began to treat the *shariah* as a single system. That alone represented a major shift from the traditional practice of *shariah* in which individual religious scholars treated each question as unique. The courts, therefore, had a hand in creating an entire lexicon of social and legal concepts about Muslims and their law.

Because many Muslims disagreed with the courts' decisions on endowments, a controversy arose over the institution. Amir Ali and others argued that the Privy Council and Anglo-Indian courts were wrong about *awqaf* which benefited the founder or her/his descendants. But they did not contest the assumptions of the jurists who made those decisions. Muslims did not point to the adaptability of *shariah*. None of them tried to show that the courts interpreted *shariah* too rigidly. They did not argue that as a code of conscience *shariah* served the changing needs of Muslims in a variety of historical contexts. They did not try to prove that *shariah* had "evolved" quite as much as the British system. They only repeated that their ancient, changeless, religious law approved of the sort of endowments condemned by the courts. Perhaps because so many of the prominent spokesmen were lawyers, trained in the traditions of British law, not *shariah*, they were unable to consider the problem in some other way.

British judges or their Muslim colleagues did not have to look far to see that the practice of *shariah* was still a lively enterprise. Thousands of ordinary Muslims still solicited opinions from the *ulama*.[140] The Muslims who became the subcontinent's political leaders may have considered questions of ritual purity or the protocol of pilgrimage trivial, but clearly many of the faithful thought otherwise. Later generations, including our own, paid more attention to the lawyers, but that did not

[140] B. D. Metcalf, *Islamic Revival*, 146–147.

elder Pirbhai in the original deed. Sir Karimbhai hired a number of lawyers to defend the *waqf*, among whom were Faiz B. Tyabji and Muhammad Ali Jinnah, also a Khojah and a rising member of the Bombay Bar. Pirbhai's son, Qasim Ali, was a member of the Khojah faction which wanted to convert the community to the use of *Sunni* law and custom. Through his lawyers, Qasim Ali attacked his father's endowment on the grounds that it was contrary to *Sunni* principles. He cited by way of example a clause in the deed of endowment which permitted the founder to revoke the endowment at a later date. This completely contravened most Hanafi opinion, which held that a *waqf* was once and for all. Qasim Ali's lawyers also attacked the provisions of the endowment which denied some members of the family their prescribed shares of the inheritance. Jinnah and the other lawyers argued that the clause permitting revocation and the non-Quranic portions given heirs were part of "Khojah custom".

Justice Frank Beaman, who heard the case, did not agree. He ruled that "Muhammad law", not custom, applied.

Usus et conventio vincunt legem [usage and custom supersede the written law] is a maxim peculiarly appropriate to the constantly shifting needs and requirements of a growing commercial community and in this country no doubt it has been extended in every direction. But there are limits to its application and I am disposed to think that those limits are passed where it is sought to be shown that the Khojas are allowed by local usage to over-ride the Mahomedan law which prohibits any Mahomedan from disposing of more than one-third of his property at will.[139]

Once again a British judge proclaimed himself the preserver of orthodox Muslim law. Unlike Hobhouse, however, Beaman had no words of praise for the Prophet as a lawgiver. Indeed, he voiced several injudicious opinions about the character of Muhammadan law. "The notions of the early Mahomedan lawyers", he wrote, were "extremely crude and primitive." The British courts managed to improve on their antiquated principles. Muhammadan law, according to Beaman, was the creation of the Anglo-Indian courts, though it suited the "conservative prejudices of good Muslims" to think otherwise. Apart from the obvious bias, Beaman did have a point: the system which the Anglo-Indian courts passed off as "Muslim" was largely their own creation.

Few judges were as blunt as Frank Beaman. In their decisions, most claimed to be doing nothing more than applying a code of law that was centuries old. At most, they admitted to settling disputed points of law like the clarification of what constituted a *valid waqf*. But, as the cases

[139] Pirbhai's case, *Bom*, XXXVI, 260.

they were dedicated to religious or charitable purposes, the judges decided whether most of the money went to the "charity" or to the family. If the sum for religious observances, etc. was thought no more "than a devout and wealthy Mahomedan gentleman might find it becoming to spend in that way",[135] the courts ruled against the *waqf*. No new text or argument swayed the judges because they relied on the precedent created by the highest legal authority in the empire.

Lawyers did present a number of new cases in an effort to get the Indian courts and the Privy Council to reverse themselves. They had no success. Even the appointment of Amir Ali to the Privy Council in 1909 did nothing to change the accepted view. Amir Ali was ignored in a higher court. One of the attempts to get a favourable ruling on family endowments was based on the appeal that the school of Imam Shafii clearly approved of them. That was, seemingly, a good strategy. If judges were mostly ignorant of the traditions of Abu Hanifa, they were totally ignorant of the Shafiite tradition. The judges, however, rejected that argument.

An appeal to "custom" seemed another way of getting around the precedent established in 1894. In theory, the Anglo-Indian courts recognized that what people did sometimes differed from what their law books told them to do. In a number of notable instances customary law prevailed. For example, the legal system of the Panjab was for the most part based on local custom rather than orthodox texts. The Khojahs were another group whose customary rules governed most of their legal transactions. In matters of inheritance, for instance, the Khojah's practices more closely resembled those of their Hindu neighbours. They did not permit females to inherit property. In 1866, a decision of the Bombay court confirmed their special status.[136] An appeal to "Khojah custom" as a justification for a family endowment was made in the case of *Cassamally Jairajbhai Peerbhai* v. *Sir Currimbhoy Ibrahim*.[137] The case showed that judges had considerable freedom in deciding what was and what was not acceptable as custom. It indicated that "custom" was often a synonym for "judicial preference".[138]

Jairajbhai Pirbhai, a wealthy Khojah leader (see pp. 71–3) established the endowment in question in 1886. After Pirbhai's death, his son Qasim Ali initiated a suit in the Bombay court to have it overturned. Sir Karimbhai Ibrahim was that last surviving custodian appointed by the

---

[135] Shaikh Ahsan-ullah's case, *Cal*, XVII, 498.
[136] F. B. Tyabji, *Principles of Muhammadan Law*, 398–399, and Dobbin, *Urban Leadership*, 113–121.
[137] *Bom*, XXXVI, 214ff.
[138] W. C. McCormack, "Caste and the British Administration of Hindu Law", 27–34, and M. Galantar, "Changing Legal Conceptions of Caste", 299–336.

the power to change the terms of trusts, to redirect their funds to more useful ends. In 1880, Hobhouse published a volume of essays and lectures on trusts. Its title, *The Dead Hand*, said much about the author's view of the institution. To British lawyers, *awqaf* closely resembled trusts. Was Hobhouse really capable of objectivity on the subject? Was he really a judicial "ringer"? Given that his views were well known, was he chosen to write opinions on Muslim endowments because everyone knew what his decision would be? Did he have a verdict before he heard the case? These are questions which the author cannot answer, though the suspicion of a rigged judgment is hard to avoid. The proceedings of the Anglo-Indian courts and Privy Council made no mention of such considerations. Judges presented themselves as defenders of Muslim orthodoxy. They claimed that their judgments were an effort to prevent deviations or softenings of the God-given law.

As Sir Charles Paul, in his defence of Abd al-Fatah, argued, both Muslim and British laws were full of "devices". Trusts and entails were permitted in British courts, so why did Anglo-Indian courts not grant Muslims similar privileges? As Sir Charles' argument implied, Muslims ought to have the same right as Britons to avoid their own publicly cherished legal prescriptions. The Privy Council and the courts did not even comment on that line of reasoning. What was more surprising was that those who defended family endowments did not give it more prominence. They might well have argued that this "modern" use of *awqaf* was an attempt by Muslims to adapt their system to suit the circumstances of the society in which they lived. In the light of Maine's evolutionary view of law, Muslims could have argued that they were developing their own system to fit the contemporary scene. Instead, they chose a conservative defence of endowments. Following Amir Ali's lead, they kept repeating that family endowments were an "ancient" and "orthodox" Muslim practice. They disagreed with the judges about their decision on one institution, but still confirmed the judges' description of Muslims as believers in an ancient and orthodox faith.

The Privy Council's decision in Abd al-Fatah's case became the definitive precedent on endowments. Thereafter, British judges who examined a *waqf* applied the standard which Hobhouse set out. If an endowment did not substantially support some public, religious or charitable purpose, the judges ruled it null and void. They overturned a number of endowments by employing that test. Decisions on what was a "substantial" portion were highly subjective. As the previous chapters noted, sums for charity and family stipends were part of almost every *waqf*. Deeds made no clear distinction between public and private. When some Muslims tried to defend their endowments by claiming that

attempts to link decisions to the Muslim tradition seemed perfunctory.

In one sense, the contradiction between Muslims and British legal history was not as stark as it first appeared. Wealthy landowners in England found ways of circumventing the rules against perpetuities. In Tudor legal language, these evasions were called "uses". Various royal statutes tried to regulate them, but over the centuries the landed elite relied on them to achieve many of the same goals Muslims had when they founded *awqaf*. The law of entail was one of the most important ways of avoiding the rigours of the ban on perpetuities. An entail was an agreement entered into by members of two or three generations of a landholding family. In it, the parties agreed to accept a specific income from an estate, but renounced the right to sell or otherwise alienate the land which formed the basis of the family's wealth. Because they were renewed every third generation and limited in force to thirty years after the death of the most junior participant in the entail, such agreements did not technically violate the rule forbidding perpetuities. Their compliance was merely *pro forma*. They were, in reality, a "device" for evading the law. Adam Smith and other legal theoreticians condemned their use, but the practice continued. An entail's intent was, therefore, not all that different from the one expressed in most *waqf*-deeds: "perpetuating the names of our father and fore-fathers" and "protecting our properties".[133] While in England legal authorities tolerated such evasions, they were not prepared to show Muslims the same forbearance.

Among lawyers in Britain, "trusts" were also much contested institutions. Today, they are usually considered as "public" or "charitable" funds, very much on the model of what Hobhouse thought a *waqf* ought to be. But trusts were (and are) not always wholly dedicated to the common good. The interests of a trust's founders often shaped its provisions to benefit the donor. For example, trusts established to support British "public" schools often benefited the family of the individuals who created them.[134] Legal thinkers hotly debated the wisdom of trusts in the middle years of the nineteenth century. On the one hand John Stuart Mill argued in support of trusts. He believed that the terms of a trust were inviolable. As much as possible, a society was bound to honour the wishes of the individuals who created them. Lord Hobhouse was a prominent spokesman for the opposing view. As a young lawyer he had made his reputation as an expert on trusts. He believed that as a society changed, the provisions of a trust sometimes became irrelevant to the needs of the moment. The government or trustees ought to have

---

[133] W. Holdsworth, *A History of English Law*, VII, 194–197, 205–207, and W. Geldart, *Elements of English Law*, 23–26, 87–88.
[134] Holdsworth, *A History*, 171–176, 184–188, and Geldart, *Elements*, 32–33.

back with one hand what he appears to put away with the other; which are to form the centre of attraction for accumulations of income ... which seek to give to the donors and their family the enjoyment of property free from all liability to creditors; and which do not seek the benefit of others beyond the use of empty words.[130]

Hobhouse's opinion made it seem that the Privy Council's sole concern was to preserve Muslim law and the reputation of Islam's "great lawgiver". But its references to gifts which established an "inalienable income for unborn generations" or the fear that endowments freed individuals from "liability to creditors" showed that the Privy Council's views were influenced by the principles of British law. Questions of debt, life-interests, inheritance and trusts were hotly debated by scholars of the British system. Their importance there, not in Muslim tradition, accounted in large measure for the keen interest of Hobhouse and other judges.

Land was once the major source of wealth for Britain's social and political elite. The gradual monetarization of the British economy forced many changes in the laws affecting land ownership.[131] In feudal England, both the king and nobles wanted stability. For the nobles, their influence depended on the possibility of controlling their estates generation after generation. The monarch needed a reliable force of political–military vassals and therefore also counted on the nobles having secure tenures. As money became the basis of power and prestige, the laws on landed property lost some of their emphasis on preserving ownership in a few select families. Statutes and court judgments began to exhibit an antipathy to "perpetuities": any legal form which permanently restricted the sale or inheritance of land. Adam Smith summed up the concern of those who took seriously the impact of the money economy: "The interest of the state requires that lands should be as much in commerce as any other goods ... When land is in commerce and frequently changes hands it is most likely to be well managed."[132] In contrast, permanence, or at least the hope of it, was fundamental to a *waqf*. Throughout the history of the institution, Muslims with wealth wanted to use it to prevent land from changing hands. British judges, or Indians trained in British law, saw Muslim endowments as a violation of a cardinal principle of the British tradition. Rather than acknowledging that Muslims operated under a different set of rules or that the history of property relations was different in the Muslim world, the Indian courts and Privy Council found a way of enforcing the maxims of British law. Their

[130] Abd al-Fatah's case, *IA*, XXII, 76ff.
[131] B. Lyon, *A Constitutional and Legal History of Medieval England*, 457–468.
[132] A. Smith, *Lectures on Jurisprudence*, 70.

Rather he paid close attention to the Prophetic anecdotes (*ahadis*) which Amir Ali referred to. He complained that these texts were of an "abstract character". He declared that Amir Ali was using them as precedents. Not surprisingly, he found them deficient. He wrote that the "opinions of that learned Mahomedan lawyer [Amir Ali]" were founded "upon precedents very imperfectly stated". Hobhouse had the power to decide what seemed clear or clouded to his seventy-five year old eyes.

Instead of directly confronting the issue of endowments, Hobhouse treated it in conjunction with two other elements of the Muslim tradition: inheritance and the power of gift. He repeated the charge that a *waqf* seemed to be an evasion of the rules of inheritance. Secondly, he contrasted endowments and gifts. On the conceptual level, they seemed to be similar transactions. Though texts of *shariah* treated them separately, Hobhouse linked the two. He noted that the *Hedaya* and *Fatawa-i Alamgiri* set certain limits on a Muslim's ability to give a gift (*hibah*). An individual could not present anyone with a gift of more than one-third of his or her property. Another qualification was that the recipient had to be a person capable of accepting the gift: they had to be alive and rational. To make a gift a receiver had to accept the offer. That necessitated that an individual be capable of indicating their approval of the transaction. Finally, an individual could make a gift only to a "stranger", which meant an individual who was not already an heir by the standards of the *Quran*. Such was the theory of gifts. Hobhouse made no attempt to determine whether Muslims actually paid heed to it. Hobhouse was in good company – few judges seemed concerned with what Muslims did. With the limits on the power of gift in mind, Hobhouse asked how it was possible that a simple gift establishing an inalienable income for generations yet unborn was forbidden by the ordinary rules on benefactions, while the simple expedient of calling such a gift a "*waqf*" set aside all of these rules? In a sense, Hobhouse was chiding Muslims for failing to answer questions no one ever asked. In summing up the Council's judgment, Hobhouse tried to show that it was based on a desire to defend the Muslims' own system.

Their Lordships have endeavoured to the best of their ability to ascertain and apply the Mahomedan law, as known and administered in India; but they cannot find that it is in accordance with the absolute, and it seems to them extravagant, application of abstract precepts taken from the mouth of the Prophet. Those precepts may be excellent in their proper application. They may, for aught their Lordships know, have had their effect in moulding the law and practice of *wakf*, as the learned judge [Amir Ali] says they have. But it would be doing wrong to a great lawgiver [Muhammad] to suppose that he is thereby commending gifts for which the donor exercises no self-denial; in which he takes

lacked. In his case, the Advocate General, Sir Charles Paul, appeared on his behalf. J. T. Woodroffe, who became Advocate General the following year, served as counsel for Rassamoy and the other appellants. Though the arguments submitted by each of them resembled those introduced in Bikani Mian's case, they did not provide the kind of detailed exposition featured in the later case.

Sir Charles defended the subordinate magistrate's ruling by referring to the government's pledge to apply the "Muhammadan law". He argued that that system did approve of endowments in the interest of the donor's own family. He added that because the institution was religious, it could not be changed. In contrast to the position adopted by Woodroffe, he claimed that Rassamoy's challenge to the *waqf* was based on current conditions and "modern notions". These contemporary considerations should not be allowed to overturn the ancient system of Muslim law. When his opponents charged that a *waqf* represented an evasion of the laws of inheritance, Sir Charles admitted that it was a "device". However, both British and Muhammadan law were "full of devices" and therefore the court ought not to disallow an institution on that ground alone.[129]

The justices of the High Court were not swayed by Sir Charles' defence of the original *waqf* and they ruled against Abd al-Fatah. Trevelyan, who wrote the opinion, noted that the deed of endowment itself proved that the dedication was "secular", not "religious". Taking the Privy Council's decision in Shaikh Ahsan-ullah's case as a precedent, he declared that the endowment served only the family's interest and did not support in any substantial fashion a "religious" or "charitable" purpose. Abd al-Fatah, once again with the moral and financial support of Nawab Abd al-Ghani, sent an appeal to the Privy Council. Councillors Watson, Shand, Morris, Hobhouse and Couch heard the arguments and decided the matter in December of 1894.

By the time the Privy Council took up the case, Bikani Mian's suit had been decided and the proceedings published. Also, Amir Ali's meticulous examination of the institution in the first volume of his *Mahommedan Law* was in print. The Councillors had ample opportunity to examine both sides of the issue. Lord Hobhouse, who wrote the Council's opinion, seemed acquainted with the range of views already expressed. However, as a representative of the highest court of appeal, Hobhouse had a special advantage. He was able to select those arguments which he wanted to refute. He did not answer all of the defenders' points or take note of all the documentary evidence which they cited. For example, he did not mention the passages from texts of *shariah*.

[129] Abd al-Fatah's case, *Cal*, XVIII, 406.

described in chapters 2–4. They included support for a school and stipend for a number of "poor persons", but most of the money went to themselves or other members of their families.

The brothers managed the property amicably for some ten years. But, towards the end of this period, Muhammad Abd ar-Rahman began borrowing heavily. In 1881, he gave Rassamoy Dhur Chaudhri a mortgage on some of the land in return for Rs. 20,250. When he failed to make payments, Rassamoy obtained a court decree and sequestered the land for debt.

While Muhammad Abd ar-Rahman obtained many loans from 125 individuals, his brother, Abd al-Qadar, made no effort to stop him. However, Abd al-Qadar's son, Abd al-Fatah Muhammad Ishaq, was disturbed by his uncle's actions. At the time, he was still under the legal age of majority. When he finally came of age, he sought the advice of pleaders working in the Sylhet district courts. He even travelled to Calcutta and sought the help of Amir Ali and the Advocate General of Bengal, Sir Charles Paul. Abd al-Fatah's grandmother (*nani*) was the sister of the current head of the family of the Dacca Nawabs, Khwajah Abd al-Ghani. Abd al-Ghani gave the youth financial support and the Nawab's name opened doors. Abd al-Ghani was also one of his uncle's creditors, having lent the spendthrift some Rs. 9,000.

With the support of those prominent men, Abd al-Fatah initiated a suit in the court of the subordinate magistrate of Sylhet in 1889. His plaint asked that all mortgaged properties be restored to the *waqf* and that his uncle be removed as its custodian. Named as respondents in the suit were the 125 people from which his uncle borrowed. His own father, his great-uncle Nawab Abd al-Ghani, his profligate uncle as well as numerous shopkeepers, moneylenders and tenants, both Hindu and Muslim, were among that throng. Having had the benefit of expert legal advice and the financial support of his great-uncle, Abd al-Fatah received a favourable verdict from the subordinate magistrate, Babu Jibun Krishna Chatterjee.

Rassamoy Dhur Chaudhri and several other defendants appealed that ruling to the Calcutta High Court. Justices L. R. Tottenham and E. J. Trevelyan heard the case in February of 1891.[128] The case was heard over a year before the full bench decided Bikani Mian's case, but Amir Ali did not have the chance to sit in judgment in this instance. Perhaps Amir Ali's personal knowledge of the suit disqualified him. Had he participated, his views would have been the same as those he expressed in the later case. Abd al-Fatah enjoyed an advantage which Bikani Mian

---

[128] For biographies of Tottenham and Trevelyan, see *Who was Who, 1916–1928*, 1052, and *Indian Biographical Dictionary*, 439.

a tomb in Bombay was "bad". Though the custodians of the tomb claimed that it belonged to a great sufi saint, Tyabji professed to see nothing special about the tomb in question. He believed that its endowment served to support the dead man's kin and was a thinly disguised attempt to preserve the family's wealth. Therefore, he overturned the endowment.[125]

Karamat Husain, who sat on the Allahabad bench from 1907 to 1912, dealt with endowments in a similar, radical way. When he considered a *waqf* which left money to provide for the upkeep and placing of lamps on the founder's tomb, he ruled it invalid. Karamat Husain ruled that a *waqf* must be for a "good purpose". This concern for a tomb he thought smacked of idolatry. Since idolatry was not a "good purpose", the *waqf* was invalid.[126] Had Karamat Husain's views on "Islamic orthodoxy" prevailed, almost every endowment in India would have fallen. Even his British colleagues found Karamat Husain's judgment too extreme and in subsequent cases they reversed his decision. Whether or not they were sustained, Tyabji's and Husain's opinions showed that Muslim judges were not of one mind on endowments. When Amir Ali and Sayyhid Mahmud claimed to be stating *the* Muslim view, they were exaggerating.

As noted in the beginning of the chapter, *Abdul Fata Mahommed Ishak (and others)* v. *Russomoy Dhur Chowdhry (and others)*[127] was the most celebrated Indian lawsuit involving Muslim endowments. Two brothers, Abd al-Husain Muhammad Abd ar-Rahman and Abu Muhammad Abd al-Qadar, created the *waqf* in question in 1868. The brothers were the sons of a successful landowner–government servant, Mawlwi Muhammad Idris Khan Bahadur, who had married into the family of the Nawabs of Dacca. When Mawlwi Muhammad died in 1846, he left his sons property in the Sylhet district worth over Rs. 300,000. In their deed of endowment, the brothers expressed their aim of "perpetuating the names of our fathers and forefathers". In order to make that possible, they founded the *waqf* as a way of "protecting our properties".

After drafting the deed of endowment, the brothers did not attempt to inform local officials of their change in status from "*zamindars*" to "*mutawallis*". In receipts and account books, they were inconsistent, sometimes styling themselves "custodians" and sometimes "owners". The provisions of their endowment were like those of the others

---

[125] *Zooleka Bibi (and another)* v. *Syed Zynul Abedin*, BLR, VI, 1058ff.
[126] Vesey-Fitzgerald, *Muhammadan Law*, 209.
[127] Report of the Calcutta court, *Cal*, XVIII, 399ff; of the Privy Council, *IA*, XXIII, 76ff, and *LI*, vol. 382, 607ff.

proved nothing. He noted that not all cases were reported. Perhaps those concerning family *awqaf* did not make it into print. Secondly, Amir Ali pointed to the presence of "Muhammadan Law Officers" in the Company's courts. Amir Ali claimed that they mediated disputes before they actually came to trial. For one reason or the other, the endowments which would have proved his position went unreported. Amir Ali failed to notice a certain inconsistency in that line of argument. If the *qazis* managed to prevent trials on family *awqaf*, why were they unable to keep the twenty "public" endowments out of court?

The final argument put forward by Amir Ali was that Woodroffe's attempt to distinguish public from private endowments was mistaken. He pointed out that texts on *shariah* made no distinction between the two. All endowments, according to "Muhammadan Law Books", "stand on the same footing".[122]

Amir Ali's views failed to persuade his colleagues. The four other justices, including W. Comer-Pretheram, the Chief Justice, agreed with the Advocate General. They ruled that a "valid" *waqf* must include the maintenance "of some religious institution or ... carry out some charitable purpose in the ordinary signification of that term".[123] Amir Ali did publish his views as the dissenting opinion. Bikani Mian's case was important for Amir Ali because it gave him the chance to publish his arguments in the Calcutta court's reports. Together with his textbook on Muhammadan law, his discussion of *awqaf* in Bikani Mian became the primary source for all of those who chose to defend their use as family settlements. In the years which followed, he did not change his line of argument. Those who agreed with him also repeated the same set of propositions. As the next chapter shows, Amir Ali eventually prevailed, but in a political, not a judicial, forum.

On the question of family endowments, Amir Ali and Sayyid Mahmud were in basic agreement. Both men knew how to argue in the style required by British law. Despite that knowledge of the British method and their introduction of material garnered from "original sources", their partners on the bench sedulously ignored their opinions. However, a number of Muslim judges also disagreed with them. For example, Justice Badr ud-din Tyabji of the Bombay High Court was as critical of family endowments as any British judge. In Abd al-Qadar's case, Tyabji took the same position as Woodroffe. He wrote that the "*waqf*" in question was not valid because it benefited the founder's family.[124] In another case, he ruled that a *waqf* dedicated to the upkeep of

---
[122] *Ibid.*, 174–175.
[123] *Ibid.*, 223.
[124] *Abdul Cadar (and another)* v. *Tajoodin (and others)*, *BLR*, VI, 263ff.

neat distinction could be made between *awqaf* which were "public", "religious" or "charitable" and those which served the "self-aggrandizement" of a particular "family". His understanding of "self-aggrandizement" was narrow. It certainly did not fit the actual use of endowments. For example, even in those *awqaf* which were public by British standards, custodians were almost invariably members of the family which created them. Since they collected salaries and had control of endowments' assets, their actions might be construed as self-aggrandizement. Custodians often did gain personally from a *waqf*. Most of the twenty cases heard by the *Sadr Diwani* involved custodians who were members of the founders' families. Despite that complication, Woodroffe asserted that these cases proved that family *awqaf* were the product of the "learned lucubrations of Muhammadan casuists [*sic*]" and not really approved by the Muhammadan law.[121]

In his comments during the trial and his written opinion, Amir Ali tried to refute Woodroffe's arguments. His view set the pattern for argument in favour of endowments like Bikani Mian's. Most of those involved in the subsequent controversy echoed either Woodroffe or Amir Ali. The latter, in his defence of the institution, produced quotations from Arabic texts which he claimed proved that "authorities" definitely approved of endowments in favour of one's descendants. But, as noted in previous cases, this approach was not very persuasive. Baillie's translation of the *Fatawa-i Alamgiri* said the same thing in plain English. Judges never paid much attention to it or to other translations. They usually pointed to Hamilton's translation of the *Hedaya* and argued that the same authorities disapproved of private endowments. They held that, at best, some "confusion" existed and therefore the courts had the power to settle the matter.

Amir Ali tried to discredit Hamilton's text by showing that his translation was in error. Hamilton, according to Amir Ali, tried to clarify his use of the term "appropriation" as an English equivalent of the Arabic "*waqf*". He added a footnote explaining that those "appropriations" were for religious or charitable purposes. The comment was not a translation of any statement in the Arabic text. Judges who ruled against family endowments on Hamilton's authority based their decision on a footnote. The weight of textbook opinion was therefore in favour of the private use of *awqaf*. Despite the validity of Amir Ali's criticism, Anglo-Indian judges continued to throw out endowments on the basis of the Hamilton translation.

As for the *Sadr Diwani* cases which Woodroffe cited as proof for recent origins of private endowments, Amir Ali argued that these cases

[121] Bikani Mian's case, *Cal*, XX, 131.

legal argument, that Muslims had carried out the Quranic prescriptions. If they did not, they were avoiding the rigours of their own "law".

No amount of historical information would have shaken Woodroffe's basic premise. He could always argue that violators of the principle did not impugn the principle itself. Nevertheless, numerous examples of Muslim non-compliance in matters of inheritance might have been introduced. The *taalluqdars* of Avadh were one contemporary instance. Muslim *taalluqdars* practised inheritance by male primogeniture, a method contradicting Quranic usage.[118] Though members of *taalluqdari* families, especially females, were unhappy with those arrangements,[119] no one inside or outside the British government accused them of being "un-Islamic". The political importance of the *taalluqdars* gave them a special status. However, other records indicated that many Muslims did not follow the regulations on inheritance rigorously. For example, the biographer of Mawlana Muhammad Qasim Nanotawi, a leader of the Deoband movement, noted that the Mawlana wanted to give away his family property because he believed he had inherited it contrary to the principles of *shariah*.[120] Was it because the Mawlana's action was exceptional that it was thought important enough to put in his biography as a mark of his piety? Indeed, as the previous chapters noted, one of the attractive aspects of a *waqf* was that it allowed an individual to name his or her heirs. The individuals who took that course did not think of themselves as evading their law or as lacking religious scruples. They believed that they were taking appropriate steps to preserve their property and their faith. But Woodroffe, it seemed, was determined to hold Muslims to a textbook version of Islam. Woodroffe, and most of those active in the courts, shared that rather static view of the faith.

Woodroffe's attack on endowments included an assertion that they were a pious method of defrauding creditors. Muslim scholars agreed with Woodroffe. Texts like the *Hedaya* and *Fatawa-i Alamgiri* held that a *waqf* created to cheat someone on a loan was bad. Nevertheless, the charge of chicanery was bound to cast the institution in an unfavourable light.

In his brief against endowments, Woodroffe employed some of the same assumptions found in Lord Hobhouse's opinion in Shaikh Ahsanullah's case. Like the Privy Councillor, he took it for granted that a

[118] T. R. Metcalf, *Land*, 200ff.
[119] Based on an interview with Begum Razia Hifazat Hosein, Lucknow, 16 April 1979. Begum Hosein is a member of the Kidwai family which produced two eminent *taalluqdari* households. She noted that in her youth girls who received some education knew that the provisions of *shariah* offered them a "fair share" of the family estate. Therefore, they resented being fobbed off with a small yearly stipend.
[120] B. D. Metcalf, *Islamic Revival*, 77.

property in Hajji Bikani Mian's endowment in lieu of a debt. Woodroffe seemed determined to prove that Hobhouse was right and Amir Ali wrong. The arguments of Amir Ali and Woodroffe so dominated the trial that the official report made the case look like a contest between these two men. Bikani Mian and his *waqf* were pushed into the background. More abstract concerns occupied the official participants and they seldom mentioned the man whose endowment provided the occasion for the legal debate.

Bikani Mian's lawyers began by arguing that "Muhammadan law" approved of endowments in the interests of the founder's family. This made the case a matter of religion. Both Warren Hastings' Regulations of 1772 and Victoria's Proclamation of 1858 showed that India's British rulers were bound to honour the "religious usages" of Muslims. Therefore, the court must uphold the *waqf* as a religious institution.

Woodroffe denied the validity of Bikani Mian's argument. He noted that the case involved a Hindu and, therefore, Muslim law was not the rule to be applied. Rather, "justice, equity and good conscience" should be the bases for any decision, not arguments of a "religious, metaphysical, or philosophical character". The government, he asserted, permitted the enforcement of Muhammadan law and the government was free to choose how much or how little of that system was valid. This case, according to Woodroffe, fell outside the limits which the government placed on the practice of Muhammadan law.

Woodroffe also contradicted the assertion that the Muhammadan system approved of endowments used as family settlements. The latter was a very recent development: "This matter of private *wakfs* is an offspring of purely modern and secular considerations."[117] To prove his point, Woodroffe did not refer to the translations of *shariah* textbooks but to the records of cases heard in the Company courts. He noted that in the *Sadr Diwani* reports only about twenty cases involving *awqaf* were listed. Of that number, only three, he argued, were similar to Bikani Mian's. Therefore, using a *waqf* to support a founder's family had to be a new tactic and therefore disapproved of by *shariah*. Woodroffe's assumption was that the ancient Muslim system did not tolerate change.

The final argument put forward by the Advocate General was based on an appeal to "Muhammadan law" itself. That system demanded a division of property among a number of heirs. Bikani Mian's *waqf* was nothing less than an attempt to evade that rule. Woodroffe was, in one sense, correct. The *Quran* (IV, 7–13) did command the partition of a person's wealth after death. However, did Muslims actually carry out that kind of division? Woodroffe assumed, at least for the purpose of

[117] Bikani Mian's case, *Cal*, XX, 128–129.

good *wakf* unless there is a substantial dedication of the property to charitable uses at some time or other.[112]

Hobhouse and the other Councillors had the same sources that Justice West had. Though translations and textbooks contained differing views, Hobhouse was not correct in his statement that no authority sanctioned *awqaf* which benefited their founders' families. Hobhouse's judgment in Shaikh Ahsan-ullah's case had only limited, immediate influence. Because he refused to issue a definitive ruling, Indian High Courts upheld several endowments which violated the Privy Council's test. For example, in March of 1892, Justices Edge and Mahmud of the Allahabad court heard the case of *Deoki Prasad (and others)* v. *Inait-ullah*.[113] As with the preceding suits, this endowment was challenged by a creditor who had seized some portion of an estate in payment for a debt. Mahmud's arguments in this case were forceful and supported provisions for the grantor's own family. Sir John Edge agreed with Mahmud and wrote that the Privy Council's ruling in Shaikh Ahsan-ullah's case did not apply because the family members receiving money from this *waqf* "might be in great want".

At this time the High Courts were not of one mind on the issue. The Calcutta court, acting in a similar case, also in March of 1892, ruled against an endowment.[114] The Calcutta court's hearing on Hajji Bikani Mian's *waqf* in August of 1892 presented an opportunity for the airing of all the major arguments on the matter of endowments.[115] Amir Ali, then serving as a justice of that court, insisted on a full bench decision in Bikani Mian's case. Amir Ali claimed to be a serious student of Muslim endowments. His researches led him to assert that *awqaf* were "one of their [Muslims] most cherished institutions, which is interwoven with their entire religious and social life, and on which rests the whole fabric of their prosperity as a people".[116] He had devoted much of the first volume of his text on *Mahommedan Law* to a discussion of the subject. Amir Ali was aware of the confusion left by the contradictory decisions of the courts. He also believed that they were formulated on the basis of scanty knowledge of Muslim sources. Therefore, he was determined to settle the matter with salvos of argument based on his extensive knowledge of *shariah*.

J. T. Woodroffe, the officiating Advocate General of Bengal, appeared in court on behalf of the creditors who had claimed some of the

---
[112] *Ibid.*, 509.
[113] *Deoki Prasad (and others)* v. *Inait-ullah*, *All*, XIV, 375, 376–377.
[114] *Meer Mahomed Israil Khan* v. *Shastri Churn Ghose (and others)*, *Cal*, XIX, 412ff.
[115] Bikani Mian's case, *Cal*, XX, 116ff.
[116] S. A. Ali, *Memoirs and Other Writings of Syed Ameer Ali*, 279.

in 1866 and the trouble did not begin until some sixteen years later.

The legal battle over Shaikh Ahsan-ullah's *waqf* started when Krishnadas Kundu obtained a decree from the subordinate magistrate of Chittagong attaching two pieces of property controlled by his sons. The brothers went before the same judge and claimed that they did not own the land in question. They were, they argued, merely employees of their father's *waqf*. The terms of that *waqf*'s foundation deed forbade the sale or seizure of any section of Ahsan-ullah's property. The subordinate judge accepted their arguments and in July of 1883 ordered the parcels returned to the brothers.

Amarchand Kundu, Krishnadas' successor, appealed the magistrate's decision to the Calcutta High Court. In 1885, the High Court reversed the lower court's decision and ordered the land surrendered to Kundu. Shaikh Ahsan-ullah's sons brought the matter before the Privy Council where Councillors Hobhouse, Watson, Peacock and Couch gave a final verdict in 1889.

Lord Hobhouse wrote the Council's opinion. In it he ruled against the brothers, arguing that Ahsan-ullah's *waqf* was an illusory religious endowment. Hobhouse's view was that a *waqf* was supposed to be a religious or charitable trust. He pointed to the leading paragraphs of the deed of endowment and noted that they all concerned the disposition of money to various members of Shaikh Ahsan-ullah's own family. Hobhouse thought that the income given for the mosques and schools was small. These benefactions, he wrote, were "customary usages" which did not represent the main object of the *waqf*. That aim, according to Hobhouse, was the "self-aggrandizement of the family". He considered all statements in the deed which indicated that the *waqf* was "in the way of Allah" as a "veil" masking the deed's real intention.[111]

The implications of Hobhouse's statements will be taken up shortly. For the moment, we note that the immediate effect of the Privy Council's decision was limited. The Law Lords decided to overturn Ahsan-ullah's *waqf*, but they avoided deciding on all endowments:

Their Lordships do not attempt in this case to lay down any precise definition of what will constitute a valid *wakf* or to determine how far provisions for the grantor's family may be engrafted on such a settlement without destroying its character as a charitable gift. They are not called upon by the facts of the case to decide whether a gift of property to charitable uses which is only to take effect after the failure of all the grantor's descendants is an illusory gift, a point on which there have been conflicting decisions in India. [i.e. Fatima Bibi's case]... On the other hand, they [the Privy Councillors] have not been referred to, nor can they find any authority showing that, according to Muhammadan Law, a gift is a

[111] *Cal*, XVII, 510ff.

originally seized for payment of Tahira's debts. In the second case, they argued that West had based his decision on the Hanafi school of *shariah*. They, Qamr ud-din and the whole family, were adherents of the school of Imam Shafii. Their status as custodians was, they claimed, recognized in that tradition. Also, they claimed that Shafiite *fiqh* definitely approved of endowments in favour of the founder's own family. They made their appeal in the usual judicial circuit and even took the case to the Privy Council in London. The Law Lords decided the second case in 1892. Though the five cousins called in experts on Shafii *fiqh* and submitted translations from Arabic texts of that school, the Law Lords ruled against them.[108]

Justice West heard another case involving a *waqf* which benefited the founder's own family in 1882. In his opinion in *Fatima Bibi* v. *The Advocate General of Bombay*, West answered the question he asked in Fatah Bibi's case.[109] In this instance, he held that a *waqf* in favour of its founder's family was valid, so long as the dedication made it clear that "the poor" or some other "charitable" or "public" purpose would ultimately get the income. An individual could distribute the funds to his own descendants provided that a stipulation was made that if and when the family line died out, the money then went to some religiously sanctioned purpose. If the courts had sustained West's opinion, his views would have helped only those Muslims aware of the decision. Many of the *awqaf* created before 1882 did not contain such a clear statement of the founder's intentions in the event of his or her line's extinction. Though West's limitation was not in conflict with the *shariah*, few founders seemed ready to face the possibility that their families might die out.

About the same time that West gave his opinion in Fatima Bibi's case, another lawsuit was brought in the court at Chittagong in Eastern Bengal. This suit concerned an endowment established by Shaikh Muhammad Ahsan-ullah Chaudhuri in December of 1864. Shaikh Ahsan-ullah was a prosperous merchant and landowner. His estate generated about Rs. 17,000 per year.[110] Shaikh Ahsan-ullah named himself and his three sons as the custodians of the *waqf*. Each of the sons received a salary in addition to a share in the income. Wives and daughters also got small allotments. The endowment supported a mosque built by Shaikh Ahsan-ullah's grandfather in the village of Paragulpur where the family owned land. In his residence in the city of Chittagong, he also maintained a mosque and two schools. The Shaikh himself died

---

[108] *Abdul Gafur (and others)* v. *Nizam Ghulam (and others)*, Bom, XIII, 638ff, and *LI*, vol. 367, 731ff.
[109] *Bom*, VI, 42ff.
[110] *Shaikh Mahomed Ahsanulla Cowdhry* v. *Amarchand Kundu (and others)*, Cal, XVII, 498ff and *LI*, vol. 340, 89.

express limitation to the use of the poor or some other inexhaustible class of beneficiaries, appears to be a question of some nicety, as to one element, at least, of which the Muhammadan doctors have differed.[105]

According to legal argot, "nice" meant "tricky" or "disputed". So far as the translations were concerned, a contradiction did exist. Hamilton's translation of the *Hedaya* did focus on the public or charitable uses of endowments. But Hamilton's translation often had only a tenuous connection to the Arabic of the original text.[106] Hamilton often reworked the English to fit his own experience and tended to interpolate his own views into passages. By contrast, Baillie's translation of the *Fatawa-i Alamgiri* reported approval for *awqaf* in favour of one's self, children or children's children.[107] The textbooks mentioned above, with the exception of MacNaghtan's, offered the same opinion and described it as the "authoritative" view. In a sense, both the textbook writers and West were wrong. The scholars of *shariah* did disagree about the use of endowments (see p. 13). But Muslims never had the equivalent of a High Court to supply a definitive ruling on what constituted a proper *waqf*. Muslim thinkers had never phrased the question in quite the same way that Justice West did. The history of endowments, which none of those involved knew in detail, showed that *awqaf* like Qamr ud-din's were common enough. From the point of view of British law, the absence of a single authoritative opinion meant that West's question was in order. Muslims had lived with the uncertainty for centuries, but the Anglo-Indian legal system was unable to tolerate such a lacuna.

Apart from the contrasting methods of British courts and Muslim scholars, West's action highlighted the difference between the concerns of the founders of endowments and those of government officials. Qamr ud-din looked at the creation of a *waqf* as a way of making sure that his estate would not be fragmented by bickering heirs and creditors. He also used it to sustain a mosque and ceremonies which represented the spiritual order. But Justice West did not concern himself with the wishes of a man dead for almost forty years. He concentrated on the point of law which the *waqf* raised.

The five cousins who lost the suit took a holiday but spent their time planning another judicial assault. They initiated another case, this time against Nizam Ghulam, who was the other part purchaser of the lands

---

[105] *Ibid.*, 88.
[106] Al-Marghinani, *Hedaya*, trans. Hamilton, 231ff; *Hidayah* (*Farsi*), 1210ff, and *al-Hidaya* (Arabic), III, 13ff; one source of difficulty was Hamilton's concern to find a "definitive" opinion. The Arabic original simply lists the conflicting views of different *Imams* without comment.
[107] N.B. E. Baillie, *A Digest of Muhammadan Law*, 557–595.

result of their purchase, those two gentlemen and their descendants became parties in several suits.

After Tahira's death in 1873, the only surviving daughter, Fatah Sahib Bibi, initiated litigation in the court of the subordinate judge of Panvel. She claimed that Tahira had no right to borrow against land which originally belonged to Qamr ud-din. That land was part of a *waqf* and therefore immune to seizure for debt. Moreover, as Fatah Bibi was the sole surviving custodian of that endowment, she was entitled to retrieve the property. The subordinate judge ruled in her favour, despite Damodar Premji's argument that he knew nothing about the property's status as a *waqf*.

Premji appealed to the district judge of Thana, who reversed the first court's ruling and returned possession to Premji. Fatah Bibi, in her turn, appealed the matter to the Bombay High Court. Although named as a litigant, Fatah Bibi died in 1875, four years before West and Pinhey heard the case. Actually, five men who were her distant relatives (descendants of Qamr ud-din's great-uncle) pursued the dispute. Though hardly close kin, they were the nearest surviving cousins and no one challenged their claim to be custodians of the endowment.

In the High Court, Premji's lawyer put forward two arguments in defence of his client's right to the disputed property. The first was a purely procedural point. The attorney noted that only a *mutawalli* was able to sue on behalf of a *waqf*. Fatah Bibi held that office by the terms of Qamr ud-din's deed, but the cousins were not even mentioned in it. They were not able to produce any other document which named them custodians. Justice West wrote that he consulted a "*mawlwi*" (Muslim religious scholar) on this matter. That man, who was not further identified, confirmed the view that only a custodian was eligible under *shariah* to act on behalf of an endowment. West assumed that a court case required that authority. Therefore, he ruled in Premji's favour on the basis of this technical argument.

In the course of the trial, Premji's lawyer raised a second, more substantial point. He referred to Hamilton's translation of the *Hedaya* and noted that the text proved that a *waqf* had to have only "charitable" objects. Qamr ud-din's endowment, so his argument ran, benefited his own family. It was, therefore, invalid from the beginning. The case was already decided, but the question intrigued West. He made note of the second argument in a *quaere* (question) appended to the decision as a judicial footnote.

Whether a *waqf* could, indeed, be created for the purpose merely of conferring a perpetual and inalienable estate on a particular family, without any ultimate were better trained and the courts more eager to establish a single rule of law.

A dispute known as *Phate Saheb Bibi (and others)* v. *Damodar Premji*[104] initiated a new phase in the history of endowments in India. Justices Raymond West and R. H. Pinhey of the Bombay High Court heard the case in 1879. The endowment they considered was created in 1838 by a man named Qamr ud-din. In his lifetime, he acquired property worth more than Rs. 50,000. In part, Qamr ud-din inherited the property from his father, who died in 1806. Along with the property, his father left Qamr ud-din a bundle of I.O.U.s and a mob of creditors. Legal battles to establish a claim against the lenders cost Qamr ud-din a number of years and a lot of money. They left him in possession, but they also gave him a rather sour opinion of the courts. In composing his deed of endowment, he declared that anyone who raised an objection to its provisions thereby lost their share of the proceeds. He ordered that all claims against his property be considered null and void.

Qamr ud-din was a landholder and petty entrepreneur. He owned a salt-works and nineteen salt pans. Presumably he sold his factory's produce to the British government which held a tax monopoly on this basic condiment. (The assumption that he was a prescient Gandhian seems unwarranted.) He also acquired control of some property through his first wife, Ayisha. Later, he married a second woman, Amina, and he had four daughters: Masa Sahib Bibi, Fatah Sahib Bibi, Tahira and Sara, two by each wife.

Qamr ud-din's deed distributed the income of his property in most of the ways noted in previous chapters. Some went to support the congregational mosque in the town of Uran which was located in the Thana district, adjacent to the city of Bombay. The money given to the mosque went to buy three pounds of oil for its lamps. Other small sums went for such observances as the monthly recitation of the *Quran* for the souls of Qamr ud-din's family. Each of the wives and her two daughters were assigned one half of all the other income. After Qamr ud-din's death in 1840, neither his wives nor his daughters made an effort to change their status on the government revenue rolls. Though the *waqf* made them "custodians", they continued to style themselves "owners". The endowment functioned smoothly for almost twenty-five years. His wives died. Masa Sahib Bibi died in 1862 and her sister Sara in 1866.

The year 1862 was a fateful one for the family in another way. In that year some of the property claimed by Tahira was seized to satisfy a debt she owed to one Hari Pandu Shet. Having obtained a decree, he promptly sold it to two men: Damodar Premji and Nizam Ghulam. As a

[104] *Bom*, III, 84ff.

The case of Wasiq Ali was probably the most noted involving an endowment heard in the Company's courts. It also was an instance when the will of the Revenue Department took precedence over the strict dictates of *shariah*. Wasiq Ali managed the richly endowed Hughli *Imambarah* (see pp. 38–9). Revenue authorities charged him with corruption and removed him in 1824. After Wasiq Ali's departure, the government began to make changes in the character of the shrine. Though a site for the ritual commemoration of the martyrdom of Imam Husain, endowment funds also maintained a small school in the building. Once British officials assumed control, they decided that the school was the most important public function of the *Imambarah*. They took charge of the curriculum. The teaching of *Quran* and the rudiments of Persian grammar gave way to a programme emphasizing the teaching of English. Hindu boys began to come to the school. Under the guidance of T. B. Macaulay and other British intellectuals, the "oriental" aspect of the school disappeared. It became, in time, the "Hooghly College", a government institution in which Hindus far outnumbered Muslims in both the faculty and student body.[101]

When Wasiq Ali entered the courts trying to get himself reinstated as custodian, he came armed with the opinions of a number of independent Muslim religious scholars in his favour. These *fatawa* pointed to the changes the government made in the endowment and condemned them as contrary to the *shariah*.[102] The *Sadr Diwani* court refused to accept the arguments and upheld the government's actions. The Hughli College remained under the control of a government sponsored committee. The court proceedings did not mention whether or not its own *qazis* supported that decision.

The records of the Company's courts showed that Muslims working for them passed over a number of issues which subsequently troubled British judges and lawyers. For example, no one ever raised the question of what the "true" nature of an endowment was supposed to be. Thus, when British judges began to investigate that matter after 1879, they had little in the way of precedent to guide them. The cases heard in the Company courts did, however, leave the impression that a *waqf* was used for "pious purposes".[103] Because most of the suits involved saints' tombs, ceremonies or other religious activities, judicial authorities easily came to the conclusion that a "valid" endowment had to sustain such things. The courts which considered the question after 1879 were, as noted above, different in many ways from their predecessors. The personnel

---

[101] Zakariah, *History of Hooghly College*, 1–10, and *Hooghly College Register*.
[102] *Wasiq Ali Khan* v. *The Government*, SDA, VI, 130.
[103] *Mir Nusrut Ali* v. *Mir Casim Ali*, SDA, I, 543–549.

active role. The British judges of the *Sadr Diwani* courts seemed willing to let their Muslim advisers, known as *qazis*, inform their decisions. For example, the reports showed that the courts allowed the *qazis* to work in the same way their Mughal predecessors had. Mughal *qazis* looked at every dispute in isolation, so did those working for the British. Though published reports of other decisions were available, the *qazis* did not refer to them and provided opinions on a case by case basis.

Almost all of the twenty cases involved a dispute over succession to the trusteeship of an endowment. The custodianship of a *waqf* was a potentially lucrative post. Custodians received a salary for their work. Also, they made decisions on the disposition of the property forming the basis of an endowment. Though in theory they could not sell or mortgage property, in practice custodians often initiated such transactions. Such activity led to relatives who were not trustees challenging the managers of endowments in court. Because most custodians were descendants or near kin of founders, the courts could not easily establish a boundary between a public trust and family interest. Not surprisingly, the *qazis* avoided so complex a matter. Rather, they limited themselves to the interpretation of the original *waqf*-deeds. Their chief concern was determining a rightful line of succession to trusteeships.

In the case of Hai un-nissa, for instance, the experts had to decide whether a woman could hold the post of custodian of a sufi shrine.[99] Hai un-nissa had, it seemed, taken over as manager and spiritual director of an ancestor's tomb. The court's Muslim scholars ruled that no impediment existed to her acting as *mutawalli*. However, she had no right to function as mystical preceptor since that would involve her unrestricted mixing with males.

Qazis were often called upon to interpret documentary evidence. They served as guides in discovering the meaning of the old Mughal decretals. As noted in earlier chapters, the Mughals distributed a variety of grants of revenue free land (*inam*) or of some portion of the government revenue in a particular district (*madad-i maash*). Descendants or disciples of the original holders sometimes claimed that these grants were actually *awqaf*. British revenue officers were puzzled by the terminology. Were all imperial grants *awqaf*? According to the texts on *shariah*, the word *waqf* did not have to be used in the dedication of property. Therefore, the *qazis* argued that imperial grants had the same intention, to promote a "good purpose", as *awqaf* and should be treated in the same way.[100]

[99] *SDA*, I, 140ff.
[100] Examples, *Kalb Ali Hosein* v. *Syf Ali*, *SDA*, II, 139–141, and *Mussumat Qadira* v. *Shah Kubueroodeen*, *SDA*, III, 543–549.

acquired some notoriety: R. K. Wilson's *A Digest of Anglo-Muhammadan Law* of 1895, Nawab A. F. M. Abdur Rahman's *Institutes of Mussalman Law* of 1907 and Faiz Badr ud-din Tyabji's *Principles of Muhummadan Law*, published in 1913. Since their authors were either Britons or British trained, all the texts were organized like their counterparts treating British law. Though some of them occasionally referred to Arabic or Persian texts, actual cases of the Anglo-Indian courts formed their major resource.

In restricting authority in *shariah* to a comparatively small number of translations and introductory manuals, the British were able to accomplish something that most Muslim rulers never had. They assigned definite sovereignty in matters of the *shariah*. Judging from the current state of Muslim law in South Asia, the British were very successful in reshaping *shariah* and remodelling the perceptions of Muslims themselves. Throughout the years of British rule, Muslims brought their disputes to the courts and accepted their rulings. Only a few Muslims objected to the "un-Islamic" character of the courts and the law. The *ulama* of Deoband tried to convince their fellow Muslims that the British courts were not the proper place for believers to seek justice. They established a special bureau at their school and encouraged Muslims to refer their questions and quarrels to it. Although many thousands sought opinions from these scholars, the majority of questions submitted concerned matters of ritual. The Deobandis solved very few conflicts involving property.[97] Because the very notion of private property in land was linked to British rule, most Muslims took their disagreements to British courts.

The gradual trend throughout the British period was to make the *shariah* a system of definite rules applied within a politically sanctioned judicial hierarchy. We now turn to an examination of the ways in which those forces worked in shaping the character of Muslim endowments.

The courts and Muslim endowments

Between the years 1798 and 1858, some twenty cases involving Muslim endowments appeared in the published reports of *Sadr Diwani* courts.[98] Though all cases were not reported, these twenty were probably representative of the issues the courts had to examine. They also illustrated the methods which the Company's courts employed in dealing with Muslim institutions. In general terms, the courts at this earlier stage of British rule were less intrusive. After 1861, the courts took a much more

[97] B. D. Metcalf, *Islamic Revival*, 146–147.
[98] *Bikani Mia* v. *Shuk Lal Poddar (and another)*, Cal, XX, 129.

sounder, more objective judgments and thereby reduce the high number of appeals. The government rejected his proposal. It eliminated jobs open to Indians and the administration wanted to avoid the disaffection which such a move created.[90]

Maine did, however, have indirect influence on Indian law. His role in reforming legal education meant that many lawyers were trained more rigorously. His major influence was exerted in the realms of legal and social theory. Most judges, barristers and administrators in India were, at least superficially, acquainted with his work.[91] Students of society found models in his work. Though some of his views attracted opposition, the basic theoretical framework remained unquestioned for many years.

Though discussions of legal theory were lively, similar intellectual energy was not spent in discovering more about the traditions of India. Few texts were translated. For Muslim law, Hamilton's translation of the *Hedaya* remained the standard until Baillie's *Digest of Muhammadan Law* appeared in 1865. Baillie's book was a partial and highly selective rendering of the lengthy compilation of Hanafi opinion known as the *Fatawa-i Alamgiri*. Though the original was much lengthier than Baillie's anthology, his translations were from the Arabic.[92]

In practice, legal textbooks were a more important source of information for judges and lawyers. The first of the genre was William Mac-Naghtan's *Principles of Mohammadan Law*, published in 1825. It tried to provide British judges with a simple statement of the rules of the Muslim system. It tried to present those things which MacNaghtan considered "essential", while avoiding "the most prolix and irrelevant discussions".[93] In H. H. Wilson's edition, MacNaghtan's text had some ninety-seven octavo pages and took the form of numbered precepts on such subjects as inheritance, sale, marriage, etc.

Later textbooks were a bit more complex. The Tagore Law Lectures, delivered at Calcutta University, produced three massive studies. Sircar's lectures of 1874 were published in two volumes in 1875.[94] Amir Ali published his lectures of 1884 in expanded form in 1892.[95] Abdur Rahim's course of 1907 appeared in 1911.[96] Three other textbooks

[90] Feaver, *From Status*, 77–79.
[91] *Ibid.*, 43, and Tupper, *Punjab Customary Law*, II, 1–10.
[92] Rankin, *Background*, 91, and J. Schacht, "On the Title of the *Fatāwā al-'Ālamgiriyya*", 475–478; this work is not a collection of *Fatawa* but a listing of the views of various masters of Hanafi *fiqh*; like the *Hedaya*, only more extensive.
[93] W. H. MacNaghtan, *Principles of Hindu and Mohammadan Law*, ed. H. H. Wilson, 15.
[94] S. G. Sircar, *The Muhammadan Law*.
[95] Ali, *Mahommedan Law*.
[96] A. Rahim, *The Principles of Muhammadan Jurisprudence*.

Indian law.[85] By and large, the Utilitarian programme was ignored. The government was slow in passing it into law. Though written in 1837, the *Penal Code* was enacted only in 1860. A plan to codify Hindu and Muslim law was never carried out. After 1857, the government was loath to tamper with the customs of Indians. Also, by that time Utilitarian thought had generated a legion of forceful negative critics. The school lost its fascination for intellectuals. John Austin, who died in 1860, was the last major legal thinker in the Utilitarian or "analytical" mode.[86]

Henry Sumner Maine was the most famous and persuasive legal theoretician of the later nineteenth century. Maine introduced the English speaking world to the use of the "historical" and "scientific" approach to law. Pioneered by German legal philosophers, the method focused on the differences between legal systems. While the Utilitarians held that human nature was the same the whole world over, Maine focused on the ways in which historical evolution made people and their laws diverse.[87] Maine was especially fascinated by the progressive development of law among the European branches of the "Aryan race". His characterization of that progress as one from "status" to "contract" became the watchword of many legal authorities in India.[88]

Maine served in India from 1862 to 1869 as legal adviser to the Governor General's Council. His Indian experience only confirmed his ideas on the character of legal and social progress. Much influenced by the linguistic theories of Max Muller, Maine believed in the unity of the Aryan race. He found in the "Hindu village" the prototypical Aryan institution, a specimen of the earliest stage of Aryan society. Europe had left the village far behind in its march of progress. His racial interests precluded any serious attention to Islamic history and institutions. However, he surely must have included them when he wrote, "the East is certainly full of fragments of ancient society. Each individual in India is a slave to the group to which he belongs."[89]

During his seven years in India, Maine had little direct influence on the practice of law there. He made several proposals which he considered practical administrative changes. One of them was to bring large numbers of British lawyers to India. They would serve as district and circuit judges in a greatly expanded lower court network. Maine criticized dependence on Indian officials. He claimed that they made the lower courts inefficient. He thought the British judges would make

[85] Rankin, *Background*, 37ff, 111ff.
[86] Feaver, *From Status*, 27–28, 45, 156–158.
[87] J. W. Burrow, *Evolution and Society*, 38–39.
[88] H. S. Maine, *Ancient Law*, 6–10, 100ff.
[89] H. S. Maine, *Village Communities in the East and West*, 13.

reflected a desire to secure the property rights of landlords and prevent the over-taxation and oppression which the British associated with Mughal rule. The definition of private property rights in land was, for better or worse, the major legacy of Whiggery.[82]

The early decades of the nineteenth century brought to prominence a group of thinkers known as "Utilitarians". Jeremy Bentham and James Mill were justly recognized as the leaders of the movement. They criticized the Whig approach to law. Mill's articles on "Jurisprudence" and "The Law of Nations" in the 1825 Supplement of *Britannica* amounted to an indictment of the British system of law. Mill's view of lawyers set the tone: "Lawyers, whose nature it is to trudge, one after another, in the track which has been made for them; and to whose eyes, that which is, and that which ought to be, have seldom any mark of distinction".[83] The Utilitarians' self-proclaimed rationality made them impatient with the intellectual hodge-podge of law. "Experience", which the Whigs touted as their fundamental principle, Mill considered a euphemism for "groping blindly in the dark". While Mill and Bentham accepted the notion that "law" was command of the state, they would have placed the power to command in the hands of a few, completely rational, magistrates. These individuals were supposed to have a scientific knowledge of the human essence. That made the views of magistrates on the highest good superior.

When both thinkers turned their attention to India, they saw a place to put their theories into practice. Mill came to have some influence over Indian affairs as a secretary to the India Company's London directors. His book, *A History of British India*, contained a lengthy attack on the indigenous legal and social systems of India. It also savaged British policy. The laws of Hindus and Muslims might have been barbaric, wrote Mill, but the remedy did not lie in installing the British system. It was overgrown with procedural technicalities and no more rational than Indian systems. Mill's alternative was the creation of an entirely new legal system for India based on his and Bentham's practical standards.[84]

Utilitarian influence was more clearly seen in the attempt to formalize Indian law in compact and clear legislative codes. T. B. Macaulay's *Indian Penal Code*, as well as *The Law of Evidence*, and the *Law of Transfer and Sale* were attempts to provide an entirely new foundation for

---

[82] Considerable debate has occurred over whether or not these legal changes actually affect power relationships: see B. Cohn, "Structural Change in Indian Rural Society", in *Land Control and Social Structure in Indian History*, 53–121, T. R. Metcalf, *Land*, 133–135, and Ray, "Land Transfer and Social Change under the Permanent Settlement", 1–45.
[83] J. Mill, "Jurisprudence", 3–4.
[84] Stokes, *The English Utilitarians and India*, 149ff.

body of rules considered part of the law of England. During the Middle Ages, most rules of law were founded on local custom, the "law of the manor". Every feudal lord kept his own "court". Rules on inheritance, land tenures and the like varied greatly from place to place. The growth of royal and parliamentary power greatly reduced that variety. The number of individuals entitled to administer the law was similarly curtailed.[80] Also, as noted above, the practice of law became professionalized. In Hamilton's day, the process was not yet complete. Common law was still a separate legal entity administered in its own courts. Well into the nineteenth century, equity, admiralty and ecclesiastical laws maintained different establishments. But the movement towards greater centralization was well under way. Therefore, in creating specific jurisdictions for Indian courts, in gradually increasing the educational requirements of legal practitioners and in seeking to collect definite codes of Muslim or Hindu law, British officials had a model in the experience of their own society.

Though the quest for legal uniformity was centuries old, few tried to explain or rationalize it before the eighteenth century. Blackstone made one of the first halting moves in that direction. He did more than catalogue rules, but spent a little time inquiring into the nature of "law". Later thinkers went far beyond his simple pronouncements, but they continued to accept many of his basic definitions. Two propositions which most legal philosophers accepted were that law was a "rule of action which is prescribed by some superior and which an inferior is bound to obey" and that "law is a rule of civil conduct prescribed by the superior power in a state".[81]

As in Blackstone's own case, legal theory in the eighteenth century had little connection to the actual practice of law. Indeed, none of the major theories had much of an impact on the operation of the judicial establishment in England. India was a somewhat different matter. As a colonial society, it was, from the legal perspective, almost a clean slate. It could, and did, serve as an institutional laboratory, a place for formulating and testing jurisprudential hypotheses. Scattered throughout the Anglo-Indian system a student of legal thought will find the marks of several theoretical trends.

The earliest influence was what became known as the "Whig" view of law and society. Though hardly a district "school", the Whigs shared an emphasis on law as a safeguard against royal tyranny. They believed that the possession of private property was the surest defence against a tyrannous state. In India, the "Permanent Settlement" of Bengal in 1793

[80] Thompson, "The Grid of Inheritance", in *Family and Inheritance*, 328–360.
[81] Quoted in S. M. Mukherjee, *Sir William Jones*, 57.

with Persian and the first translation was intended for Muslims in the Company's employ as well as for Britons working in the courts.[75] But most of the latter did not know Persian very well and so Charles Hamilton began an English version based on the Persian text.[76] He published his work in four folio volumes in 1791. For seventy years, it remained the only complete English translation of a text on *shariah*. Judges constantly referred to it, despite many complaints about its accuracy.[77] Law schools in India and Pakistan still use it as a textbook.

Hamilton's "Preliminary Discourse" to the translation contained a number of observations about the text and about Muslims for whom it was supposedly an authoritative guide. The "Discourse" emphasized the practical value of the text, since "a very large portion of subjects under the British government in India are Mohammedans, upon whose attachment to their rulers much of the prosperity of our Asiatic empire must necessarily depend".[78] Although Hamilton considered Muslim loyalty crucial to the continuance of the British dominance, he did not have much respect for the Muslim system of justice described by the *Hidayah*:

however sagaciously it might be formed for the sudden extension of dominion, during an age when mankind were involved in the darkest gloom of superstition and ignorance, the Mussulman system, civil and religious, is but wretchedly adapted to the purposes of public security and private virtue. We may observe, with some degree of laudable exultation, its obvious inferiority in every useful view to that excellent system which we profess, and which is so admirably calculated to promote the temporal good of mankind as well as their eternal happiness![79]

Hamilton's dim view of the Muslim system was widely shared by British administrators, not only in his own time, but in the century and a half for which the "Asiatic empire" endured. His opinions contained more than cultural pride. They reflected a stress on law that was part of British intellectual life. Most of the great minds of the imperial age had something to say on the subject of law and its place in social life. British legal institutions were themselves undergoing significant alteration. India and its laws had a place in the formulation of British legal discourse. Usually they provided negative examples on which thinkers like Hamilton drew.

A major trend in Britain was towards increasing specificity in the

[75] Burhan al-din al-Marghinani, *Al-Hidayah, Fārsī Tarjumah Kardā*, 1–12.
[76] Pandey, *Introduction*, 142, and Cohn, "From Indian Status", 623–625.
[77] Ali, *Mahommedan Law*, I, 244–256.
[78] Hamilton's Preface to *Hedaya*, xxvii.
[79] *Ibid.*, xxvii–xxviii.

bore the marks of the Christian past. More importantly, they ignored Muslim rulers' frequent unwillingness to apply the *shariah*'s standards to the management of the state. They ignored the possibility that Muslims, like everyone else, often fell short of their own ideal of perfection. "Secularity" was, perhaps, a concept too deeply rooted in the European experience to be useful when describing Muslim history. Nevertheless, history showed that Muslims were "secular" in the sense that they did not constantly, invariably or primarily behave in a religious fashion.

Though British experts, both before and after MacDonald, wrote confidently about the *shariah*, British legal authorities remained basically ignorant of the Muslim literature on the subject. Very few texts on *shariah* were translated. The "orientalism"[71] encouraged by Warren Hastings and popular in limited government circles produced only two major translations. William Jones provided an English rendering of a short treatise on inheritance, *Al-Sirajiyyah*, which was published in Calcutta in 1792.[72] Jones was an excellent example of the first generation of British scholar–administrators. A student of Latin and Greek, he began his study of the Orient with Persian and Arabic. In time, he developed a deeper interest in Sanskrit and Hindu civilization. His interest in these matters had a practical side. As a judge of the Calcutta Supreme Court, he planned to codify both Hindu and Muslim "laws". He did not live long enough to make a serious start on the project.

A second early translation had more influence. It was a text known as *Al-Hidayah* (*The Guidance*), originally composed as a *qazi*'s handbook by Burhan al-din al-Marghinani in the twelfth century A.D.[73] It was general and simply written, covering the *shariah* from the point of view of Abu Hanifa's school. It paid the most attention to the opinions of two of that master's pupils: Abu Yusuf and Imam Muhammad. As a summary of other texts and an introduction, the *Hidayah* was popular with students. However, it was only *one* text in a much larger body of literature known and used by Muslim scholars in India.[74]

The translation of the *Guidance* was undertaken in two stages. First, at the request of Warren Hastings, a number of Muslims employed by the Company compiled an Arabic text of the book. Then they translated it into Persian, which was the language of the Mughal court, imperial administration and polite society. Muslims in India were more likely to know Persian than Arabic. Because their initial contacts were with the Mughals, British officials, including Hastings, had some acquaintance

---

[71] Kopf, *British Orientalism*, 1–49.
[72] *Al-Sirajiyyah, or the Mahommedan Law of Inheritance*, trans. W. Jones.
[73] Al-Marghinani, *Hedaya*, trans. C. Hamilton.
[74] J. H. Harrington, "Remarks upon the Authorities of Mosulman Law", 475–512, and W. H. Morley, *The Administration of Justice in British India*, 257–310.

One reason for the lack of attention to the impact of Anglo-Indian courts on *shariah* was the tremendous influence which they exercised on how people looked at the Muslim system. The list of terminological associations mentioned in the beginning of this chapter still provides the scholar's stock of concepts describing *shariah*. Those conceptualizations were brought forward in time, but they were also read backward into the pre-British past. Historians of "law" in the age of Muslim dominance fully accepted them. Just as some have looked upon the Mughal empire as an embryonic form of the British raj,[68] legal historians have found in Mughal India a fully articulated judicial system. They have described the "jurisdictions" of various courts and officials. They have outlined a process of appeal. The results of their labours have been many studies of "law" in Muslim India, but descriptions of the actual workings of *shariah*, especially with regard to property and its disposition, have been rare.[69]

How then did the British describe the Muslim law they sought to apply? Granting that *shariah* was accepted as law, British authorities found an analogy to the European experience by noting that it was "religious law", similar to the canon law of the medieval church. To the British, the connection between *shariah* and the faith of Islam seemed much more intimate and obvious than the ties of Christianity to common law or equity. That emphasis on "religion" was evident in the Regulations of 1772 and it remained a basic administrative category throughout the British period. Though writing in the early years of the twentieth century, D. B. MacDonald summed up the point in a way that was consonant with earlier perceptions:

in Muslim countries, Church and state are one indissolubly, and until the very essence of Islam passes away, that unity cannot be relaxed. The law of the land, too, is, in theory the law of the Church. In the earlier days at least, canon and civil law were one. Thus, we can never say in Islam, 'he is a great lawyer; he a great theologian; he, a great statesman'. One man may be all three, almost he must be all three, if he is to be any one.[70]

The British categorized the life of Muslims in terms which were historically significant (and value-laden) for themselves. Their views ignored the many ways in which their own system of law and society still

---

[68] Blake, "The Patrimonial–Bureaucratic Empire of the Mughals", 77–94.
[69] M. B. Ahmad, *The Administration of Justice in Medieval India*; M. Akbar, *The Administration of Justice by the Mughals*; W. Husain, *Administration of Justice during the Muslim Rule of India*; and K. M. Yusuf, "The Judiciary in India under the Sultans of Delhi and the Mughal Emperors", 1–12.
[70] D. B. MacDonald, *The Development of Muslim Theology, Jurisprudence and Constitutional Theory*, 4.

eral Party and a close associate of John Morley.[65] His connection to Indian or Islamic law was based solely on his tour of duty in Indian government. Training and experience in British law informed his decisions.

Laws and theories of law

Judges did not have to have an intimate knowledge of *shariah* to make the courts work. Their task was simplified by the basic premise with which the Anglo-Indian courts operated: that the *shariah* was a system of law similar in some ways to that of the British. When the East India Company's Regulations of 1772 mentioned the administration of justice, they indicated that the courts would apply only the "laws" of Hindus and Muslims. Something more complex actually occurred. Rather than applying already existing legal codes, the courts mixed British legal notions and indigenous traditions. They applied principles garnered from the reading of a very few Hindu and Muslim texts in institutions whose procedures were modelled on British courts. In effect, they created a legal system.

To date, scholars have provided a much clearer account of how that process worked with regard to *dharmaśastra*. Genuinely historical studies of the British impact on *shariah* have lagged behind. Like *shariah*, *dharmasastra* was part of a vision of a perfect society. Its literal meaning, "science of righteousness", pointed to its concern with all activities. Like its Muslim counterpart, many of the *dharmasastra*'s injunctions were not enforceable. Also, texts on this "science" exhibited considerable differences of opinion among savants. Regional variations and local customs were often at variance with textual prescriptions. Even Hindu kings did not enforce all of it. During the centuries of Muslim rule, the state avoided meddling with it and it was further localized. When British authorities took over the enforcement of *dharmasastra*, they smoothed out the irregularities, supported some opinions over others, subjected it to the rule of precedent and made it metropolitan rather than local. Under the British aegis, it also became less fluid, more like a legal system on the British pattern.[66] British courts transformed *shariah* in a similar way. As with Hindu law, they "overgeneralized on what they knew and assumed uniformities where none existed".[67]

---

[65] *Dictionary of National Biography, Second Supplement*, II, 272–273, and L. T. Hobhouse, *Lord Hobhouse*.
[66] J. D. M. Derrett, *Religion, Law and the State in India*, chapter 9.
[67] Cohn, "From Indian Status", 618.

divisions within the law and the importance attached to enactments of the British–Indian government were only the most obvious expressions of that control. Other, more symbolic aspects of legal practice – the etiquette of the courts with its "M'Lords" and "my learned friends", the gowns of the judges or lawyers, even the architecture of the court buildings – reminded all participants of British forms and traditions.

An individual advocate's talent was a less tangible element in the practice of law in the Indian courts. For example, the High Courts' methods placed a premium on an attorney's forensic skills. Every High Court Bar had its share of men who were known as "winners". These men attracted a larger share of clients and higher fees. Moti Lal Nehru's early reputation was based on his status as a "winner" in the Allahabad court. The wealth he acquired provided the material base for his own and his son's political careers.[64] In choosing lawyers, clients seemed to base their decision on their representative's record of wins and losses. Few of them expressed any sort of "communal" preference. A Muslim litigant, arguing a case under Muhammadan law, was apt to pick a winning Hindu or Englishman to represent him. Such choices indicated that personal conviction was not required of a lawyer. The same attorney might strive to overturn a Muslim endowment one day and the next, in another case, direct his talents to the defence of a similar endowment. Personal conviction was not required, indeed it was discouraged in the interests of legal objectivity. In that matter alone, a major distinction existed between a lawyer in the British tradition and a learned man of Islam. For Muslims, just knowing the rules of *shariah* was not enough. A learned man was supposed to be a pious man.

The Privy Council was, as noted, the highest legal authority in the British empire. It was also the most "British" in terms of its personnel and procedure. Until Amir Ali's appointment to that body, the panel was made up entirely of British jurists. Arthur Hobhouse, who served from 1881 until his death, was an appropriate example of a Privy Councillor, since he wrote the definitive judgments on Muslim endowments. Born in 1819, he had a distinguished academic, legal and political career. Having taken a first in classics at Balliol College, Oxford, he went on to Lincoln's Inn and was called to the Bar in 1844. Though he spent most of his career in the courts of England, he did serve one term as the Law Member of the Indian Legislative Council. After his appointment to the Privy Council, he heard some 200 appeals, 120 of which originated in India. As a politician, he was a leading member of the Lib-

---

[64] *Allahabad High Court Bar Association, Centenary Volume*, 85–89, and R. S. Khare, "Indigenous Culture and Lawyers' Law in India", 71–96.

office or in the courts."[60] When reform came in the 1850s, one of its most fervent exponents was H. S. Maine, now best remembered as a legal theorist. Under Maine's leadership, lectureships and required examinations came to the Inns of Court. Even so, officials and Indian lawyers expressed concern that attending the Inns was a short cut to a legal career in India. Many believed that the legal education given in Indian universities was superior, especially with regard to the indigenous legal systems of India.[61] Their doubts, however, did nothing to change the character of the profession in India. Like their British counterparts, Indian lawyers were an elite caste.

Several grades of legal practitioners existed in India. They ranged from the barristers, who had been called from the British Bar, through the advocates and *Wakils*, trained in Indian universities, to the lowly "*mukhtar*", allowed to practise only in subordinate criminal or revenue courts.[62] Those who attended Indian universities faced a one to two year course covering all of the subjects familiar to students of British law: jurisprudence, contracts, torts, evidence, procedure and criminal law. An examination of the textbooks employed for teaching these subjects in Indian schools showed that all of them had British authors. In addition to that portion of the course, students worked on legal matters specifically related to India. Those included the various codes (e.g. *The Indian Penal Code*) enacted by India's British rulers. Also, subjects such as land tenure and the Indian version of equity received special attention. The concentration on the law of property reflected the practice of the courts where that litigation was most common. Only a small part of the syllabus was devoted to the study of Hindu and Muslim laws. Only four textbooks on these subjects were listed and two of these had British authors.[63]

Legal training's most immediate goal was to teach the laws actually in use. Therefore, the Indian universities insisted that students be well read in the published reports of the courts. This kept them current on trends in decisions, interpretations and types of litigation. It also initiated them into the arcana of legal argument. Since the principle of *stare decis*, precedent, held an important place in Anglo-Indian law, knowledge of the previous decisions of the courts was essential.

The programme of study just outlined demonstrated the central, formative place which British law had in the Indian legal system. The predominance of British authors in Indian legal syllabuses, the topical

[60] G. Feaver, *From Status to Contract*, 18–25.
[61] (UP) *JP Civ, Confidential* (1911), no. 331, letter of Lord Crewe dated 26 May 1911.
[62] *Ibid.*, undated letter of Dr Tej Bahadur Sapru.
[63] *Ibid.* Sapru's letter provides a topical syllabus and reading list used in Allahabad University's law course.

Anyone called to the Bar in England, Scotland or Ireland was automatically admitted to the Bar in India. Social prestige definitely went to those who were "England trained". Most High Courts had two Bar associations, one for the members of the British Bar and another for the locals. Many Indians, including Gandhi and Jinnah, had attended the Inns of Court.

Because the Inns of Court and the law courses which the British established in India trained so many future leaders, a few paragraphs should be devoted to the character of the legal profession in England. Lawyers, as a distinct professional class, emerged gradually in the late fifteenth and sixteenth centuries. Before that period, England had several different court systems. Most of those were local, maintained by feudal lords, each of whom had his own "court". The church courts were staffed by clerics. However, as litigation outside local and church courts became more common, the need arose for specialists who knew how to manage the rules applied in the Royal and Chancery courts.[59] The specialists, in their turn, developed a vested interest in creating and maintaining a system which they monopolized. Thus, the clergy gradually ceased to control the law courts and lay legal experts appeared.

Lawyers remained a fairly exclusive group, even without the benefit of ecclesiastical sanction. Because their training consisted of an apprenticeship to someone who belonged to the profession, their numbers were limited to a favoured few. By tradition, candidates for the Bar had to be associated with one of four "Inns of Court" located in London's Chancery Lane. The Inns were not schools, and had begun life as residence halls. During the Reformation and Renaissance periods, they were best remembered as the sites for many balls and gala feasts. Until the middle of the nineteenth century, lawyers attended no lectures and took no examinations. The only requirement for an aspiring barrister was that he eat a prescribed number of meals at the Inn.

The character of legal training changed very slowly. Blackstone was appointed the first professor of law at Oxford in 1785. Cambridge established a chair of law about the same time. But in both cases, incumbents were usually time-servers, more interested in keeping their London practice than in teaching the law. With few exceptions, they were underpaid and uninterested. Not surprisingly, the state of British legal education before 1850 was described as "a very melancholy topic... The law student was obliged to get his knowledge of law by means of undirected reading and discussion and by attendance in chambers, in a law

---

[59] Thompson, "The Grid of Inheritance", and C. Howell, "Peasant Inheritance Customs in the Midlands", in *Family and Inheritance*, 328–360, 112–115.

ment in a will, then a *Shiah* ought to have the same right." That was a dubious argument from the perspective of any school of *shariah*, but the British controlled the courts and they made the law. In criticizing Mahmud's earlier judgment, Sir Arthur Wilson, a Privy Councillor, wrote that Mahmud had introduced "fresh logical inferences newly drawn from old and disputed texts". Wilson believed that the original decision was based on an "extremely dangerous principle", namely "That new rules of law are to be introduced because they seem to lawyers of the present day to follow logically from ancient tests however authoritative".[56] Since Mahmud had learned not only his law but his Arabic in England, Wilson may have had a point. Mahmud may well have drawn new principles from his texts, but that did not mean that Wilson and his colleagues were correct in their views. A little later, the chapter will provide other examples of the ways in which British judges decided what was Muslim law. For the moment, the point seems clear that broad learning and clever argument based on Muslim sources were not ultimately decisive in the system of justice the British administered in India.

Sayyid Mahmud's career on the Allahabad bench ended sadly when he was forced to resign in 1893. He was accused of severe and chronic drunkenness. Though even his friends acknowledged his alcoholism, Mahmud himself denied the charge. He claimed that the Chief Justice, Sir John Edge, who was jealous of him and hated him, used his power to bring about the dismissal.[57]

In India's High Courts, lawyers had a prominent place. Government honours, social prestige and wealth made the legal profession an attractive career for large numbers of Indians. Of the 592 students who attended Aligarh College between 1877 and 1911, 151 found their way into some branch of the legal profession. The law was second only to government service (317) in the number of graduates it drew.[58] Also, the law became a stepping stone to a political career. Gandhi, Jinnah, Moti Lal Nehru, Jawaharlal Nehru and scores of less famous politicians entered the *pandāl* by way of the courtroom. The courts of India were the nursery school of India's nationalist movement. The next chapter will focus on the influence which the practice of law exerted on politicians' views of India, its political, economic and communal needs and wants.

Indians had two paths to a career as a lawyer. The first was to take their legal training in England. The second was to attend one of the Indian university courses in law. The first option had advantages.

[56] *Ibid.*, 254.
[57] Robinson, *Separatism*, 433, and "Mahmood Number", 266–300.
[58] Lelyveld, *Aligarh*, 323, and B. B. Misra, *The Indian Middle Classes*, 326–332.

a total of twenty-nine men served as justices of the Allahabad High Court. Of that number, only four were Indians: Sayyid Mahmud, P. C. Banerji, C. Rustamjee and Karamat Husain. The two Muslim justices did get to submit their opinions, but in the end the full bench seldom accepted them.

The career of Justice Sayyid Mahmud provided an instance of the minimal influence which Muslim judges exerted. Sayyid Mahmud was the son of Sir Sayyid Ahmad Khan, in itself a claim to prominence. He went to Cambridge University where he read Latin, Greek and "Oriental" languages. He also studied law in England and was called to the Bar there. On returning to India, he practised in the courts and became a subordinate district magistrate. After a brief stint as a temporary judge of the Allahabad court, he became a permanent justice in 1883.[53] Mahmud's contemporaries generally acknowledged that he had one of the best minds ever applied to the practice of law in India. Having studied Arabic at Cambridge, he made extensive use of that language in his opinions on Muslim law. Moreover, his judgments were written with a clarity and vivacity rare in a rather dense literary genre. His opinion in the case of Agha Ali Khan was a good example of both his style and learning.[54] In this case, the point at issue was whether or not a member of the *Shiah* sect could create an endowment which had effect only after the founder's death. The only translations of *shariah* texts covered the views of the Hanafi school of the *Sunni* sect. Indeed, not until 1842 did the courts even recognize a distinction between *Sunni* and *Shiah*. Hanafi opinion generally accepted an endowment which became effective when its creator died. But what was the *Shiah* view?

Using Arabic texts by *Shiah* scholars, Sayyid Mahmud showed that *Sunni* and *Shiah* had very different notions about the character of an endowment. For the former, a *waqf* was a unilateral disposition of property. But the *Shiah* scholars held that a *waqf* was a contractual engagement, requiring an offer and the acceptance of that offer. Therefore, argued Mahmud, the *Shiah* tradition required that the transfer of property into a *waqf* occur at once. The transaction could not be made dependent on some future, uncertain event, in this case the death of the founder.

Sayyid Mahmud's opinion in Agha Ali Khan's case was accepted initially, but seven years later both the Allahabad court and Privy Council overturned it.[55] British judges came up with a short and simple counter to Mahmud's painstaking exposition: "If a *Sunni* could create an endow-

[53] *Indian Judges*, 306.
[54] *Agha Ali Kan (and another)* v. *Altaf Hasan Khan (and another)*, ALL, XIV, 430ff.
[55] *Baqar Ali Khan* v. *Anjuman Ara Begum (and another)*, ALL, XXV, 236ff.

on the Bombay High Court.⁵⁰ He was a member of the Tyabji-Fyzee clan who belonged to a small branch of the *Ismaili Shiah* sect known as Sulaymani Bohras. The Bohras in general, and the Tyabji-Fyzees in particular, were deeply involved in the commercial life of Bombay. Having acquired a fortune in trade, many members of the family took up careers in the courts.⁵¹ As a young barrister, Faiz often found himself pleading a case before his father, while his cousins represented the opposing party. Later, he too became a High Court justice.

At least in theory, an expert in *shariah* was a scholar of the "Arab sciences" as well as a pious Muslim. In Indian history, as noted previously, learning in *shariah* was passed from generation to generation within one family. Amir Ali and the others did not come from families which preserved that learning. They were landholders by background and "modern" by education. The effects of the latter can be seen in the textbooks they wrote. Their format followed that of law books in English. "*Shariah*" received relatively little attention apart from some Arabic quotations. The reported cases of the Anglo-Indian courts were their primary source. Amir Ali's texts contained many Arabic and Persian quotations, but he always translated them with the terminology of British law. Not many traditionally educated Muslims accepted Amir Ali's claim to authority in matters of *shariah*. Shibli Numani, for example, dismissed Amir Ali as an ignoramus who knew only enough Persian to impress an Englishman.⁵² Though the majority of India's Muslims were *Sunni*, Amir Ali was a *Shiah*. Faiz B. Tyabji belonged to the tiny Sulaymani Bohra sect. They, and other men like them, were certainly not representative or learned in the faith. Yet they claimed to be spokesmen for the "Muhammadan community" and experts in its "law". By education, temperament and taste, they more closely resembled their British colleagues whose style of dress and speech they closely imitated. Indeed, the recognition they received from British judges and lawyers accounted in large part for their status as "representative Muslims".

Although most of the *ulama* did not accept Amir Ali and the rest in the ranks of the learned, they must certainly have seemed scholars to the British judges who were usually completely ignorant of Arabic, Persian and Urdu. Ironically, Muslim judges appeared to have little real influence on the decisions of the High Courts. British judges were always the majority on the bench. For example, between 1876 and 1910,

---

⁵⁰ *Indian Biographical Dictionary*, 442–443.
⁵¹ T. Wright, "Muslim Kinship and Modernization", in *Family, Kinship, and Marriage among Muslims in India*, 217–238, and Hollister, *The Shi'a of India*, 273–305.
⁵² Shibli Numani, "Purdah awr Islam", in *Maqālāt*, I, 103–120.

taken in to lead in a case about *waqf* or *debutter*. Not many people in this country have any settled notion of what we are doing in India administering law to Indians, nor have means of readily acquiring any well-founded notion of how we come to be doing so or of the principles which we apply. Certain I am that when I went in 1918 to India to engage upon the task, I had the smallest amount of information and no real explanation of many facts of great historical importance.[48]

By training and background the British justices of the Indian High Courts did not understand Indian institutions or "legal traditions". Shortly we will see that very little in the way of source material existed which could make up for the lack. Like Rankin's own book, much of what was available concerned Anglo-Indian, not Indian, law. A few Indians did serve in the High Courts. Many Indian lawyers practised in them. Did they serve as informants, a living source for information about Indian custom?

Amir Ali, Abd ur-Rahim and Faiz Badr ud-din Tyabji were prominent justices. They were also the authors of textbooks on Muslim law. All of them decided cases involving Muslim endowments and included a discussion of them in their texts. Examining their backgrounds will help to answer the question posed above. Amir Ali and Abd ur-Rahim were born into comparatively wealthy families of Bengal Province and were educated at Calcutta University. That university was established and regulated by the British. Its syllabus was determined by the British or British trained educators who carried on their teaching primarily in English. Amir Ali and Abd ur-Rahim both obtained their legal training in England.[49] F. B. Tyabji was a native of Bombay educated in a similar fashion.

The ancestors of Amir Ali arrived in India in the 1740s as soldiers in the army of Nadir Shah. When he returned to Iran, one of Amir Ali's forefathers stayed in India. Since he was a *Shiah* and a recent immigrant from that sect's heartland, he found a welcome in the court of the Nawab of Oudh, himself a *Shiah*. When the last Nawab went into exile in Calcutta in 1856, Amir Ali's family accompanied him. Amir Ali had considerable success at the Calcutta Bar and became a justice of the High Court in 1890. In 1909, he became the first Indian to have a place as a Law Lord of the Privy Council.

Abd ur-Rahim's family came from Midnapore district in West Bengal. His family followed a common pattern of combining *zamindari* holdings with careers as employees of the British. He became a justice of the Madras High Court in 1908 and received a knighthood in 1919.

Faiz B. Tyabji was the son of Sir Badr ud-din Tyabji, who had a seat

[48] Rankin, *Background to Indian Law*, vii.
[49] *Indian Judges*, 219–253, 457–488.

long standing hatreds, arguments and misunderstandings. Yet, the subordinate magistrate had to wade through petitions which were "prolix, verbose, as well as argumentative"[46] and select a point of law on which to decide a case. In choosing a single judiciable matter, the magistrate exercised personal discretion. He was apt to fix upon a legal point which ignored other legal options hidden in a mass of personal conflict. But, once he decided the legal point, all subsequent litigation centred on it to the exclusion of other issues. For example, suits on endowments frequently entered the courts indirectly, as plaints appended to a series of unrelated issues. The question of endowments was one among others involving inheritance, preemption or debt. High Court justices heard cases on Muslim endowments because district magistrates decided that this controversial institution deserved examination by a superior court.

Most High Court justices were British. A few of them were men who had worked their way up through the "judicial line" of the I.C.S. Such appointments were probably the one hopeful prospect on magistrates' otherwise bleak horizons. Justice Frank Beaman, who sat on the Bombay High Court in the early years of the twentieth century, was one of the lucky few. He had served in half a dozen subordinate courts in the Sind. He was not a trained lawyer, but his self-tutoring must have been thorough, for it earned him a seat on this prestigious court. His appointment was also exceptional in that Beaman, like the image of justice herself, was blind. In formulating his judgments, he used a combination of memory, dictation and notes taken in an improvised Braille. Years later, the older barristers of Bombay remembered that he compensated for his lack of sight by exercising an especially sharp tongue.[47]

Most High Court justices came from the ranks of the British Bar. A Chief Justice was generally knighted before assuming his place at the centre of the bench. Sir William Comer-Pretheram and Sir John Edge were two examples of British barristers appointed to Indian courts. They were trained in England and each acquired a reputation by practising in British courts. Many, if not most, British justices were almost completely ignorant of Indian institutions and traditions. The candid admission of G. C. Rankin, a Chief Justice of the Calcutta court, is worth quoting as a summation of the issue.

I have been impressed at times with the peculiarity of the fate of very learned and able friends of mine who, as the reward of exceptional knowledge and skill in the business matters of England and Scotland, are suddenly required to turn a large part of their attention to Indian appeals. What, at first, do they think of them or make of them? What is their approach? So too with learned counsel

---

[46] Murtazai Bibi's case, *AA*.
[47] P. B. Vachha, *Famous Judges, Lawyers and Cases of Bombay*, 91–93.

floods.[45] Documents which were submitted tended to be almost too perfect. Account books showed that receipts and expenditures matched each other to the last *pais*. The suspicion that some of the evidence was cooked up was hard to avoid. Even when legitimate, the quantity of documentation was staggering. Once again, the district judge had to weigh it and decide what was worth forwarding to the High Court in the event of an appeal.

Biased testimony and dubious documents were not uniquely Indian problems. The courts of England had to deal with their share of forgers and liars. The circumstance which was singular was that Indian cases were tried under a system of law formulated according to British notions of justice. Though the disputes arose in an Indian social context, they were settled in a completely different milieu by judges who were ignorant of or unsympathetic to the original point of conflict. As cases passed upward to the High Courts on appeal, they entered a realm in which the distance between judge and litigant was even more pronounced.

District judges established the value of the property involved in a civil suit. When creditors brought a debtor into court, the latter tended to underestimate the value of his property, perhaps in the hope that the court would consider it too small a sum and refuse a decree. Creditors, in their turn, overvalued the property. The disparity between creditors' and debtors' claims forced judges to depend on the government's revenue assessment when determining the worth of land. They took the yearly assessment and multiplied by ten. In the case of houses or other buildings, value was determined by their state of repair and whether they were made of baked brick or mud.

Perhaps the most important function of the subordinate magistrate was establishing the legal point at issue in any suit. But deciding where the legal dispute lay usually took a little work. Many plaintiffs believed in a shotgun approach to litigation. They sometimes entered as many as ten or twelve separate pleas. In another case involving a woman's marital status, the plaintiffs raised other issues totally unrelated to the question of whether the woman was wife or mistress. They argued that "family tradition" excluded female control of the estate. They claimed that the supposed widow was in collusion with people who were "enemies and plunderers" of the family's wealth. They also argued that the suit was undertaken merely to harass the *pardah* observing women who had control of the property (a point which seemed to contradict one of their other pleas). The plaintiffs' lawyer entered a number of similar allegations. As noted in the previous chapter, suits were often the fruit of

---

[45] *Sheikh Mahomed Ahsanulla Chowdhry* v. *Amarchand Kundu (and others), LI*, vol. 340, 89.

Those opting for the judicial line faced the prospect of a succession of dim and dusty courtrooms. Attracting the brighter members of the Civil Service proved a constant problem for provincial judicial departments. Those who opted for the rigours of a life in district courts had only a basic knowledge of the law. As late as 1911, the U.P. government considered a number of plans to provide British magistrates with additional legal training. Notably, none of the options discussed concentrated on training in Indian legal traditions. Rather, they focused on the laws of procedure and equity, which even in India derived from British law.[42]

Whatever their strengths or weaknesses, subordinate judges performed several crucial tasks. They had to hear and report on the testimony of witnesses. Because the British system emphasized a contest between aggrieved parties, between "plaintiff(s)" and "defendants(s)", each side in a suit usually called upon as many of their friends as possible. In a typical case, the litigants called as many as forty or fifty witnesses.[43]

In sifting through the testimony of each witness, judges must have noted how the needs of the moment affected individual memories. An instance of this selective recall was the testimony of Mufti Ikram-ullah, who appeared in a case in which a widow seized her late husband's property in lieu of receiving her marriage gift (*mehr*) of Rs. 21,000. The widow's opponents claimed that she had never married the deceased but was only his "mistress". Ikram-ullah was a witness in the widow's defence. He claimed that he clearly remembered that a marriage took place, though he did not remember whether he actually attended the ceremony. He did not remember the names of anyone else who might have been present at the festivities. But he did recall that the *mehr* was exactly Rs. 21,000![44] The cases involving endowments described later in this chapter involved the testimony of thousands of witnesses. Therefore, though their role was seldom acknowledged, subordinate magistrates, by deciding which testimony to accept, influenced the kind of information the High Court justices received.

Subordinate magistrates also had responsibility for collecting documentary evidence: deeds, affidavits, account books, letters and the like. Two major problems were attached to that process. There was either too much or too little of the evidence. Litigants often claimed that important deeds or revenue receipts had been burned, buried or lost in

---

[42] (UP) *JP Civ* (1911), File 160, nos. 4–9.
[43] *Murtazai Bibi* v. *Jumna Bibi*, *AA*; for a description of a district magistrate's work, see P. Mason (under pseud. P. Woodruff), *Call the Next Witness*.
[44] *Syeda Bibi (and another)* v. *Mughal Jan (and others)*, *All*, XXIV, 231ff, and *AA*.

emperors. In his youth, his education was of the most general sort, stressing Persian literature more than anything else. He followed an uncle into the Company's employ. He learned the law by actually administering it.[39] Sayyid Ahmad never learned much English, so he had little formal knowledge of British law. Also, his family maintained no tradition of deep learning in *shariah*. As the next chapter will show, he picked up a bit of both systems, but not because the job required such scholarship.

The Supreme Courts, which were intended for British use only, did import trained lawyers, but the judges of the *Sadr* courts were British employees of the Company. During the East India Company's experiments in educating its servants at Fort William College and at Haileybury College, lectures on British law were part of the course of study.[40] As noted below, not much was available for the study of Indian legal systems. Not even the staunchest defenders of Company rule contended that this training produced legal scholars. But Company courts employed both Muslims and Hindus who were supposed to be experts on their respective "laws". The records did not indicate whether they were drawn from the ranks of the *ulama* and *pandits* or whether they were more ordinary government employees assigned to that duty.

After the reform of the courts in 1862, educational qualifications for subordinate judges became ever more rigorous. By the end of the nineteenth century, Indians, who made up the majority of the magistracy, had to have knowledge of English and a B.A. to gain appointment in provincial judicial services. Alongside the Indians who served as district magistrates were some British members of the Indian Civil Service. When they served as subordinate judges, they did so as part of their preparation for their role as "Guardians". Britons, and the few Indians who made it into the I.C.S., had a short course in law as part of their training in England. The knowledge imparted was neither broad nor deep and concentrated on the laws of evidence and procedure. On arriving in India, these fledgling officials worked as subordinate magistrates by way of introducing them to the people and the territory.[41] Most of them expected that after a year or two they would move up and out.

Several years into his career, each officer was presented with a choice about his future. He could take either the "administrative line" or the "judicial line". Administration was much more popular, exciting and prestigious. Those who chose it could look forward to the possibility of a commissionership or a post in a provincial or viceregal secretariat.

---

[39] G. F. I. Graham, *The Life and Work of Syed Ahmed Kahn*, 1–9.
[40] D. Kopf, *British Orientalism and the Bengal Renaissance*, 64.
[41] P. Mason, *A Shaft of Sunlight*, 71–72.

trained in institutions which the British established and controlled. In subordinate courts, proceedings were conducted in the local vernacular. English was the only language used in the High Courts. Lawyers argued in English and all written evidence was translated into it.

When a case went to an appellate court, the lower tribunal sent along a "paper book". The paper book included the opinions of the magistrate, transcripts of the testimony of some (but not all) witnesses and any other documents thought relevant to the legal point at issue. Paper books were, therefore, hefty tomes. The expenses of preparing them, of translating them into English and of printing them were considerable. Next to stamp charges and attorneys' fees, they were one of the major costs of lodging an appeal. However, because the High Courts heard no oral testimony, paper books provided the basic material on which justices decided a case.

By concentrating on documentary evidence and legal argument, High Courts dealt with suits in far less time than the subordinate courts. Appeals were usually handled in four or five sittings scattered over a month or two. Two or three justices were sufficient for most disputes, but when a particularly important point of law was at issue, all the justices took part under the presidency of the Chief Justice. High Courts managed to process as many as a thousand or fifteen hundred appeals each year. Even so, lawsuits were lengthy affairs, often consuming four or five years, with most of that time spent waiting for hearings. Lawsuits were often multigenerational. If one of the original participants died during the proceedings, his or her heirs carried on with the litigation.

"The Rule of Law" in place of the "Rule of Men" was the constantly repeated ideal of British law; an ideal which the British did consider fit for export to India. Yet, the nature of the courts placed many responsibilities in the hands of the men who made them work. Aspirations aside, their background, training and personalities influenced the way in which the law was administered. Having briefly discussed the institutions, this chapter turns to the officers of the court and their backgrounds.

Judges and lawyers

In the days of Company rule, most of the individuals who worked in the courts were not professional lawyers. The Indians who acted as judges in the district courts were the products of the "*Kacahri*," which acted as both office and training school. Sayyid Ahmad Khan, later a knight, Legislative Councillor to the Viceroy and founder of Aligarh College, began his career in the Company's judicial service. Sayyid Ahmad belonged to a family which had been in the service of the Mughal

precedent. As the suits involving Muslim endowments showed, the last item came to have considerable authority for judges forced to decide issues of "native law". The system of court reporting was greatly enhanced in the wake of the reforms of 1862. The Company's courts had published reports of their decisions, but comparatively few were noted and the descriptions were brief. Each of the High and Chief Courts appointed official reporters and published their decisions in handsome, leather-bound volumes. They reported more cases in greater detail. In theory, each of the courts was independent, but in practice they knew of each other's important judgments and used them as precedents.

Each court served two purposes. They were courts of original jurisdiction for the cities in which they were located. In the bustling commercial centres of Bombay, Calcutta and Madras, the number of cases brought to them was considerable. In the Allahabad court, located in a small city in the agrarian hinterland, this kind of litigation was rarer. Each of the courts also served as the appellate body for all of the subordinate courts of their provinces. High Courts were, as noted, independent. They maintained slightly different traditions governing procedure and the composition of the bar, but in all significant aspects they were similar.

Appeals from the High and Chief Courts were directed to the Privy Council in London. Certain members of that body of royal advisers were designated Law Lords. Though not all were actually peers, most of them had lengthy careers in the practice of British law. As noted, the Queen or King confirmed the decisions of the Law Lords by issuing a proclamation. This gave to their deliberations special importance. They established precedents for all of the courts of the empire. The Privy Council's judgments were the ultimate product of a single hierarchy of legal authority which stretched from the lowliest district magistrate in India to the monarch's chosen judicial experts in the empire's capital city.

In India, the parties' place of residence and an estimate of the monetary value of the property involved or the gravity of a criminal offence determined which subordinate court took a case. *Munsif*'s courts handled petty crimes and small claims. At the next level, every district had a number of subordinate magistrates who dealt with suits involving larger sums of money or serious criminal infractions. Finally, the district magistrate represented the highest legal authority for a given area.

The higher a case went in the judicial hierarchy, the more British that system became. While subordinate magistrates and lower court lawyers were mostly Indians, higher court officers were either British or Indians

goods". The government, through the courts, was willing to enforce decrees which required the confiscation and sale of property. To win, once and for all, seemed possible. Something in that approach appealed to more adventurous spirits. "The courts", as Percival Spear wrote, "were to the public a great penny in the slot machine whose workings passed man's understanding and from which anything might come except justice."[37] Thus, part of the courts' popularity lay in the status of the lawsuit as a spectator sport. Entire villages found the intricacies of the new system a favourite topic of conversation and a source for further entertainment. Years after the settlement of a case, participants, their kin and neighbours could recall in detail the course of litigation.

Within a very few years, Indians made themselves masters of legal manoeuvre. They learned that the adversary character of British justice had its charms. Whatever the ultimate result, an old enemy was discomfited by merely bringing a suit. No matter how baseless or contrived a suit was, one's opponents were forced to spend time and money in their own defence.

In the years following the Revolt of 1857, the organization of the courts changed. In 1862, the government eliminated the distinct but overlapping jurisdictions of higher level courts. Supreme Courts, with their civil, ecclesiastical and admiralty benches, were abolished, along with the *Sadr Diwani* and *Nizamat Adalats*. Four "High Courts", established in Allahabad, Bombay, Calcutta and Madras, absorbed their functions. The government's aim in making these alterations was to regularize and simplify even further the judicial system. The home government contemplated similar reforms in the British courts, but did not make them until 1873. As was often the case, "rationality" and "efficiency" were easier to attain in the colonies.

High Courts were royal courts, established by charter of the crown. The queen or king appointed the justices. The Government of India offered advice on nominations. In addition, Lahore and Nagpur were the seats of "Chief Courts". The Viceroy–Governor General chartered them and selected their judges. As in the days of Company rule, no real separation existed between the political and judicial arms of the state.

The reorganization of 1862 also obliterated the last, nominal vestiges of Mughal tradition. The courts' Persian titles disappeared. More importantly, all remaining Hindu and Muslim "experts" who advised British judges on their respective "laws" were retired in 1864.[38] From then on, the judicial personnel of the Anglo-Indian courts learned about "Muslim" or "Hindu" law from translations, by experience and

[37] P. Spear, *The Twilight of the Mughals*, 95.
[38] B. Cohn, "Some Notes on Law and Change in North India", 88ff.

Indians themselves apparently had no difficulty in recognizing the difference between the Company's courts and their "traditional" agencies. Indeed, Indians developed a taste for pursuing their intermural conflicts in those new arenas. Throughout the years of raj, the number of Indian litigants in the courts increased steadily. The British believed that their own honesty and impartiality drew the crowds. In retrospect, several other aspects of the Anglo-Indian judicial style might have accounted for that popularity.[33] For one thing, British courts delivered absolute decisions. The victor in a lawsuit appeared to gain all the spoils.

Definitive judgments were rarer in other Indian methods of conflict resolution. For example, arbitration was a well-known approach to resolving disagreements. In contrast to the Anglo-Indian institutions, arbitration had the advantage of being cheap. Even British officials recognized the value of this method and from time to time made efforts, without much success, to encourage its use.[34] A willingness to compromise was the basis of arbitration. Often, in the bitter family disputes described previously, heightened passions made mutual concessions unlikely. Also, the stakes were sometimes too high to permit satisfaction with a part when the whole seemed attainable.

The decisions of village or caste councils (*panchayats*) and of Hindu or Muslim religious leaders had some of the advantages as well as the disadvantages of arbitration. Though relatively inexpensive, they tended to shy away from making awards which satisfied one party but aggravated another. Living in the midst of the disputants, they were inclined to seek first an amicable compromise. Barring that, they deferred judgment, hoping that the contestants would cool off or lose interest.[35]

Violence was another "traditional" method of conflict resolution. Though the British tried to limit the resort to mayhem, they never entirely succeeded in eliminating this direct means of dealing with a rival's claims. Often, British influence merely inspired the substitution of the iron tipped, bamboo quarter staff, the *lāṭhī*, for swords and muskets.[36] The proverb "jis ki lathi, us ki bhains" ("who has the stick owns the buffalo") still rang true in much of rural India. However, the existence of police and criminal courts restrained individuals. A charge of murder or assault might follow even the successful application of force.

In contrast to other means, the British courts literally "delivered the

---

[33] Pandey, *Introduction*, 136, and (UP) *JP Civ* (October 1894), nos. 12–18; (July 1896), nos. 8–9.
[34] (UP) *JP Civ* (August 1891), nos. 1–4.
[35] Cohn, "From Indian Status", 615ff.
[36] Malihabadi, *Yādōn*, 28.

marriage, caste and other religious institutions".[31] This chapter will describe later the process by which the British decided what "law" to apply. For the moment, it concerns itself with the institutions which enforced it.

Hastings' policy directly involved British officials in the administration of justice. Subsequent Governors-General followed his lead and in the 1790s the court system took on the institutional shape it retained for almost seventy years. At the lowest rung of the Company's judicial ladder was an official known as an *"amin"*, who in Mughal times was a local revenue agent, not a judge. Under the Company, *amins* were usually Indians who had no special training, but were recruited and educated along pre-British lines. District courts (*zila'*-courts) and courts of appeal handled cases brought up from the *amins*' jurisdictions. They were located in district towns and in the major cities of the province: Murshidabad, Patna and Benares. The highest appellate courts were located in Calcutta. The *Sadr Nizamat Adalat* (*Nizam*'s Chief Court) reviewed appeals in "criminal" cases and the *Sadr Diwani Adalat* (*Diwan*'s Chief Court) examined "civil" appeals. Later, this system, with some regional variations, was brought to the other provinces. The Revenue Department retained special jurisdiction for any issues arising from the collection of the land tax. A parallel system of "Supreme Courts" located in the three Presidency Towns was supposed to serve the British and minorities like Armenians and Jews. Though, in theory, banned from the Supreme Courts, Indians of all faiths brought suits in them.

The use of Persian titles in courts established for Indians showed that the British were still wary of straying too far from what they considered "traditional" forms. But the creation of hierarchically arranged tribunals whose sole function was the adjudication of arguments and the punishment of crime was itself a major departure from the practices of the past. A *qazi*, for example, did not have to have a special place to hear disputes. He could do that in a mosque or even in the homes of disputants, so long as the presence of witnesses precluded the chance of collusion.[32] Moreover, as noted above, *qazis* shared authority in these matters with other members of the imperial elite. No clear line of appeal connected local officials with the emperor, the ultimate source of justice. The Company's courts had their jurisdictions clearly laid out. The government guaranteed the superiority of metropolitan tribunals over local institutions. Thus, the Company's organization of the courts and their procedure followed more closely the model of the British Isles than it did that of Mughal India.

[31] G. C. Rankin, *Background to Indian Law*, 2.
[32] Al-Marghinani, *Al Hidayah*, trans. C. Hamilton, 334ff.

hand when they assumed the task of enforcing order and settling disputes among their newly acquired Indian subjects.

The Anglo-Indian courts

From the beginning, the growth of the Anglo-Indian legal system was tied to the acquisition of political power In 1757, as a reward for their help in making Mir Jafar governor of the Bengal province, the British gained control over the district known as the "Twenty-four Parganahs" which surrounded their base at Fort William. As the semi-independent ruler (*zamindar*) of the area, the East India Company collected the imperial revenue. In addition, it had the right to punish petty crime and the obligation to settle disputes among sub-tenants and cultivators. Charters of George II had already established royal courts in Fort William, but they were supposed to be for the exclusive use of resident Britons. Therefore, the Company's agents handled the "natives" according to what they thought was the custom of the country.

The Mughal emperor, Shah Alam, enlarged the British role in dealing with disagreements among Indians when he was forced to make the Company the chief treasurer (*Diwan*) of Bengal in 1765. Though the governor (*Nawab*) had charge of maintaining order, the *Diwan* supervised the work of the *qazis*. When they received the appointment, the British wished to avoid direct involvement in that aspect of the administration. The Company's officers hoped to turn a profit from the office with a minimum cost in money and effort to themselves. The attempt to stay in the background by allowing Indians to run the government failed. Within a very few years, Indians were complaining that *qazis* were corrupt and oppressive.[29] In response to those charges, the directors of the Company ordered the first of many changes in the style of their rule.[30]

Warren Hastings, appointed governor of Fort William in 1772, took a very different approach to the Company's administrative role. Determined to "stand forth as *Diwan*", Hastings ordered British officers to supervise directly the collection of revenue and settlement of disputes. In his Regulations of 1772, he raised the question of what legal standard would be used in resolving arguments between Indians. One of the Regulations announced that the Company's officers would apply "the laws" of Hindus and Muslims in all matters pertaining to "inheritance,

---

[29] B. N. Pandey, *The Introduction of English Law into India*, 136–141.
[30] B. B. Misra, *The Central Administration of the East India Company*, provides a meticulous description of changes in the structure of the courts.

the sultan. After Sultan Ibrahim's departure, Shah Qasim asked, "who was that snake-charmer?"[24]

Whether sufis were friendly or contemptuous towards the state, they provided an independent source of guidance in matters related to the *shariah*. Each sufi leader (*pir*) had his following of disciples and devotees. For them, the *pir* took the responsibility of supplying arbitration and moral precepts. Many Muslims preferred *pirs*' opinions and decisions to those supplied by state officials or religious scholars.[25]

Muslims in India came from many different ethnic groups, from *Sunni* and *Shii* sects, from dozens of economic and social backgrounds. The *Shii* immigrant from Iran was a Muslim, but so was the Bengali fisherman, the Panjabi Jat farmer and the Arab merchant of Gujarat. Many different "Muslim communities" existed side by side in India, each of them practising its own distinctive brand of *shariah*.[26] In the history of Islam in India, no one paramount authority managed the enforcement of a single recognized code of law.

Even at the height of their influence and power, the Mughals did not, apparently, consider forcing a single version of *shariah* on India's disparate Muslim population. The Emperor Alamgir I (Awrangzib) gained some notoriety by ordering the compilation of a textbook containing the opinions of scholars in the Hanafi tradition. Known as the *Fatāwa-ī 'Alāmgirī* or *Fatāwa-ī Hind*, this collection of Hanafi *fiqh* circulated throughout the Muslim world. However, the compilation of this text was not part of some scheme to impose its views on all Muslims. Rather, it appeared designed to enhance imperial control of religious scholars.[27] Alamgir, that most "orthodox" of rulers, shared his predecessors' desire to bind the *ulama* to the imperial authority and to deny them independent status.

With the waning of Mughal power in the early years of the eighteenth century, the local officials charged with keeping order and mediating disputes began neglecting their responsibilities. *Qazis* started selling their *madad-i maash* grants to the highest bidders, even when the purchasers were not Muslims. They and the *Kotwals* openly accepted bribes to guarantee a favourable decision. They made no pretence of following either *shariah* or imperial regulation.[28] Thus, political chaos threw Muslims back, even further, on their own resources in matters of *shariah*. Also, the lack of effective institutional control gave the British a freer

[24] Eaton, *Sufis of Bijapur*, 123 (slightly altered).
[25] Ashraf, *Life and Conditions*, 50–51, 101–102.
[26] E.g. C. L. Tupper, *Punjab Customary Law*, II.
[27] M. Bakhtawar Khan, *Mir'āt 'al- 'Ālam*, I, 49–50.
[28] B. Cohn, "From Indian Status to British Contract", 615; on the breakdown of state control over *madad-i maash* grants, conversations with Irfan Habib, Aligarh, July 1979.

mosque.[19] They were tied to the state by the obligation they accepted of mentioning the ruler's name during the Friday prayer. They also took on other official responsibilities. Individuals bearing the title "*qazi*" acted as military commanders and provincial governors.[20]

In the Muslim states of India, *qazis* did not have sole authority for matters of public order or the disposal of property. An officer known as the *Kotwal* heard disputes and enforced state policy. Disputes involving land revenue, imperial grants and the succession of heirs were decided by the local representatives of the imperial treasurer (*Diwan*).[21]

Religious scholars in the subcontinent were heavily dependent on the state of their livelihood. They were not united by training or background. They came partly from Central Asia and from Arabia and Iran. Indian converts to the faith also had a place in the ranks of the learned. In practice, the depth of their learning varied greatly. Their education was largely a matter of studying with a master who taught only a few students, usually his own sons or the sons of friends and near relations. Progress in learning consisted of reading a comparatively small number of set texts. Without printed books, teachers and students did not have large numbers of books. They often made do with fragments of texts. Serious scholars had to travel in search of other books and new teachers. Most pupils had a very general grounding in Persian literature and a smattering of Islamic religious sciences in Arabic. They did not always find work as teachers or *qazis*. Well into the British period, the *ulama* remained unspecialized in learning and occupation. Some were clerks, some teachers, government employees and even soldiers.[22]

As elsewhere in the Muslim world, the pious often looked askance at scholars who took government employment. Sufis were sometimes ostentatious critics of the *ulama* and the state.[23] Sufis did not have a single response to their rulers. Some of them gladly accepted support from kings, but many stories circulated about the sufis who did not. The following encounter between a saint, Shah Qasim Qadiri, and the ruler of Bijapur, Sultan Ibrahim II, illustrated that tendency:

On Friday Sultan Ibrahim arrived at the Jami mosque [the congregational mosque] in all his majestic grandeur and decked in his jeweled crown. After prayers, the sultan moved toward Shah Qasim who, however, made no notice of

---

[19] "Life of Guru Nanak", in *Shri Guru Adi Granth*, trans. E. Trumpp, 20–30.
[20] For example, the ancestors of the Mahmudabad Rajas of Avadh were *qazis*: see T R. Metcalf, *Land*, 7.
[21] Cohn, "The Initial British Impact on India", 419.
[22] B. D. Metcalf, *Islamic Revival*, 5–95, and M. Zaki, "Organization of Islamic Learning under the Saiyids and Lodis", 1–9.
[23] A. Rashid, "The Treatment of History in Muslim Sufi Writings", in *Historians of India, Pakistan and Ceylon*, 113–134.

ship.¹³ Abu Hanifa's critical attitude towards the state was not unique among the "*shariah*-minded".¹⁴

Truly pious Muslims seemed very reluctant to identify the *shariah* too closely with any one institution. Their caution arose in part from their disgust with high-living and high-handed kings. But something of Islam's moral seriousness also expressed itself in their refusal. As Malcolm Kerr put it:

This lack of positivism in allocating procedural sovereignty both in constitutional and legal theory appears to follow from the jurists' awareness of the need to protect the idealism of their concept of ultimate sovereignty [which rests with God] from the corruptions to which it would inevitably be exposed from a positive process of interpretation and application. A noncognitive, ideal moral value would lose something of its purity in the course of being interpreted by less-than-ideal facilities. If, however, the interpretive process is not clearly spelled out in positive terms, then the ideal is safe from corruption by virtue of the simple fact that no interpretation that does take place is necessarily authoritative.¹⁵

Some religious scholars did make a private peace with the state and their consciences. They sought a way of healing the breach between those whose chief concern was the purity of the faith and those who were supposed to be its public guardians. Influenced, perhaps, by the powers of coercion and patronage which kings commanded, they argued for co-operation with the state by saying that an evil monarch was preferable to anarchy.¹⁶ But such compromise often ended up by splitting authority in Muslim states. The government controlled most aspects of public life while the influence of *shariah* was limited to the private domains of ritual and family life.¹⁷

The *shariah* practised in the Muslim kingdoms of India was a product of the strains and compromises outlined above. The sultans and *padishahs* appointed *qazis* for most of the cities and market towns in their empires. They supported them with grants known as *madad-i maash* which allowed the *qazi* a portion of the state's land revenue.¹⁸ *Qazis* were supposed to hear disputes, but they were also the local guardians of the faith, the individuals who led communal prayers at the central

---

¹³ Von Grunebaum, *Medieval Islam*, 167.
¹⁴ Hodgson, *Venture of Islam*, I, 238, 318, 351.
¹⁵ M. H. Kerr, *Islamic Reform*, 11 (parenthetical remark added).
¹⁶ Zia ud-din Barni, "*Fatawa-i Jahandari*", in *Sources of Indian Tradition*, I, 463–465.
¹⁷ Hodgson, *Venture of Islam*, I, 341–348.
¹⁸ Ahmad, *The Administration of Justice in Medieval India*, 102–104, Akbar, *The Administration of Justice by the Mughals*, 3–12, Habib, *The Agrarian System*, 298–312, S. Moosvi, "*Sūyūrghāl* Statistics", 282–298, and S. A. Rashid, "*Madad-i Ma'ash* Grants under the Mughals", 98–108.

generic term for scholars' responses to questions submitted by the faithful. In it the scholar quoted appropriate verses from the *Quran*, anecdotes describing the Prophet's words or deeds and the opinions of the masters of *shariah*. If the matter was not clearly resolved by reference to any one of those sources, the scholar discussed the problem further. Often the sources lent themselves to divergent interpretations and the scholar felt entitled to provide his own opinion.[10] If the individual who submitted the question in the first place was not satisfied with the *fatwa* he received, he was at liberty to consult as many of the learned as he wished. Individuals had no formal compulsion to accept any one opinion.

An official, known as a "*Qazi*" (the term was derived from an Arabic word meaning "to decide") existed as the state sponsored spokesman on *shariah*. This office went back to the days of the early Caliphate. The first caliphs followed the example of the Prophet and settled disputes among the faithful in person. But as the empire grew and the physical distance between caliph and believer increased, the need arose for local adjudicators. As a matter of course, most Muslim rulers appointed and supported *qazis*, but they also maintained other officials to settle the arguments of their subjects. They frequently meddled in the *qazis*' business and refused to enforce their judgments.[11] Moreover, pious Muslims often held the *qazis* and their sponsors in contempt.

In the history of *shariah*, the state represented a formidable, but contradictory, force. In the aftermath of the Arab conquests, the needs of the political system and the ideals of the faith came into conflict. For the community of faith, *shariah* was the standard of behaviour and belief. Governments, however, were run on the commands, sometimes the whims, of their rulers, by bureaucratic regulation and by the demands of internal or foreign policy. As early as the Ummayad (A.D. 661–750) and Abbasid (A.D. 750–1258) caliphates, the practice of the state often seemed contrary to the ideals of the community of faith.[12] By praying in public mosques or appointing *qazis*, caliphs and sultans made a public display of their attachment to Islam. However, their actions often reduced such performances to pious frauds. Individuals genuinely attached to the faith often refused to cooperate with the state. For example, Abu Hanifa had to be flogged before he would accept a *qazi*-

---

[10] For examples of the form, see Jennings, "Loans and Credit", 206, and Abd al-Hai, *Fatāwa-yi 'Abd al-Hai*, 15–20.
[11] J. S. Nielsen, "*Mazālim* and *Dār al- 'adl* under the Early Mamluks", 114–132, and Petry, *Civilian Elite*, 24.
[12] G. E. Von Grunebaum, *Medieval Islam*, 142–144; for India, K. M. Ashraf, *Life and Conditions of the People of Hindustan*, 28–33, 49.

mining which view was authoritative. Among the *Sunni* the four *Imams* and their immediate disciples enjoyed a certain prestige. They were known as "*mujtahidīn*", a term which indicated that the depth of their learning and piety gave special significance to their opinions. Even so, scholars in later generations felt free to dissent from the views of earlier authorities. For the *Shii*, a *mujtahid* possessed not only learning and piety, but also a superior authority derived from physical descent from Ali which gave unique intuition into the *shariah*'s true intent. While the *Shii* asserted that every generation had its authoritative leaders, the *Sunni* tended to restrict that honour to the four *Imams* and a few of their immediate followers.

After the two or three generations who shaped *shariah* and *fiqh* as religious sciences (*'ulūm*) passed away, responsibility for continuing their application fell to the body of learned and holy men: the *ulama*. Among the *ulama*, *shariah* and *fiqh* were inseparable from the practice of other Islamic disciplines such as Quranic commentary or theology. Some academic specialization existed, but in practice almost any scholar felt able to issue an opinion. When it came to earning a livelihood, scholars pursued a number of different occupations. Many were teachers or held government posts, but a significant number made their living as cloth or grain merchants and bookbinders. One noted scholar was apparently a seller of wineglasses![8] Thus, in contrast to the professional lawyer of the British legal tradition, an expert in *shariah* had to have broad learning in the basics of his faith and visible piety. He did not have to earn a living through the practice of *fiqh*.

The basic form in which the science of *fiqh* was exercised was in response to a problem (*mas'lah*) posed by one of the faithful. The form of the question and its answer (*jawab*) acquired a stereotypical cast.[9] The question began with the phrase, "What do the masters of the faith say?" That was followed by a description of the point at issue couched in wholly general and impersonal terms. The persons involved were referred to by using the Arabic word "*fallān*", meaning "someone", "anyone", or the names of the stock characters of Arabic grammar, "Zayd" and "Umar", were employed. The question might have involved a matter of ritual purity, inheritance or the etiquette of performing the pilgrimage, but it was usually stated in purely abstract terms. Often the questions did not concern real problems but described only hypothetical situations.

Fatwa, a word derived from a verb meaning "to inform", became the

---

[8] Cohen, "The Economic Background and Secular Occupation", 16–61.
[9] Makdisi, *The Rise of Colleges*, 109–110; Arabic retains the *hamzah* while standard Urdu orthography drops it.

Complete agreement on *shariah* was prevented by sectarian and regional differences among Muslims. Sects differed, sometimes violently, about the nature of the path. The best known division was between the *Sunni* and *Shii*, but even within them different approaches to the *shariah* developed. Among the *Sunni*, for example, four "schools" (*mazāhab*) of interpretation gradually emerged.[7] Each of them traced its origin to the exposition of *shariah* offered by one of four "leaders" (*Imams*): Abu Hanifa (d. A.D. 767), Malik ibn Anas (d. A.D. 795), ash-Shafii (d. A.D. 820) and Ahmad ibn Hanbal (d. A.D. 855). Each of these men gained notoriety for their knowledge and piety. Since their knowledge embraced all aspects of the faith, their opinions on *shariah* were not the result of specialized scholarship. Indeed, Ahmad ibn Hanbal and Malik ibn Anas were most famous as collectors of Prophetic anecdotes (*ahadis*). Abu Hanifa was a theologian (*mutakalim*) and his only surviving books deal with scholastic theology (*kalām*), not *shariah*. In practice, each of the *Imams* had a regional following. The school of ash-Shafii was associated with Egypt, that of Abu Hanifa with Iraq and ibn Hanbal with Arabia. Of the four, that of Abu Hanifa was the most widespread geographically.

The *Imams*, and those who followed them, developed a branch of learning called "*fiqh*". The word "*fiqh*" meant literally "to understand" and this described accurately the task which these men set for themselves. They worked at applying the *shariah* to the actions of individuals. To determine whether or not a particular course of action was proper for a Muslim, they examined it in the light of series of tests. The first test was the revealed word of God, the *Quran*. But the *Quran* was a fairly short book. It discussed only a few things in detail. The example of the Prophet's life (*sunnah*) was, therefore, a second source of guidance. If *Quran* and *sunnah* did not provide a specific solution to a problem, then the practitioners of *fiqh* had to fall back on tests which required some form of human judgment: analogy (*qiyas*), informed opinion (*ra'y* and *ijtihād*) and the consensus of the community (*ijma*). Thus, the practice of *fiqh* did not so much involve the application of a particular rule, but the search for religiously appropriate modes of behaviour. As noted above, that search was characterized by differences of opinion among those who applied the *shariah*.

In the application of *shariah* few formal standards existed for deter-

---

[7] Schacht, *An Introduction*, J. N. D. Anderson, "The Nature and Sources of Islamic Law", and G. E. Von Grunebaum, *Classical Islam*, supply standard introductions. The account below is over-simplified since other schools existed and similar divisions existed among the *Shii*.

rect form of prayer, marital relations, ritual hygiene, crime, punishment, inheritance and much more in detail.

The *shariah* does contain "rules" in the sense that it sets forth models for individual behaviour, but these cover a much greater range of activity than Euro-American law regulates. The individual rules governing any single matter are significant only in the context of the whole practice of the faith. Taken as a whole, *shariah* provides a guide to conscience for believers, since by nature many of its injunctions are unenforceable. Therefore, *shariah* has always been as strong or as weak as the conscience which accepted its guidance. History is full of examples of individual Muslims who persuaded themselves that obedience to one or another rule was not essential for either eternal salvation or temporal happiness. Regulations were ignored or reinterpreted to allow for nonconformist behaviour. A classic example was the prohibition of the use of alcohol. Some drank without giving a defence for their action. Others claimed that the *Quran* mentioned only "wine" and said nothing against beer or brandy. Similarly, tradition forbade the taking of interest. Yet in the past loans at interest were common and given with the approval of religious authorities.[3]

Arguments among Muslims over different aspects of the *shariah* were (and are) common. Should one, when ending the daily prayers, say "*Amin*" in a soft or loud voice? Disagreements on that issue have even sparked riots.[4] Usually they inspire spirited debate. As the study of *shariah* developed as an organized intellectual discipline, disputation among scholars was encouraged and given a prominent place in their training.[5] A trivial, though revealing, example of this process concerned men's whiskers. While the wearing of a beard, because it imitated the Prophet, was acknowledged as a pious act, a question arose about moustaches. Could one wear them at all? Some scholars held that they were not permitted. Others said they were, but had to be trimmed short. Still other views were that they should be trimmed only at the ends or in the middle.[6] Debate resulted in collections of opinions, but not a single, completely dominant rule of law. As the first chapter (see pp. 13–14) noted, Muslims disagreed on whether a *waqf* was an acceptable way of disposing of property. Though Muslims almost universally agreed that *shariah* was important, many interpretations of the *shariah* coexisted. A saying of the Prophet was often quoted to give sanction to the diversity of opinions: "After my death there will be seventy-two sects among the Muslims, but I will be in the seventy-third."

---

[3] Jennings, "Loans and Credit," 168–216.
[4] *Ata-ullah (and another)* v. *Azim-Ullah (and another)*, *All*, XII, 430ff.
[5] Makdisi, *The Rise of Colleges*, 106–120.
[6] "'The Beard' by Abu Tālib al-Makkī", trans. E. H. Douglas, 100–110.

(*ummah*). Yet a basic difference existed between the views of the faithful and those of colonial legal practitioners. The Muslims knew they fostered ideals not yet attained. They knew too well that reality was fragmented, far less edifying than their vision of perfection. By contrast, colonial jurists had greater power than ever the pious enjoyed. The courts could enforce principles of unity in thousands of instances. They could sharpen concepts and give them greater currency. Judges and lawyers operated in hierarchies of authority within which ideas travelled with relative speed. They could do more to ensure the spread of their perception of Muslim orthodoxy.

That modern scholars, both Muslim and non-Muslim, carry on their research within a framework of similar legalist notions bears eloquent testimony to the success of the colonial courts. Scholars still apply wholesale the conceptual vocabulary of the British legal system when describing *shariah*. Even Muslims explain that *shariah* is "Islamic law". That Muslims everywhere and at all times use that law, that it is ancient, religiously inspired and rigorous remain textbook maxims.

In opposition to the common view, this chapter begins with a brief description of *shariah* which avoids the conceptual vocabulary of British law. It shows that significant differences exist between that system and the *shariah*, especially in the areas of codification and enforcement. The chapter then describes the process by which British colonial courts contributed to *shariah*'s transformation to a legal system. Before continuing the story of endowments and how they fared in the Anglo-Indian courts, the chapter describes these courts. It also describes some aspects of the social backgrounds and training of the individuals who worked in the courts. Next, it discusses some of the different theories of law common in judicial circles. Finally, it returns to an analysis of court suits on endowments as an example of how *shariah* became Islamic law.

Tensions between theory and practice in the development of *shariah*

Shariah is the common pronunciation of an Arabic word which has the literal meaning of "a water hole", or "a path of water", hence "a clear path".[2] Such colourful desert imagery does provide some insight into the role which *shariah* is supposed to play in Muslim life. For the devout Muslim, it should be *the path* to peace and order in this life and salvation in the next. Almost every aspect of private and public life is important enough to be included in its purview. Books on *shariah* discuss the cor-

---

[2] E. W. Lane, *An Arabic-English Lexicon*, IV, 1535, and R. Dozy, *Supplément aux Dictionnaires Arabes*, I, 748.

approach to applying an alien code was remarkable. Fundamental to its work, as well as to that of other judicial bodies, was the assumption that what Muslims called "*shariah*" was equivalent to what British judges called "law". Following the supposition of an essential similarity between the two, judges made a series of further terminological connections. They identified the *Quran*, the example (*sunnah*) of the Prophet and the writings of Muslim religious scholars as the "sources" of Muhammadan/Muslim law. Scholars of *shariah*, most of whom wrote in the eighth and ninth centuries of the Christian era, became "legal authorities", the Muslim counterparts of Coke and Blackstone. Treatises written by these learned and pious men became "legal textbooks", their opinions (*fatawa*) "precedents". *Qazis*, official guardians of the *shariah* appointed by Muslim rulers, became "judges" and the *ulama* "lawyers". Thus, in making their decisions British judges did not approach *shariah* on its own terms, but with concepts derived from the practice of British law.

The methods employed by the courts in cases like Abd ul-Fatah's had both specific and general dimensions. In narrow legal terms, they helped to establish a "law of *waqf*". Though political action in 1913 reversed one aspect of that law, politicians and judges left most of it intact. Beyond that, the courts' judgments had influence in a wider political and social context. For example, when "representative" institutions of government appeared in British India, lawyers made a habit of becoming politicians. Legal concepts and terminology worked their way into political discourse. They provided the categories used in defining social groups for political purposes. Moreover, the end of colonialism did not eradicate their influence. The independent states of South Asia appropriated most of the substantive law and all of the judicial apparatus of the raj. In legal and political spheres, Muslims and non-Muslims in the subcontinent still operated within the conceptual universe of nineteenth century British lawyers.

With regard to Muslims in South Asia, three basic assumptions informed the work of the courts. The first was that Muslims constituted a single community which possessed a single set of laws governing almost every personal, social and political activity. The second was that Muslims were "orthodox", which was to say that they were punctilious in matters of law and ritual. The third assumption was that their orthodoxy made Muslim law static and essentially conservative, unresponsive to changing historical circumstances.

Colonial courts did not create those assumptions out of thin air. They were certainly embedded in the Great Tradition of Islam. For centuries pious Muslims cherished similar notions about their community of faith

5

Creating a law of Muslim endowments

"The Law" is often taken as a given, and its development largely explained in terms of its own internal logic. This perspective, however, makes the historian uncomfortable, for it implies that the logic of the law is separable from the society in which it operates.   John Brewer

Though they stood at the apex of the British empire's judicial pyramid, the Law Lords of the Privy Council dispensed with the usual panoply of periwig, gown and sash. The simplicity of the image which their Lordships presented, dressed in ordinary suits, meeting around a plain table in an unadorned room, gave little indication of the power they possessed. Since the sovereign invariably issued a special decree confirming their judgments, their word was, quite literally, law.

On three separate days in November and December of 1894, five of the Law Lords turned their attention to a case involving a number of persons living in the Sylhet district of north-eastern Bengal Province. The case came labelled in the customary shorthand of judicial reporting: "*Abdul Fata Mahommed Ishak (and others)* v. *Russamoy Dhur Chowdhry (and others)*".[1] Their Lordships never met the parties involved. As a court of appeals, the Privy Council heard no witnesses. It produced a decision based on lower court records, its own members' knowledge of the law, their lengthy judicial experience and the arguments of advocates representing the opposing parties.

Because Abd ul-Fatah's case involved an institution with an Arabic name, "*waqf*", Councillors knew at once that the case required a verdict according to what they called, "Muhammadan law". Their Lordships' knowledge of that system was limited to what could be learned from a few translations of Arabic or Persian books and a few law school textbooks. The advocates who argued the case had the same meagre store of technical learning. Despite these obvious deficiencies, the Law Lords had no hesitation about providing judgments binding on all Muslims living in India and the rest of the British empire.

Apart from the irony of making a group of elderly British lawyers the ultimate authority in matters of Muslim doctrine, the Privy Council's

---

[1] *Cal*, XVIII, 399ff, *IA*, XXIII, 76ff, and *LI*, vol. 382, 607ff.

cessors had not done, he must have thought himself well within his rights. The gift was provided in consideration of the spiritual powers of his sainted ancestor, powers which were his by inheritance. Why should it matter that he helped his relatives or failed to keep immaculate accounts? It mattered because the government said it did. That concern for proper management, defined in a narrow sense, had influence beyond government circles. Later, when endowments became a political issue, some Muslim leaders adopted the British criticisms. They pointed to government involvement as proof that most *awqaf* needed closer supervision, supervision they would happily provide.

This chapter reviewed the sources of disagreement over endowments. These conflicts led to the government's involvement in the matter. The roots of the trouble, family arguments, debts or peculations were not new phenomena, nor were they uniquely "Indian" or "Muslim" problems. But the government changed the institutional context in which these things were examined. It was not just that old battles could be fought with new weapons, but that endowments were examined and analysed in novel ways. Through the processes of legal and political controversy the emphasis shifted away from the individual Muslims affected by endowments. The thousands of Hamid ud-dins, Pir un-nissahs and Shaikh Ahsan-ullahs faded into the background. In their place, the Muslim/Muhammadan community became the centre of attention.

for instance, has seen a large house divided by a barbed-wire topped wall running through the centre of rooms and the courtyard because a nephew and his paternal uncle were squabbling in the courts. At some point, people pursued argument for its own sake.

Besides the courts, other British government institutions got involved in issues related to endowments. An increase in the number of lawsuits was one result of that involvement. Officials took a special interest in the management of any endowment with some formal connection to the government. For example, the Revenue Department of the United Provinces stepped in to regulate a tomb/sufi guest house (*takyah*) located in the market town of Bahraich. A sufi saint, known as "Mian Sahib", died there about 1620. This saint's spiritual power acquired a reputation and his tomb drew pilgrims from the area. The Mughal governor took an interest in Mian Sahib's shrine and in 1733 gave it the right to the government's revenue on a tract of wasteland. In time, Bahraich expanded and occupied land mentioned in the governor's grant. In 1861–1862 the British replaced the original donation in order to facilitate the growth of the town. They offered the shrine the income of two villages, revenue free. Their combined worth was about Rs. 7,000 per year. Having given the "gift", officials wanted to make sure that the custodians spent the money in ways they thought compatible with the shrine's "religious" purpose. They wanted most of it distributed among the poor or used to support sufis or hold celebrations on the saint's death anniversary. However, they were convinced that the head of the shrine, Hamid ud-din, was spending too much for his own and his family's benefit. They also noted that Hamid ud-din seemed to be following in his predecessor's footsteps, since they had carried on in the same way. Hamid ud-din built a fine house for his brother, Ikram Ali. Moreover, Ikram Ali and a cousin entered the lumber business, with the trees of the granted villages furnishing their stock in trade. The authorities claimed that Ikram Ali indiscriminately felled trees, and that he even used fruit trees and made no effort to replace them.[51]

The revenue officials wanted Hamid ud-din removed as manager. In his stead, they passed the management over to the "Sayyid Salar Tomb Committee", an organization which they considered a model of honesty. The government pressed a court suit to achieve its aims and the courts ruled in its favour. The Revenue Department incurred some Rs. 2,500 in court costs which it charged to the shrine.[52]

Hamid ud-din, the custodian, probably did not pay much attention to the propriety of his actions. Since he had done nothing that his prede-

[51] (UP) *Judicial (Civil) File*, no. 487 of 1912.
[52] *Ibid.*

1823, a man named Muhammad Ali Jamadar, who lived in Patna, set aside a one-*anna* (one-sixteenth of a *rupee*) share in the income of a village to build and maintain his own tomb. To ensure the correct management of the endowment, he gave his eldest son, Khuda Bakhsh, a document making him and his eldest male descendants superintendents of the tomb. Eventually Khuda Bakhsh's son, Rajab Ali, assumed the responsibility. However, by the time his son, Mehdi Husain, took over as custodian, old Muhammad Ali Jamadar's memory was beginning to fade.

Mehdi Husain probably began to think that his own needs and those of his family were more important than the upkeep of his great-grandfather's tomb. He started appropriating the income for himself. But a cousin, Walid Ali, brought a suit against him claiming that Mehdi Husain was a thief. The court agreed with the challenge and appointed Walid Ali custodian in place of his cousin. Walid Ali's concern for honest management did not go beyond the walls of the courtroom. Having spotted an easy mark in a long dead ancestor's, presumably neglected, tomb, Walid Ali also began to filch the endowment's proceeds.[49]

Other members of the family, in their turn, noticed what Walid Ali was up to. A venerable old lady, a daughter of Khuda Bakhsh known as Pir un-nissah, claimed her right as a direct descendant of the first custodian and ousted Walid Ali. She acted as *mutawalli* until 1878 when advanced age forced her appoint two male kin in her place. In 1880, Walid Ali brought yet another suit against them in the court of the subordinate judge of Patna. The case finally reached the Calcutta High Court. There the whole matter was left undecided by a legal technicality. The original deed restricted control to male descendants. While the court agreed that Walid Ali was unfit, it was not sure that Pir un-nissah had any right to appoint custodians.[50] A mere one-*anna* share in the income of a single village was not worth all the time and money spent fighting over it. After so many years of bickering, the dispute probably provided an excuse for a game of beggar-your-brothers.

The courts became just another arena for the pursuit of family arguments. Records indicated that while the courtroom struggles took place, opposing parties continued to share the same household. How can this domestic continuity in the face of formal contention be explained? One possibility was that the participants did not take the legal disputes very seriously. More likely, their proximity further embittered the contestants. The warfare continued on the home front as well. The author,

[49] *Walid Ali* v. *Ashruff Hossain (and another), Cal,* VII, 732ff.
[50] *Ibid.*, 735.

to a conspiracy hatched between him and Amarchand. Rahim-ullah, according to his younger brother, was acting on the "evil advice" of his wife's family and listening to people who were "great enemies" of their father. Ahsan-ullah claimed that all the loans were collusive and meant to defraud him and his sons.[47]

Ahsan-ullah aimed much of his anger at his elder brother. He hurled epithets at him, not the moneylenders. Such inter-mural recrimination was a common feature of disputes over endowments. Opposing parties did not recognize, apparently, that great and impersonal economic forces contributed to their difficulties. Their irritation had an immediate, identifiable source within their own families.

Deeds of endowment themselves laid the ground for family strife. As noted in chapter 2, these documents established inequalities of income and authority. They favoured one son over another. If the family had sons, daughters, widows and wives had to make do with a pittance. Nephews, paternal or maternal uncles, in-laws and other distant kin had only a residual interest in the endowment. The strategy of narrowing the number of beneficiaries and limiting their control made sense to the founders, but it aggravated the disadvantaged. The aggrieved had a weapon in the British courts. Even if a legal challenge to the endowment ultimately failed, at least they had struck a blow.

Suits instituted by excluded relatives seldom failed. The courts often overturned endowments. The British courts, as it turned out, took a very strict view of the inheritance regulations contained in the *Quran* and texts of *shariah*. A daughter, for example, had a chance to gain a piece of the family's property in place of a tiny monthly allowance. She could enter the courts with some hope of success. Moreover, as the legal profession in India proliferated, scores of pleaders, *wakils* and advocates may have engaged in a form of ambulance chasing. These legal practitioners enhanced their own incomes by informing prospective clients of their rights.[48] They knew that the British courts, when confronted with a choice between upholding a *waqf* or dividing an estate according to the letter of the *Quran*, almost always chose the latter course. The system of court reporting and the tendency of law schools to focus their teaching on disputed points of law kept the legal profession informed about current trends in judicial interpretation. Not surprisingly, conflicts between family members entered the courts. Sons sued their mothers and brothers their sisters. The courts became a new stage on which to act out personal, inter-family antipathies.

Another source of conflict was the management of endowments. In

---

[47] *Ibid.*
[48] Murtazai Bibi's case, *All*, XII, 271.

Endowments and family strife

Abd ul-Fatah's paternal uncle, Muhammad Abd ur-Rahman, borrowed heavily against an estate which he and Abd ul-Fatah's father converted into a *waqf* in 1868. The uncle got a loan of some Rs. 9,000 from his mother's brother, the Nawab of Dacca, Khwajah Abd ul-Ghani. He also had over one hundred other creditors to whom he owed amounts of between Rs 100 and 150. Among that number were a dozen Muslim shopkeepers and tenants. Russamoy Dhur Chaudri's loan of Rs. 20,000 made him the largest among a total of 125 creditors. Moreover, Abd ul-Fatah was suing all of them, along with his uncle, the Nawab of Dacca, and his own father.[44] The procedure of the courts concentrated on the economic facts to the exclusion of the more personal ones. As chapter 6 will show, the courts' approach influenced that of politicians in the early decades of the twentieth century. They interpreted the issue, like some officials, as one involving the communal interests of "Hindus" and "Muslims".[45]

Endowments and family strife

As just indicated, questions of debt were tied up with tensions and conflicts within a family living off an endowment's proceeds. The circumstances surrounding the case reported as *Shaikh Muhammad Ahsan-ulla Chowdhry* v. *Amarchand Kundu*[46] showed how internal bickering and debt were connected. Shaikh Ahsan-ullah's father created this *waqf* in 1864. At that time, the eldest of the founder's sons became custodian. When he retired from that post, he passed it on to his younger brother, Rahim-ullah. The youngest brother, Ahsan-ullah, received only a stipend and was completely excluded from the endowment's management. Rahim-ullah soon began borrowing, using the *waqf* properties as collateral. As usual, he owed money to several different individuals. Amarchand Kundu was only one among them. In court, Ahsan-ullah claimed that his brother engineered the loans and subsequent confiscations for his own benefit. Ahsan-ullah's lawyers pointed out that under the terms of the original deed, females were prevented from assuming control of the estate. Rahim-ullah had no sons. Therefore, the youngest brother argued that Rahim-ullah intentionally wasted the endowment's wealth because his heirs would not get control of it. Also, Rahim-ullah had stopped the religious ceremonies the endowment supported and used those funds for his own benefit. Rahim-ullah's behaviour was attributed

---

[44] Abd al-Fatah's case, *LI*, vol. 382, 607ff.
[45] "A Memorial of Certain Muhammadan Gentlemen Resident in England...", (NAI) *HJP A* (March 1909), nos. 163–164.
[46] Shaikh Muhammad Ahsan-ullah Chowdhry's case, *LI*, vol. 340, 89.

The expense of a lawsuit in time and money may have encouraged debtors to delay their payments. Perhaps they hoped that creditors would grow tired of the struggle. For example, between 1891 and 1895 5,320 cases involving debt were heard in the courts of the United Provinces, but 1,562 of the sales they ordered never took place because the debtors paid up at the last possible moment.[37]

Moneylenders were themselves not eager to pay the costs of suits and forced sales. They were often content with yearly interest payments. Often no particular advantage came their way from taking over land. If the debtor's relations with the agriculturalists were good, the moneylender came on the scene as a suspect stranger. If the former owner and his tenants got on badly, the lender acquired someone else's headaches. They also knew that dispossessed landowners were not easy to get rid of. They sometimes stayed on as subordinate tenants or intermediaries. In short, they had reason to avoid recovering the principals of their loans. A resort to the courts probably pointed to financial pressures on the lender or to the debtor's refusal to make even interest payments.[38]

Debt remained a topic of interest for judges and administrators. Some of them expressed the view that Muslims were particularly victimized by Hindu moneylenders.[39] The endowments discussed here provided little to confirm such a simplistic opinion. Muslim landholders were themselves lenders and mortgage holders.[40] Income derived from mortgages was included in endowments' receipts. Muslims lent money to Hindus and ended up in possession of the latter's property.[41] Muslims owed money to other Muslims, family members and professional lenders. Loans between Muslims did carry interest charges and proved that Muslims did not avoid its use.[42]

Official impressions about Hindu encroachment on Muslim landlords[43] were partly encouraged by the character of court reporting. For example, the best known *waqf*-related case was *Russamoy Dhur Chaudhri* v. *Abul Fata Mahomed Ishak*. If that title was the only bit of information possessed, then it indeed looked like an instance of a Hindu loan shark circling in on a foundering Muslim landlord. Only a close examination of the records revealed the complicated loans and family intrigues which lay behind the dispute.

[37] (UP) *JP Civ* (August 1891), nos. 1–4; (October 1894), nos. 18–21; (November 1892), nos. 1–4.
[38] Musgrave, "Rural Credit", 221–222, 227–229.
[39] F. N. Wright, *Report on the Settlement of Cawnpore District*, 3ff.
[40] Hamid Ali's case, *AA*.
[41] Murtazai Bibi's case, *AA*.
[42] *Nizam Ghulam (and others)* v. *Abdul Gafur (and others)*, *LI*, vol. 367, 757–758.
[43] S. M. Moens, *Report on the Settlement of Bareilly District*, 134ff.

Costs to the appellant

Item	Cost		
	Rupees	Annas	Pais
Stamp for memorandum of appeal	160	0	0
Stamps for copies of the above	1	8	0
Stamp for the *wakalatnamah*	2	0	0
Advocate's fee	327	12	0
Printing and translation charges	338	15	3
Charge for admission of a "paper book" consisting of documentary evidence	14	9	3

Total of claimed expenses Rs. 844.12.6

Costs to the respondent

Item	Cost		
	Rupees	Annas	Pais
Stamp for *wakalatnamah*	2	0	0
Advocate's fee	327	12	0
Printing and translation charges	413	9	3
Charges for admission of the "paper book"	14	9	3

Total of claimed expenses Rs. 757.14.6

High Courts were courts of appeal. They did not hear witnesses. Their decisions were based on an examination of the lower courts' proceedings and on other documentary evidence. The "paper book" contained any of those items which the litigants thought relevant. As noted, they had to bear the costs of printing it. Also, they paid for the translating of all materials into English. The majority of the High Court judges were British and usually unable to deal with evidence not in their native tongue. The costs noted above seemed to be typical in terms of the percentage of the property's value they absorbed.

The "Law Lords" of the Privy Council in London were the highest legal authority in the British empire. An appeal to that body involved spending a small fortune. In one suit, first heard in the Sylhet district court then in the Calcutta High Court, the estimated worth of the property was Rs. 300,000. Costs in the Calcutta court amounted to Rs. 3,796. In addition, the courts ordered the losing party, the respondent, to pay the appellant Rs. 3,916.8 in compensatory damages. The Privy Council, to which the loser appealed, required the posting of a Rs. 4,000 bond before it considered the case. Translation and transmission of appropriate documents to London added another Rs. 2,950 to the bill. Finally, the participants had to secure the services of special lawyers in London who argued the case before the Council.[36] Pursuing a lawsuit at any level in the legal system was obviously expensive. It contributed to the burden of debt which Indian landholders carried.

[36] *Abdul Fata Mahommed Ishak* v. *Russamoy Dhur Chowdhry*, *LI*, vol. 382, 602.

Costs to the first defendant

Item	Cost		
	Rupees	Annas	Pais
Stamp for *wakalatnamah*	1	0	0
Pleader's fee	212	0	0
Stamp for petition	1	0	0
Stamps for copies of the above	12	8	0
For summoning witnesses	14	8	0
Money order commission	0	6	0
Diet money for witnesses	50	0	0
Fees for filing of records from previous suits	17	8	0

Total of claimed expenses Rs. 309.6.0
Charged disallowed by the court 0.8.0
Total costs incurred by the first defendant Rs. 308.14.0

Once again, the court decided that all parties should share the costs, with the first defendant paying Rs. 203.7.0 and the plaintiff Rs. 105.7.0.

Costs to the second defendant

Item	Cost		
	Rupees	Annas	Pais
Application	1	0	0
Penalty because above was disallowed	0	8	0
Stamp for *wakalatnamah*	0	8	0
For summoning witnesses	2	0	0
Money order commission	0	4	0
Diet money for witnesses	1	0	0
Pleader's fee	50	0	0

Total of claimed expenses Rs. 55.4.0
The second defendant paid Rs. 45.8 and the plaintiff Rs. 9.4.

Most of the costs mentioned above were self-explanatory. The government required that pleas, and copies of them, be submitted on paper bearing a stamp of value commensurate with the suit's estimated worth. A *wakalatnamah* was a document giving power of attorney to the litigants' pleaders, sometimes called *"wakils"* (literally "agents"). Each of the parties was responsible for providing for the travel, lodging and food of the witnesses summoned. In this instance, the defence obviously summoned more witnesses, or hardier eaters, than the plaintiff. Since even the district court was often miles away from home and cases spread out over months, the amount spent on witnesses could be considerable.

The suit was appealed from the district court to the High Court in Allahabad and heard in 1911. The participants listed their expenses as follows:[35]

---

[35] *Ibid.*

cessions to land held in *awqaf*. A small revenue payer like Mujawar Husain was caught between a government bent on the full realization of its due and tenants determined to pay as little as possible. Not surprisingly, most *waqifs* realized the importance of meeting their tax obligations. Deeds of endowment invariably contained a provision that the revenue should be paid first. Many like Mujawar Husain were willing to take out loans to pay it. But getting a loan was only a temporary respite followed by court suits, sales and seizures. According to the authorities on *shariah*, a *waqf* was supposed to be immune from confiscation. The British government recognized no such limitation.

The courts of British India had a twofold connection to the problem of debt. On the one hand, they enforced laws which demanded that debts be paid, even if land had to be taken away from its owner and sold. On the other hand, the costs incurred in court disputes created debts. Court charges were heavy and had to be met to get a decision. Often, borrowing was the only way for a litigant to get the cash to fight a suit.

For those involved in a court dispute over an endowment, the expense of a suit must have been uppermost in their minds. The section which follows provides some idea of the size of these costs by describing those produced by two different controversies carried on at all three levels of the colonial judicial system.

Court fees were determined by estimating the value of the property involved in the suit. In our first case, the court placed the worth of the estate at Rs. 13,558.13.8. The subordinate judge of Shahjahanpur first heard the case in 1909. The plaintiff and the defendants reported their costs in the case as follows:[34]

Costs to the plaintiff

Item	Cost		
	Rupees	Annas	Pais
Stamp for the plaint	245	0	0
Stamps for copies of the above	15	12	0
Process fees	2	0	0
Stamp for *wakalātnāmah*	1	0	0
Diet money for witnesses	14	8	0
Application	2	0	0
For summoning the witnesses	6	0	0
Money order commission	1	0	0
Pleader's fee	212	8	0
Inspection of records	0	12	0

Total of claimed expenses Rs. 500.8.0
Charged disallowed by the court Rs. 6.0.0
Total cost incurred by plaintiff Rs. 494.1.0

The court apportioned these expenses with the plaintiff paying Rs. 158.1 and the defendants Rs. 336.

[34] Based on Mazhar Husain Khan's case, *AA*.

Marriage in India was a social as well as an economic matter, an investment which warranted the spending of large amounts of money. Marriages established social alliances between families and kin groups. Also, they were opportunities to assert family status. A cheap wedding reflected badly on the contracting parties. The exact nature of the "household expenses" was not reported. As for the house and the *imambarah*, Mujawar Husain probably thought of them as necessities.

In Mujawar Husain's case, the need to pay the government revenue was the largest single reason for borrowing. Concentrating on frivolous expenditure, few officials admitted the possibility that their own taxes created the need to borrow. The British government tended to believe that its revenue demands were lighter than those of its predecessors. When the British settled the revenue demands, and during subsequent resettlements, they often reduced the sums which the Mughals established. The figure which they reduced was known as the "*jama*'". But under the Mughals, and others, the *jama* was more a statement of hopeful expectation than of actual tax receipts. In Mughal records, another figure, known as the "*ḥāṣil*" (literally "what is obtained"), more closely indicated the moneys taken in. The British reduced the first unrealistic figure, but they tried hard to collect the lower sum in full.[29] The Mughals and their ilk were extortionate, but they did face some constraints. In their time India still had a great deal of unoccupied land. Peasants often moved when pressed too hard.[30] Cultivators, *zamindars* and village headmen became adept at concealment and resistance. All of these things limited the ability of pre-British states to get every *rupee* they asked for.

The British seemed more efficient at obtaining what they demanded. They surpassed the Mughals in monopolizing the use of force and eliminated their subjects' chance to obtain concessions through armed opposition.[31] Also, they tried to eliminate cheating. A gradual increase in population and government encouragement to cultivate "wastes" put more pressure on available land.[32] The government was willing to relent only in periods of serious drought or flood. Even then, it gave only paltry easements. During the famine years of 1876–1877, 1890–1891, 1896–1897 and 1899–1900, the revenue demand was either met in full or missed by only a few percentage points.[33]

Unlike the governments of Muslim states, the British offered no con-

[29] E. Whitcombe, *Agrarian Conditions in Northern India*, 140–160.
[30] Habib, *Agrarian System*, chapters 6 and 7.
[31] T. R. Metcalf, *Land*, 173–179.
[32] Whitcombe, *Agrarian Conditions*, 83–97, 120–135, 226 n. 67.
[33] *Ibid.*, 147ff, and B. Chandra, "Reinterpretation of Nineteenth Century Indian Economic History" in *Indian Economy in the Nineteenth Century*, 67.

able Hajji Bikani Mian listed four individuals as major creditors. One of the four, Rup Lal Dass, was a close personal friend and business associate. Bikani Mian's deed of endowment appointed him as financial adviser to his heirs.[24]

Bikani Mian's creditors also challenged the image of the moneylender as a professional. Of the four, only one listed his occupation as *"Mahajan"* (lender). The other three combined trade and landholding with moneylending.[25] Almost anyone with some spare cash could be a petty lender.[26]

When searching for a loan, a would-be borrower went first to family members. Friends were next in order of preference. Only when these sources were exhausted did one approach a stranger. That pattern was evident in the experience of Mujawar Husain Khan of Allahabad. His father had drafted a deed of endowment on 8 May 1878, five days before his death. As Mujawar Husain was still a child, his mother acted as custodian until he came of age and took charge. The estate consisted of several plots of land located in the Arail *parganah* of Allahabad district and in the Haswa *parganah* of Fatehpur district. The profits, after taxes and management costs, were reported as Rs. 858.12.30 per year. In addition, two groves of fruit trees were connected to the family's residence in Allahabad city. Two *imambarahs*, one of masonry (*pukka*) and the other of mud brick (*kacca*) were attached to the dwelling and considered part of the value of the holding.[27]

Soon after reaching adulthood, Mujawar Husain began to borrow, using the endowment's land and buildings as collateral. On 17 November 1892 he borrowed Rs. 500 from a relative. The money went to cover the costs of his own wedding. In the following three years he kept borrowing and the names of more individuals were added to the list of his creditors. He owed the most to Mul Narain, described as a *khatri* moneylender. On five separate occasions between January 1893 and July 1895, Mujawar Husain got loans from Mul Narain. He borrowed a total of Rs. 700 to pay for "household expenses". Another Rs. 700 went to build a new house and a new *imambarah*. Finally, he borrowed a total of Rs. 2,000 to meet the government's revenue.[28]

Mujawar Husain's reasons for borrowing did not seem all that foolish.

---

[24] *Bikani Mia* v. *Shukh Lal Poddar*, *Cal*, XX, 120, and *AC*.
[25] *Ibid.*, *AC*.
[26] P. J. Musgrave, "Rural Credit and Rural Society in the United Provinces, 1860–1920", in *The Imperial Impact*, 216–232, and D. Washbrook, "Law, State and Agrarian Society in Colonial India", 649–721.
[27] *Hamid Ali (and another)* v. *Mujawar Husain Khan*, *All*, XXIV, 257ff, and *AA*.
[28] *Ibid.*, *AA*.

officials faced not only mutinous soldiers, but also mobs of disaffected cultivators and *zamindars*. Some of them assumed a connection between the riots and the dislocations caused by debt-related land transfers.[19] Thereafter, the administration continually discussed ways of handling indebtedness. A few argued on pure economic principle that landholders mired in debt deserved whatever fate the Market decreed. The government had no right to intervene to defeat the rights of creditors.[20] Wastrels must always give way to the thrifty.

Other officials, perhaps the majority, argued from a different point of view. They feared the political consequences of seizures for debt. They held that British rule rested on the government's ability to manipulate the landlords, India's "natural aristocracy", and on the good will of the peasantry. The loss of their support endangered the raj. In practice, different branches of the government worked at cross-purposes. The courts tended to operate according to impersonal economic principle. Judges routinely granted decrees to creditors. At the same time, political officers legislated exemptions aimed at insulating landholders from the full force of the Market and the courts. An early attempt to aid larger landlords occurred in the province of Avadh. There, the government established a close relationship with a group of landed magnates known as "*taalluqdars*".[21] Those individuals, some 272 in number, received special legal protection which prevented their losing their estates.[22] That was only one in a long series of legislative and administrative acts which protected land groups, including both large landlords and yeoman cultivators. The Bundelkhand Encumbered Estates Act was an example of an act meant to help *zamindars*, while the Punjab Alienation of Land Bill favoured cultivators deemed politically significant.[23] Perhaps because the administration was itself divided on the economic wisdom of such measures, the relief granted was sporadic and haphazard. When passed, these laws affected select geographical areas or particular sets of landholders. The protection they offered was never extended to all landholders in every region of British India. Most of the *waqifs* mentioned here were not among the privileged few benefiting from administrative solicitude. They had to face the consequences of their debts.

Examining the records of endowments casts some doubt on certain aspects of the administration's understanding of the problem of debt. For example, it was clear that debt was not an impersonal activity. The parties involved knew each other, perhaps were friends. The redoubt-

[19] Stokes, *The Peasant and the Raj*, 159–184.
[20] Note of C. Bernard in (NAI) *HJP B* (October 1879), nos. 44–45.
[21] T. R. Metcalf, *Land*, 191ff, and Stokes, *The Peasant and the Raj*, 205.
[22] T. R. Metcalf, *Land*, 230–235.
[23] N. G. Barriar, *The Punjab Alienation of Land Bill of 1900*.

kings", but such incantations did not create patron–client attachments. Tenants, judging from the records, were usually a nuisance. They were no more eager to pay rent than their city cousins. Even though most landlords used toughs to persuade cultivators to meet their obligations, peasant families, armed with sticks and supported by village brethren, often succeeded in defying their landlords. Failure to realize expected income seemed a constant source of worry.[15]

Defaults always brought a shortfall in endowments' incomes. If violence failed, a landlord had to sue. Even the largest of them were forced to take recalcitrant tenants to court.[16] The superior resources which the richest commanded reduced a court action to a troublesome expense. Perhaps the deficit could be made up by squeezing more pliable subordinates a little harder. But for the more modestly wealthy, litigation was a strain on limited incomes. Court suits and rent stoppages contributed to indebtedness which was a major source of trouble for endowments.

Debt and indebtedness

Debt was one economic transaction which seemed easily discussed in purely abstract terms. A few British officials maintained a strictly theoretical perspective on it. When they noticed that many landlords and cultivators borrowed heavily, they looked for an economically intelligible explanation for their behaviour. While searching, administrators developed a scenario which they thought explained the problem. Debt, they believed, was the creature of huge expenditures on frivolous activities such as weddings.[17] Landlords especially, but cultivators as well, seemed prone to wasting their assets in useless display.[18] Like children, they delighted in baubles and carnivals. The attempt to live in a grand style drew them to the moneylender's door.

Moneylenders also became the objects of official caricature. A crafty merchant (*bania*) was just the sort of person to take advantage of fun-loving, slightly dim gentry and peasants. When the profligates proved unable to make their payments, the moneylender went to the courts and forced a sale of land. Then, at the auction, the merchant bought the estate and became an absentee landlord. Some considered that the typical pattern of landowner–moneylender relations.

The Revolt of 1857 gave the government more reason to worry about the consequences of merchants buying land. During the disturbances,

---
[15] E.g. *Biba Jan* v. *Kalb Husain*, *All*, XXXI, 145ff.
[16] T. R. Metcalf, *Land*, 238–250.
[17] T. G. Kessinger, *Vilyatpur*, 153–155.
[18] F. W. Porter, *Final Report of the Settlement of the Allahabad District*, 13, and H. K. Gracey, *Final Report of the Settlement of the Cawnpore District*, 10ff.

The problems faced by rural landholders were similar to those of the city dwellers. Though relations between landlord and tenant differed from region to region in India, Muslim landlords, no matter where they lived, faced a similar difficulty: they were seldom connected by kinship to their tenants. Their problem was better understood when contrasted to the status of North India's *raja*-landlords. A *raja*, as in the case of some Jats or Rajputs, was often the head of lineage group. His subordinate tenants, sometimes even his cultivators, were part of the kin network.[10] They were not always honest or eager to pay rent to their wealthy relative, but at least the *raja* had those fraternal ties to use as a lever. Even after the *rajas* became landlords, the familial connections remained. Few Muslim landlords enjoyed that advantage. Tenants were not usually of the same lineage and often they did not share the landlord's faith.

Estates were, as described above, composed of fragments of land scattered here and there over one or more districts. Therefore, each tenant or cultivator paid a comparatively small amount of rent. For instance, three of Mughal Jan's tenants were described as follows: one was Amir Khan, a Pathan cultivator who paid Rs. 14.4 per year; the second was Ghisa, a butcher who farmed part-time and paid Rs. 12; finally, Chunru paid Rs. 10.[11] When property was placed in a *waqf*, its income still came in small amounts from dozens of different individuals. The largest landowners had managers and accountants to supervise collections. Some deeds of endowment mentioned the payment of these "establishment charges".[12] But most of the endowments discussed here were created by petty landlords. They did the collecting themselves. Since they lived in towns, not on their holdings, a yearly or twice yearly visitation was necessary to get hold of the rent.[13]

Tenants were useful on occasion. The names of the three mentioned above were recorded because they showed up in court to testify on Mughal Jan's behalf.[14] The records, however, rarely mentioned such expressions of loyalty. The deeds invoked the traditions of peasant deference with phrases conjuring up "little kingdoms" and "little

---

[10] R. G. Fox, *Kin, Clan, Raja and Rule*, and M. C. Pradhan, *The Political System of the Jats of Northern India*.
[11] *Syeda Bibi (and another)* v. *Mughal Jan (and others)*, *All*, XXIV, 231ff, and *AA*.
[12] These expenses included the salaries of accountants and peons and varied with the size of the holding. Mehrban Ali had a large estate and his charges were over Rs. 2,100 yearly: see Mujibunnissa's case, *LI*, vol. 441, 701. The costs for Altaf Ali Khan's holding were less than Rs. 100 per year: see *Mazhar Husain Khan* v. *Abdul Hadi Khan*, *All*, XXXIII, 480ff, and *AA*.
[13] Murtazai Bibi's case, *AA*.
[14] *Ibid.*

poorer families. This step, however, sometimes made it more difficult to collect rent. Each tenant paid a fairly small sum. When one of them consistently refused to pay up, the "landlord" had little choice but to initiate legal action. The remedy was often worse than the original affliction. The machinery of the courts was cumbrous and expensive. By the time it moved to the landlord's aid, the tenant scampered off. The landlord lost his rent and the money spent on legal fees. Getting tenants, then making them pay, absorbed so much time and trouble that endowments were often without the funds to pay their beneficiaries or provide for religious institutions and ceremonies.[4] Some custodians tried to solve that problem by offering long-term, low-rent leases. In Calcutta or Bombay, a new leaseholder had a chance to turn a profit by knocking down the old houses and putting up new ones. In that way, an entrepreneur collected higher rents, while holding a forty or fifty year lease at minimal cost.[5] The only benefit which the endowment received was the gain of a more secure income. But the sum was often much lower than the one originally set aside by the deed. Someone or something had to bear the loss.

Urban landlords who by ill luck held less than choice lots were unable to negotiate new leases, even on unfavourable terms. For example, Begam Gauda Bibi's houses in Calcutta were located in an area infamous as a cholera breeding ground. Tenants were hard to get. The individuals who actually occupied her houses came from the lowest economic strata, unwilling or unable to come up with the rent.[6] Even if municipal authorities wanted to clean up such places, the endowment's funds had to meet the cost of improvements. Shahzadi Begam's endowment had to lay out Rs. 1,224 to pay for sewage pipes for her houses.[7] Another *waqf* had to spend Rs. 500 to build privies which met the Calcutta Corporation's standards.[8] The beneficiaries of these endowments must have believed that it was money down the drain.

Declining incomes from urban properties or expenditures for civic improvements were more than financial losses. Individuals did not receive their assigned incomes. The continuance of the religious aspects of endowments was also endangered. Yet, the impulse to fulfil completely the terms of a *waqf* was so strong that custodians borrowed money to make up for deficits.[9] That procedure carried its own risks to the future of an endowment.

---

[4] Khair un-nissa's *waqf*, *OC*, w. 38 of 1907, and Mirza Ali Busrawi's *waqf*, *OC*, w. 34 of 1902.
[5] *OC*, w. 34 of 1902.
[6] *OC*, w. 45 of 1905.
[7] *OC*, w. 51 of 1915.
[8] Manu Bibi's *waqf*, *OC*, w. 43 of 1909.
[9] *Ibid.*, and *OC*, w. 51 of 1915.

maintain the webs of privilege and responsibility, the ceremonies and holy places, the things that the founders cared for while living.

Did they really believe that such permanence was possible? Certainly some of the deeds admitted the possibility that all might not go as planned. A disaster could occur: the family line might die out. But a mention of these misfortunes was usually prefaced with a "*Khudā nah khwāstah*": "God forbid"! Legal deeds were not vehicles for the expression of cosmic doubt or philosophical musings on the vagaries of fate. Their language gave the impression that the spiritual and material order of their founders would endure.[3] However, as the first chapter noted, endowments had a way of generating conflicts which disrupted and destroyed the endowments themselves.

As chapters 2 and 3, this one covers the perspective of those most intimately involved in strife over endowments. Though the forces which disrupted the smooth functioning of *awqaf* were developed in a larger economic and social context, people usually saw their problems in highly personal terms. Confronted with a loss of their income, they were not inclined to curse economic laws. They were far more likely to fix the blame on their enemies. Most of the disputes discussed here ended up in the law courts. The courts' handling of these quarrels will be discussed in detail in the next chapter. The views of the courts came to be more influential than the feelings or perceptions of those directly concerned in challenging or defending a given *waqf*. However, when the judges set about the formulation of their understanding of what an endowment was, they did so on the basis of what they saw or did not see in looking at the kinds of disputes described below.

Rents

The income of most endowments derived from cash received as some form of what British law considered "rent". Rent was defined as money paid by a person or persons in consideration for the use of property *owned* by someone else. The source of the rent was either land or houses in the possession of the person who created an endowment. The crucial problem in either case was collecting that rent.

In towns and cities, declining property values presented a serious threat to rent collection. As a house aged, it became harder to attract high rents and high-status, presumably more reliable, tenants. As noted above, a house was often large, intended to serve wealthier people with many retainers and relatives. One way of dealing with a decline in a house's value was to cut it up into apartments and rent these to several

---

[3] *Mujibunnissa (and others)* v. *Abdul Rahim and Abdul Aziz, All*, XXIII, 243.

4

The unsettling of endowments

> In this world, we worry about our daily bread.
> At the thought of heaven, we must tremble
> in expectation of Judgment Day.
> "Prosperity" is only a word, we find it not
> in this world or the next.   Mir Sawda

Deeds of endowment were couched in the language of eternity. Their material and spiritual purposes were supposed to be fixed "always" and "forever" (*hameshah*). The arrangements made for distributing their income were intended to go on "through the generations" (*naslān b'ad naslān*).[1] The hope they expressed for permanence flew in the face of the experiences of their authors. After all, these men and women constructed endowments which suited the various political and economic changes they witnessed. They saw old kings depart and new ones arrive. They dealt with new laws derived from British customs which replaced older notions of how to accumulate and spend wealth. Though they tried to preserve some of the values of pre-British societies, in the end they had to take account of the different context in which those values operated. Each endowment was an attempt to balance the status of a "chief" (*rais*) and the demands of the "little kingdom" (*riasat*) with those of a system which labelled founders "landlords" and their domains "estates". Every *waqif* wanted his or her offspring to inherit the fruits of that ingenuity.

In both the temporal and spiritual realms endowments sought to preserve the world of their founders. As was usually a senior generation's wont, they put sage advice in their deeds designed to help their heirs keep that world intact. They counselled thrift and the need to reinvest profits. They warned against luxury and bickering.[2] Following the former and shunning the latter would enable the next generation to

---

[1] Urdu and Persian, sometimes following Arabic usage, have several ways of expressing temporal duration. In addition to *hameshah* ("always"), one can use "*behudūd*" meaning "without limit". Another way of expressing continuity was to speak of "generations" (*naslan*) or of "progeny" as in "*awlād bah awlād*". All of these phrases appear in deeds of endowment. For an example, see *Murtazai Bibi* v. *Jumna Bibi*, *All*, XII, 265.
[2] *Muhammad Munawar Ali* v. *Rasulan Bibi*, *All*, XXI, 337.

became a public issue towards the end of the nineteenth century, the reformers got more attention. The opinions of those who ignored or contradicted the reformers were too diffuse, perhaps too rooted in local concerns, to merit such attention. The reformers were better organized. The British government also assisted, since its colonial policies made religion one of the key social concepts. Also, since some officials blamed Muslims for the Revolt of 1857, the government was more sensitive to those views which seemed to stir the community. The British were therefore inclined to listen to the reformers, perhaps more closely than many Muslims did. As the endowments themselves demonstrated, Muslims had a variety of religious concerns not condoned by reformers.

The two previous chapters described some of the spiritual and temporal concerns of Muslims who founded endowments. They showed that in both spheres the founders' families came first, then an ever-widening circle of individuals who were, in some sense, "familiar". When founders took notice of such trans-local institutions as a reformist movement or the government, they usually did so with an eye to their involvement close to home. Their endowments were meant to make permanent the role that founders exercised while they lived, to enhance and preserve their memory. They were a very human attempt to oppose the forces of time.

Sir Sayyid's approach to Islam emphasized the "rational" dimension of the faith. He and his disciples criticized beliefs and practices which seemed to them superstitious. Those categories included sufi miracle-mongering, elaborate ceremonials and anything which hinted at idolatry, such as the construction of ostentatious tombs.[63]

The practices described above did have some defenders. Many of those who spoke in favour of *fatihahs* and the like were simply affirming the validity of what their ancestors had done. A few, for instance the scholars associated with the Barelwi movement, formulated a theological argument that local beliefs and practices were not contrary to the faith so long as they did not contradict such basic notions as the oneness of God.[64]

Movements which claimed to reform, restore or revitalize the practice of Islam in India were a feature of the spiritual landscape from the seventeenth century onward.[65] British rule in India actually opened up new arenas for reformist activity. For example, the introduction of modern printing greatly increased the number of periodicals and books published in English and the vernacular languages.[66] Printing presses speedily reproduced and distributed reformist tracts. Newspapers reported the sayings and doings of prominent reformers. Railroads enabled them to travel all over India more easily and more quickly. All of these developments meant that there were new pulpits to thump and plenty of preachers ready to make a fist.

To what extent did these preachers really represent or influence the mass of Muslims in India? From the evidence which *waqfnamahs* provided, most people ignored the reformers. *Fatihahs*, *majalis*, elaborate weddings or funerals and so many other beliefs and practices which the reformers fulminated against remained the things supported by endowments. That was as true of the *awqaf* founded between 1900 and 1910 as it was of those established forty or fifty years before. More than thirty years of preaching by Deobandis and Ahl-i Hadisi apparently had little effect. Two hundred years after Shah Walli-ullah began to criticize those practices, many, if not most, Muslims carried on with them. Of course, the reformers did attract some followers, but their opinions did not predominate.

The points of view of reformers and the Muslims who created endowments were clearly different. Yet, as the examination of endowments

[63] Justice Karamat Husain was a notable example of this approach, see p. 144; also, see the arguments of Sayyid Abd ur-Rawf and Nawab Abd ul-Majjid Jaunpuri in Biba Jan's case, *All*, XXXI, 138ff.
[64] B. D. Metcalf, *Islamic Revival*, 296ff.
[65] I. Habib, "The Political Role of Shaikh Ahmad Sirhindi and Shah Walliullah", 36–55.
[66] Robinson, *Separatism*, 77–78.

Holi or Diwali which Muslims also participated in. Those were occasions on which everybody, even poorer families, spent money for food, clothing and entertainment. The events supported by endowments were special because they occurred repeatedly throughout the year. Ordinary families could not afford to celebrate all of them. Only a family of substantial wealth which wanted to assert social dominance was able to keep so many and to distribute the food or gifts to people. Such rituals were not simply spiritual events. They were also periodic confirmations of the temporal order.

Despite *fatihahs*, *milads* and Muharram being for Muslims among the most popular liturgical events, some religious leaders objected to certain aspects of their performance. Shah Walli-ullah, the eighteenth century reformer, condemned *Sunnis* who joined *Shiis* in the rites of the Imams Hasan and Husain. He also criticized the holding of elaborate *urs* celebrations. No one, he asserted, can intercede with the Almighty. Walli-ullah believed that such festivals were the result of the baleful influence which India's infidels exerted on Muslims.[60] In the nineteenth century, the *ulama* of Deoband repeated Walli-ullah's criticisms. They joined him in looking askance at *urs* and *fatihahs* which included anything more than a simple recitation of the *Quran*'s opening chapter. Deobandis did urge their followers to be polite to fellow Muslims (excepting *Shiah*). They did accept invitations to such events, but took a dim view of any ostentation, even in weddings. They were also against elaborate ceremonial to mark the Prophet's birthday. Like Walli-ullah, Deobandis believed that the *Shiah* were heretics and therefore opposed any participation in the rituals of Muharram. The Deobandis were not alone in complaining about the idolatrous elements in Muslims' common practice of the faith. Those who associated themselves with a group known as the "Ahl-i Hadis" and some of those influenced by Sir Sayyid Ahmad Khan joined them in condemning elaborate or expensive *urs*, *fatihahs* and weddings.[61]

The Ahl-i Hadis, like the Deobandis, claimed to be the spiritual heirs of Shah Walli-ullah. As the name of the group indicated, they stressed a purified version of Islam which found its model in the life of the Prophet as that was reported in Hadis literature. The Prophet's example was their guide and they wanted to eliminate any practices or beliefs not confirmed by it. By the standards of the Ahl-i Hadis, most aspects of Sufism, developments in *shariah* and all the popular observances mentioned above were historical accretions, not part of the pristine faith.[62]

[60] A. Ahmad, "Political and Religious Ideas of Shah Waliyullah of Delli", 22–30.
[61] B. D. Metcalf, *Islamic Revival*, 264ff and 364ff.
[62] *Ibid.*, 296ff.

un-nissah's *waqf* provided as much for her *fatihah* as it did for the *milad*.[56]

The *urs*, literally "the marriage", actually the death anniversary, of the sufi saint Abd ul-Qadir Gilani (who died in Baghdad in A.D. 1166) was popular throughout India. Gilani, known as "Pīr of Pīrs", founded the Qadiriyyah order of sufis and this *silsilah* was well represented in India. As they spread throughout the subcontinent, his disciples proclaimed his powers of intercession.[57] Dozens of other saints were popular. Which ones founders chose to remember depended partly on their place of residence and partly on their personal attachment to the cult of one saint or another.[58]

A few festivals were exceptions to the round of birth and death anniversaries. *Shab-i barāt* was one of the most popular of these. On that night, the 14th of the month of Shaban, people believed that their fate for the coming year was determined. On the night of the 13th a vigil was held in honour of a family's dead. The 14th itself was an occasion for joviality featuring feasting and fireworks in the evening.[59]

The importance of the rites of Muharram was noted above. Muharram and all of the festivals – those connected with scriptural Islam or popular Islam or with the family – had in common the preparation and distribution of food. The offering and eating of food established a bond between individuals. However, the relationship created was not one of equality. To accept food, to eat someone else's food, was an indication of submission or dependence. To offer it was an assertion of social superiority. The distribution of food was part of the symbolism of unequal exchanges which marked so much of India's social and political life. The meaning of the relationship was even enshrined in the polite discourse of Urdu. A social or political superior was addressed as "feeder of the poor" (*bandah-parwar*) or "the slave's sustainer" (*bandah-nawāz*). The centrality of food in these ceremonies demonstrated that they were more than figures of speech. A leader, even if her or his sphere of influence was limited to a single *muhallah*, reinforced the bonds of loyalty by feeding dependants or inferiors on many occasions throughout the year. The close attention paid to births and deaths within a *rais'* family pointed to a concern to maintain symbolic links between that family and its clients. It may also account for the absence of provisions for festivals such as *'Īd ul-fiṭr*, the feast marking the end of *Ramazan*, or of *'Īd uz-zuhā*, the commemoration of Abraham's sacrifice, or for popular Hindu festivals like

[56] Mazhar Husain Khan's case, *AA*.
[57] Sharif, *Qānūn-i Islām*, 192–194; more than half the endowments surveyed made provision for this festival.
[58] *Ibid.*, 195–202.
[59] *Ibid.*, 202–204.

during the burial, on the third and fortieth days and also each year on the anniversary of death. Eventually, the commemoration of death became quite elaborate. Sometimes several reciters of the *Quran* were hired to repeat the Holy Book with the intention of gaining spiritual merit for the dead person's soul. In addition, at the time of death and on the various remembrances of it, some families prepared sweets or other special foods, offered some to relatives and friends, then distributed the rest to the poor. Very rich families also gave away clothing.[51]

Most *waqfnamahs* left money to pay for the *fatihahs* of close relatives and of the founders. Farhat un-nissah's provisions for this ceremony were representative in terms of the amount of money allocated and the relatives remembered. Her dead husband and three female relations each had Rs. 10 set aside for their yearly commemorations. Farhat unnissah ordered that Rs. 25 be spent on her own *fatihah*. Another Rs. 30 went to retain two reciters of the *Quran* to appear at the ceremonies.[52] Shaikh Ahsan-ullah's *waqf* provided Rs. 25 to commemorate the death of any adult member of the family, but only Rs. 10 went for the anniversary of a child's death.[53]

Deeds showed that weddings in the family also called for feasting and the distribution of gifts. The amounts endowments spent to celebrate nuptials probably reflected the sums which founders spent while they lived. Shaikh Ahsan-ullah, for example, ordered Rs. 100 to celebrate a daughter's marriage and Rs. 250 for that of a son. At the birth of a son in the immediate family, Rs. 25 was set aside to pay for the reciting of the *Quran* and the distribution of food. The birth of a daughter called for the spending of only Rs. 15.[54] In Shaikh Ahsan-ullah's family, women received equal consideration only in death.

Endowments supported ceremonies on the birth and death anniversaries of important religious figures. The *milād-i sharīf*, the anniversary of the Prophet's birthday, was mentioned in many deeds. On this occasion, the *Quran* was repeated, poems in praise of the Prophet sung and food prepared. In some places in India, especially in areas like Lucknow which had significant *Shiah* populations, *Sunnis* sometimes tried to turn the *milad* into a rival of the rites of Muharram.[55] But *Sunnis* did not spend nearly as much on them as the *Shiah* did on *majalis*. Also, more than other festivals, the *milad* had to compete with family rites. Farhat

[51] J. Sharif, *Qānūn-i Islām*, trans. G. Herklots, 89–108.
[52] Mazhar Husain Khan's case, *AA*.
[53] Shaikh Mahomed Ahsanulla's case, *LI*, vol. 340, 125.
[54] Ibid.
[55] A. H. Sharar, *Lucknow: The Last Phase of an Oriental Culture*, trans. E. Harcourt and F. Hussain, 89–90.

community with an awareness of the larger world beyond the Bombay City limits. Most deeds of endowment did not display a similar sense of extra-local events and institutions. But Pirbhai, like the Dacca Nawabs, occupied the economic, social and political summit which made his broader perspective possible. Although the views of such men differed from those of most *waqifs*, later, when Muslim endowments became an all-India political issue (see chapter 6), their opinions carried greater weight than those of the majority of those who had created *awqaf*. When the Governor General's Legislative Council considered endowments, the Nawab of Dacca and the merchant-*rais* Pirbhai had tremendous influence in shaping the concepts used in discussing the issue.

For the majority of endowments, the focus on the donor's home areas and kin groups meant that they were not impersonal acts of charity. Donors and recipients knew each other. The poor or the students who accepted free meals or a little cash or who attended the mosques and *imambarahs* were aware of the source of the donation. Personal bonds of loyalty, affection and deference were constantly reinforced. Also, in this way, the local *rais* imitated on a smaller scale the kings and princes who were always expected to support the same kinds of activity. Just as royal patronage brought fame, respect and honour to great kings, local patronage brought similar rewards to the little kings who claimed a prominent place in the life of a neighbourhood or town. Relations between the donor and recipients were certainly not equal. However, the humble expected the great to distribute part of their wealth in the form of gifts of food, clothing and entertainment. Thus, donations confirmed mutual, asymmetrical bonds between a *rais* and his subjects.

Rituals and ceremonies

Just as mosques and *imambarahs* were often part of the donor's dwelling place, many religious ceremonies mentioned in deeds of endowment were connected with life in the founder's family. One of the most frequently supported activities was "*fatiḥah*". The *Fatihah*, literally "the opening", was the first, short chapter of the Holy *Quran*. Even during the Prophet's lifetime, Muslims used it as a prayer. At important events, at a marriage for instance, its recitation solemnized and confirmed the proceedings. The reading of the *Fatihah* eventually became part of the funeral ritual of Muslims. It was repeated at the graveside. Also, on the third and fortieth days following someone's death, relatives and friends assembled again at the grave to recite it for the benefit of the departed's soul. In India, the custom arose of having the whole of the *Quran* recited

practices did not represent a pure form of any single doctrine. For centuries, no one, least of all the Khojahs, worried about all the inconsistencies. All of that changed, however, in 1844 when the Agha Khan, fleeing punishment for fomenting an unsuccessful rebellion against the Persian king, arrived in Bombay.

Once the Agha Khan saw his Indian followers at close range, he decided to bring them into conformity with his version of Ismaili orthodoxy. When the Agha Khan began his reform, several dozen families defied his attempt to gain direct control of the community's spiritual leadership as well as of its considerable material assets.[46] In the 1860s and 1870s, the dissidents claimed that they were moved by a desire to do away with "ancient superstitions" in the Khojah creed and replace them with "orthodox" *Sunni* teachings.[47] The latter part of the nineteenth century witnessed many movements which transformed personal antagonisms into sectarian, communal or reformist crusades. Jairajbhai Pirbhai was a prominent figure in the Khojahs' internal wrangle.

Pirbhai was active among the Khojah reformers. He was also a leader of an organization known as the Anjuman-i Islam. The Anjuman was partly a political association and partly a club for rich Muslim merchants interested in "reform". The Anjuman's programme included the establishment of schools on the British pattern. Somewhat paradoxically, it also encouraged Bombay's Muslims to adopt the Urdu language, though most had Gujarati or Marathi as their mother tongue. Though composed of professionals and merchants, the Anjuman glorified the cultural and political achievements of the Abbasi and Mughal empires.[48] Pirbhai's son, Qasim Ali, continued his father's work and became active in the Muslim League.[49]

Pirbhai's *waqf* reflected the cosmopolitan character of life in Bombay. Like Calcutta, Bombay had a large population of British merchants and the usages of British law sometimes influenced Muslim endowments. Pirbhai's deed was written in English in 1886. It created what the deed called the "Jairajbhai Pirbhai Khojah Benevolent Trust Fund".[50] Despite the British legal jargon, its provisions resembled those of the *awqaf* previously discussed. Some eighteen members of Pirbhai's immediate family received the bulk of the income as stipends. In addition, sums of money were directed to further the activities of the reformist Khojahs and the Anjuman-i Islam.

The endowment created by Pirbhai mixed a keen interest in a small

[46] Ibid., 366ff.
[47] C. Dobbin, *Urban Leadership in Western India*, 90–130, esp. 118–120.
[48] Ibid., 229–246.
[49] Rahman, *From Consultation*, 69.
[50] *Cassamally Jairajbhai Pirbhai* v. *Sir Currimbhoy Ibrahim*, Bom, XXXVI, 214ff.

number of kinship groups: Yusufzai, Afridi, etc., which in turn included smaller lineages. For instance, individuals could identify themselves as members of the Alikhel branch of the Adamkhel lineage of the Afridi tribe.[41] Funds in a number of endowments went to institutions which mostly served the members of one of these groupings. Farhat unnissah's school, as noted, educated students who were mostly from the Alizai Pathan lineage in which she claimed membership. Others, like Sayyid Mehrban Ali, gave donations to the poor members of their status group, in his case Sayyids.[42]

Many other social–religious communities benefited from endowments. For example, the brothers Sabu and Harun Saddiq belonged to a group known as "Memons". The Memons originally lived in Gujarat where they accepted Islam after coming into contact with Arab traders and missionaries. After their conversion they maintained a separate, caste-like identity. They intermarried, often lived in the same neighbourhoods and associated primarily with other Memons. The brothers Saddiq lived in Bombay. In the endowment which they created, Rs. 500 per month went to support hospitals, mosques and schools which specifically served their community. The alms they gave through their *waqf* were supposed to go only to poor Memons.[43]

The endowment created by Jairajbhai Pirbhai of Bombay was another example of patronage oriented to a fairly restricted community. Pirbhai was a Khojah. The Khojahs were scattered along India's west coast, but they were particularly well represented among the merchants of Bombay. The Khojahs were converted to Islam by members of the Ismāʻīli branch of the *Shiah* sect. They also retained many of the customs of their pre-Muslim past. In matters of inheritance, for example, their practices more closely resembled those of their Hindu neighbours.[44] Their beliefs and rituals were very eclectic. Their own texts referred to Imam Ali, the cousin and son-in-law of the Prophet, as an incarnation of the Hindu deity Vishnu.[45] At the same time, a *Sunni* prayer leader traditionally presided at the mosque located in their graveyard in Bombay. Their attachment to the Ismaili style of Shiism was expressed primarily by their allegiance to an Irani nobleman known as the Agha Khan. The Khojahs believed that the Agha Khan was the direct descendant of the Seventh Imam, hence the living guide to paradise. They sent him donations and from time to time members of the sect made the journey to Iran to pay their respects. Their beliefs and

[41] Malihabadi, *Yādōn*, 28.
[42] Mujibunnissa's case, *LI*, vol. 441, 701.
[43] *Abdul Rajak* v. *Bai Junababai*, *BLR*, XIV, 298.
[44] Decision of E. Perry J. (11 October 1841) in *SCR B*, IV, 707ff.
[45] J. N. Hollister, *The Shiʻa of India*, 356.

shrines and holy men were a common part of religious life. Despite the important place they held, the deeds of endowment studied here seldom offered significant support to living sufi masters or to the shrines of famous saints. When allowances were given to them, the amounts were comparatively small. For example, a patroness in Calcutta gave one "Ali Shah Sahib" the same sum given to one of the "poor ladies" living in her house.[34] Perhaps the founders of endowments believed that these individuals already had control of a sufficiency of *awqafs*. More likely, they contributed to sufis and their shrines in irregular fashion by sending money when important events such as births or deaths occurred, or by presenting cash gifts when actually visiting a shrine.[35]

By comparison, the amounts provided to benefit the residents of a donor's neighbourhood or town were much larger than those given to sufis. For example, Begam Yemnabai of Ghogari *muhallah* in Bombay gave money to dig a well there. She also set aside money in her *waqf* to pay for the shrouds and graves of poor Muslims attending the *muhallah*'s mosque. The poor were also supposed to receive a monthly ration of sugar cakes distributed at the mosque.[36] Other endowments left money for similar activities. Some provided free meals for students of *Quran* or the religious sciences.[37] Others gave meals or a little cash to those keeping the *Ramazan* fast.[38]

Endowments sometimes gave money to larger groups which were in some sense extensions of the family or neighbourhood: a particular lineage, status or sectarian group (in practice, the three often amounted to the same thing) to which the founder belonged. Among those were the four "*ashraf*": "noble" or "genteel" groups. First were Sayyids, who claimed descent from the Prophet. Mughals were the second *ashraf* group and were descended from the Mongol tribes which entered and conquered India. Third were Shaikhs who tried to stretch their family trees back to early Arabs, but who were usually made up of Indian converts or the products of mixed marriages between Indians and foreign-born Muslims. The Pathans were the last group and were associated with the peoples of Afghanistan. However, each of these groups was further subdivided.[39] Sayyids were sometimes of Arab descent and sometimes Irani. Mughals belonged to different regional groups such as "Kabuli" or "Bukhari" Mughals.[40] Pathans belonged to one of a large

[34] *OC*, w. 53 of 1915.
[35] S. K. Rashid, *Wakf Administration*, 114–115.
[36] *Asoobai v. Noorbai*, BLR, VIII, 245–246.
[37] Maulvi Muhammad Illahabadi's *waqf*, *OC*, w. 42 of 1908.
[38] Manu Bibi's *waqf*, *OC*, w. 43 of 1909.
[39] Imtiaz Ahmad, "The *Ashrāf-Ajlāf* Dichotomy", 268–278.
[40] *Tārīkh-i Adabīyat-i Mussalmānān-i Pakistān-o Hind*, VII, 92.

mad Taqi tried to assert his power, he quickly encountered the opposition of the donor's family. Though Muhammad Taqi took the matter to the British courts, the founder's daughter managed to defeat him and she kept hold of the property.[28]

Individual members of the learned class had only a residual role in endowments. Founders sometimes consulted them when drafting their deeds.[29] Also, a few founders stipulated that in the event that their family line died out, or disputes arose among descendants or custodians proved unworthy, then the "authorities of the time", i.e. the *ulama*, had the power to step in and appoint new *mutawallis*.[30] However, religious scholars did not receive substantial or immediate benefits from most endowments.

The organization of the *ulama* in India lent itself to the local style of patronage displayed by endowments. By way of contrast, the first chapter noted how the school of al-Azhar in Cairo acted as the pivot point for Egyptian religious scholars. No comparable centre was part of the Muslim experience in India. Several different cities developed reputations as the homes of famous religious scholars. In Delhi, Shah Walliullah founded a school which his son and grandsons maintained. However, at the same time, another family created the equally famous Firangi Mahal at Lucknow and many scholars associated themselves with that tradition of learning.[31] Janpur also produced a large number of noted scholars.[32] Some of the smaller towns, like Ciryakot and Kandhla, also had families which enjoyed a reputation for scholarship lasting through several generations.[33] New schools, like Deoband, emerged in the later nineteenth century. Each of the schools or the scholarly families fostered a slightly different approach or specialized subject. Those they trained sometimes took up residence in a different region of the subcontinent. While the students might have maintained personal respect for their teachers, this dispersion of scholars served to create many more centres of religious scholarship. Which, if any, group the individual *rais* supported was partly a matter of his place of residence and partly a matter of personal preference. With a few notable exceptions, *waqifs* seemed most interested in the scholars in their immediate vicinity.

For most Muslims in India, as well as for many non-Muslims, sufi

---

[28] *Agha Ali Khan (and another)* v. *Altaf Hasan Khan (and another), All*, XIV, 431–432.
[29] For example, Sayyid Muhammad Jawwad Mohani, *Risalah-i Waqf alā 'al-Awlād-o Naql-i Dastawīz-i Waqfnāmah Murattabah-i* . . ., 15–16.
[30] E.g. Mujibunnissa's case, *All*, XXIII, 245.
[31] B. D. Metcalf, *Islamic Revival*, 16ff.
[32] Muhammad Khair ud-din, *Tazkirat ul Ulama*, trans. Muhammad Sana Ullah.
[33] Lelyveld, *Aligarh*, 240–241.

candidates who received them.²⁵ The officials of the educational service would have happily accepted the proceeds of the endowment, but they balked at the Nawab's insistence on assuming personal control of the school and the scholarships. The education department gave the matter lengthy consideration and soon both they and the Nawab forgot about it. Nawab Ali was acting like a *rais*. Patronage was worth while to him so long as it enhanced the leadership he exercised in his corner of Mymensingh.

A few *waqifs* offered civic patronage of the sort familiar to India's British rulers. Sayyid Mehrban Ali spent Rs. 60,000 on building an iron bridge in Galaothi. He gave a further Rs. 3,000 to construct a dispensary there. His *waqf* had a provision granting Rs. 1,200 per year to keep the clinic going.²⁶ The Nawabs of Dacca were also conspicuous public benefactors. In addition to the Rs. 65,000 they distributed annually among the poor, they provided the city of Dacca with its electrical and water systems.²⁷ A bridge, hospital or water-mains were simply more "modern" specimens of the kind of beneficence the *rais* traditionally offered. They served to increase the donor's prestige. In British India this kind of civic mindedness drew official approval. The knighthoods conferred on two of the Dacca Nawabs and Sayyid Mehrban's C.B.E. were the government's rewards. They did not confer any real power. But they had symbolic value and guaranteed the holder ready access to officials.

The Dacca Nawabs or Sayyid Mehrban Ali had a sense of the wider world beyond their home turf. Associating themselves with the British administration or with the school at Deoband demonstrated their breadth of vision. Most *waqifs*, however, were more firmly rooted in a single neighbourhood or town. Their perspective and their patronage rarely extended beyond them. For example, the support offered to religious scholars was usually local. Members of the learned class who served in mosques or who taught in *madrasahs* received stipends from the gentry. But the gifts bestowed on the *ulama* were indirect, given through the mosque or school. Scholars seldom got direct control over property included in endowments. Even when they did, they sometimes had difficulty in establishing the right to manage a dedication. In the endowment created by Muhammad Ali of Kanpur in 1863, the income from four villages and two houses was supposed to support an *imambarah* managed by Muhammad Taqi, a *Shiah alim*. But when Muham-

---

[25] (Beng) *PEBGD*, File 11 (May 1887), nos. 62–63; also (September 1887), nos. 103–105; finally, those of December 1887.
[26] Mujibunnissa's case, *LI*, vol. 441, 701.
[27] B. C. Allen, *Dacca*, 181–182.

apparently remained committed to supporting the kind of education they knew best: the one which took place in or near their own homes.

The Deobandis did try to tap into networks of old-style patronage. They wanted to create a number of small, locally supported *madrasahs* connected to Deoband. Graduates of Deoband would staff these schools and ensure the linkage.[22] They only succeeded in attracting the support of a few wealthy individuals like Sayyid Mehrban Ali who founded a Deoband affiliated school in his home town of Galaothi.[23] The chief difficulty with their scheme was that the branch schools were too dependent on an individual patron. When, as in Sayyid Mehrban's case, the patron died and his endowment was challenged in the courts, the *madrasah* ceased to exist. While dependence on a single sponsor hampered the Deobandis' ambitious plans, it was not so crucial to the type of education offered by Farhat un-nissah's school. If her establishment faltered or failed, another *rais* was always ready to devote a veranda or a spare room to teaching the *Quran* and the rudiments of Persian.

When *waqifs* did display an interest in the new-style educational institutions, it was typically when these were located in their immediate vicinity. Shaikh Ahsan-ullah of Chittagong, for example, maintained a fairly large school in the village where he owned land. The school employed four or five teachers and its curriculum included the teaching of English, Bengali, Persian and the *Quran*. For a time the school received a grant from the Bengal government's education department.[24] The Shaikh's control over the school was obvious in the support which he gave to his own children as well as the children of relatives and tenants. He paid the tuition for any child connected to his family. Even when the government dropped its grant, he continued to pay the costs of the school out of his own pocket.

The close connection between support for education and the local importance of a *rais* was also illustrated by the case of Nawab Ali Chaudhry of Mymensingh in Eastern Bengal. In 1887, the Nawab offered to establish a *waqf* in favour of a school located in the Tangail subdivision of Mymensingh district, the Nawab's home area. The Nawab volunteered to dedicate property worth over Rs. 50,000 which yielded a yearly income of over Rs. 3,000. A condition governing the *waqf* was that the school be renamed the "Nawab Ali Jubilee School" in his honour and to commemorate Victoria's fiftieth anniversary as sovereign. Also, the Nawab Ali would assume overall management of the school. Finally, he offered to provide fifteen scholarships, provided that he could select the

---

[22] B. D. Metcalf, *Islamic Revival*, 125ff.
[23] *Mujibunnissa (and others) v. Abdul Rahim and Abdul Aziz, LI*, vol. 441, 701.
[24] Shaikh Mahomed Ahsanulla's case, *LI*, vol. 340, 129–136.

mathematics; religion teachers made do with much less. The British created a new standard of polite and practical learning. Sir Sayyid and a few others began to create educational institutions which accepted that change.

The "reformist *ulama*" associated with the theological school at Deoband (founded 1867) initiated another kind of restructuring of the older style of education. The syllabus known as the *Dars-i Nizamiyyah* was the focus of their endeavour. The training given in Farhat un-nissah's school merely prepared students for the study of the subjects contained in the *Nizamiyyah*. Usually only the very few who specialized in religious learning undertook its course of study. The *Nizamiyyah* syllabus included the "Arab Sciences" of Quranic exegesis (*tafsīr*), scholastic theology (*kalām*) and other subjects directly concerned with the foundations of the faith of Islam. In practice, the *Nizamiyyah* tended to teach these topics in Persian translation rather than Arabic. It also embraced, somewhat gingerly, the "Foreign Sciences" associated with Hellenistic learning: logic (*mantiq*) and philosophy (*falsafah*). The Deobandi reform consisted of de-emphasizing the Persian and "foreign" elements and concentrating on the study of Arabic, the Prophetic traditions (*ahadis*) or the application of *shariah*.[20] Like the Aligarh reformers, the Deobandis tried to institute a system of regular attendance at classes. Students also took a series of examinations which evaluated them and passed them on to higher levels of instruction.

Just as the Aligarh and Deoband schools both tried to reshape the curriculum and organization of learning, they also shared an interest in developing new sources of financial support. Farhat un-nissah's contribution to learning was local and direct. It served a few neighbourhood boys. It gave them an education which had little to do with the visions of either Aligarh or Deoband. Therefore, the reformers' cultivation of different types of monetary backing was a necessary part of their attempt to realize their ambitions, ambitions which the likes of Farhat un-nissah probably did not share. Aligarh made an appeal to the British government and did receive grants in aid. Both schools appealed directly to Muslim princes like the Nizam of Hyderabad, with some success. Also, both tried to develop support among the local elites whose contributions were transferred to a central location often distant from their homes. *Awqaf* formed only a small portion of the fiscal resources of both Deoband and Aligarh.[21] Most wealthier Muslims who created endowments

[20] B. D. Metcalf, *Islamic Revival*, 31, 90–91, 100.
[21] *Ibid.*, 96–99, and Lelyveld, *Aligarh*, 134–142; both institutions received some support by way of *awqaf*. The Nizam of Hyderabad provided a *waqf* for Deoband and Nawab Azmat Ali Khan of Karnal established one for Aligarh in 1907; see *Muhammad Rustam Ali (and another)* v. *Mushtaq Husain (and others)*, *IA*, XLI.

among non-Muslims. Also, despite the competition from "modern" schools, many Muslims continued to send their sons to schools which taught the old curriculum by the old methods of recitation and memorization.[15]

Members of the government's education service were very critical of both the curriculum and organization of *maktabs* and *madrasahs*.[16] Officials convinced that British educational institutions provided the standard found it difficult to approve of schools in which neither students nor teachers felt compelled to attend. They also found fault with the methods of instruction in which teachers seldom explained the meaning of the words that students learned. Moreover, instruction in mathematics, the physical sciences and history was usually absent. Government inspectors condemned that kind of training as inefficient and impractical. Their complaints gave rise to the belief that Muslims were, on the whole, educationally backward.[17] Some expressed the fear that Muslims would lose government jobs to non-Muslims. Although the number of Muslims in the provincial services actually increased, as did the number of Hindus, the official conviction that Muslims were losing the race for government preferment was widely publicized and convinced some of the need for educational reform.[18]

A number of Muslim leaders, most notably Sir Sayyid Ahmad Khan, partly shared the government's dim view of *madrasah* education. In establishing the Muhammadan Anglo-Oriental College at Aligarh, Sir Sayyid managed to combine some aspects of the *madrasah* style with others taken from British "public schools". Aligarh removed students from their home environments, in contrast to schools like Farhat un-nissah's which left them with their families. Also, Aligarh tried to require regular attendance at classes. The Aligarh curriculum emphasized learning the English language and studying other subjects which India's British rulers thought important. In that way, Aligarh retained something of the spirit behind the *madrasah* education. As Persian was the language of the Mughal court and government, so English was that of the British raj. In Farhat un-nissah's school, the High Traditions of Islam had little influence beyond the memorizing of the *Quran*; the *Quran* teacher received only half the salary of the Persian master. At Aligarh, theology and Quranic commentary also received little encouragement.[19] Greater monetary rewards awaited those who taught English or

[15] *Ibid.*
[16] E.g. (Beng) *EDP* (June 1865), nos. 29–30.
[17] Robinson, *Separatism*, 39–46.
[18] Lelyveld, *Aligarh*, 100–101.
[19] D. Lelyveld, "Religion at Aligarh, or What to Make of a Diminished Thing?", unpublished paper.

year for teaching Persian. Shaikh Muhammad Firuz, a reciter of *Quran*, got half that sum for teaching the Holy Book to the boys. Finally, a servant for the school got Rs. 36 annually.

In March of 1899, twenty boys were recorded as attending Farhat unnissah's school. Most of them included the title "*Khan*" in their names, indicating that they claimed Pathan ancestry. As the Begam's deed described her as a Pathan and since the *muhallah*'s name "Alizai" was that of a Pathan lineage, most of the students were probably connected to the donor by real or fictive kinship. However, the fathers of three of the boys did not use the appellation "*Khan*". The records described two of these men as "weavers" and the third as a maker of glass bangles. Obviously, a few of the area's poorer residents sent their sons to the school.

Five of the twenty boys were in the process of memorizing the Holy *Quran*. The method of learning the scripture was for each student to learn a few verses by heart each day. Another five were working on primers which taught the Arabo-Persian alphabet or the basic rules of Persian grammar. The rest were working on one of four or five Persian literary works. The poet–sage of Shiraz, Sadi, was studied through three books: the *Karimah*, the *Bustan* and the *Gulistan*. Each of these books contained stories conveying some moral *desiderata*: be honest or do not be stingy. Poetry was used to restate, reinforce or illustrate these values in easily memorized couplets. Another popular text which was studied was the *Anwar us-Suhaili* (*The Lights of Canopus*), a series of Aesop-like fables which conveyed moral lessons. The Indian style of Persian considered Sadi's works and the *Anwar* models of literary diction.

Outside the *Quran*, that syllabus contained little that was distinctly "Islamic".[14] In Mughal times, indeed even in the second half of the nineteenth century, Persian was the premier literary language. Perhaps more importantly, the Mughals and the British, until 1832, conducted government business in it. After Persian lost its political importance, it remained important in the cultural sphere. It provided the themes and formal conventions for much of the poetry written in Indian vernaculars. Many of the elite continued to believe that a taste for and interest in Persian poetry was essential for anyone laying claim to genteel status. Both Muslims and non-Muslims attended schools like Farhat unnissah's to acquire the rudiments of Persian.

In the second half of the nineteenth century, with the rise of more sharply defined communal identities, Hindus began to abandon some of the traditions of the Mughal elite and enrol in schools established on the British model which concentrated on the learning of English. Even then, the appreciation of Persian literature never completely died out

[14] Robinson, *Separatism*, 39.

lifetime, he built a mosque and an *imambarah* on one of them. In his *waqf*, he directed that Rs. 6,000 be spent annually to support the mosque and the ceremonies held in the *imambarah*. His custodians also had the power to build another mosque should any money be left over.[8]

The easy transition between household and holy place was illustrated by the endowment created by the courtesan Najiban, mentioned earlier. In North India, ladies of the evening traditionally expressed considerable religious fervour, especially during the month of Muharram. During the first ten days of the month, they did not entertain gentlemen in their usual fashion. Instead, they held mourning rites for Husain. Famous courtesans vied with each other in providing the best reciters of elegies or the most elaborate replicas of the martyr's tombs.[9] Najiban had sponsored these pious assemblies in her home in Bareilly for many years. As she approached extreme old age, she founded a *waqf*. One of its provisions was that her house be turned into a permanent *imambarah* and the ceremonies continued.[10]

Although the special commemoration of the death of Husain was associated with the *Shiah* sect, deeds of endowment showed that individuals who identified themselves as "*Sunni*" sometimes supported *imambarahs* and the mourning rites of Muharram.[11] They also showed that these ceremonies occurred throughout India. Muslims in Bombay, Calcutta and the north left money to pay for *taziyahs* and reciters of elegies.

Schools were also located in the households of wealthier Muslims. Many endowments contained some provision for a teacher or referred to the support of a "*madrasah*". No single archetype for such schools existed. The word *madrasah* was applied to small, very informal schools as well as to large and highly organized establishments. Some of the smaller schools were called "*maktabs*",[12] but the founders of endowments clearly preferred the use of the more elegant term, *madrasah*. Judging by the amount of money usually given for these schools, the one established by Begam Farhat un-nissah was probably fairly typical.[13] Farhat un-nissah lived in the Alizai *muhallah* of the town of Shahjahanpur. The school met in her house and the costs of supporting it were therefore minimal. Only Rs. 24 per year went to provide oil for the lamps, pens and slates. Two men taught there. Mati-ullah Khan received Rs. 120 per

---

[8] *OC*, w. 34 of 1902.
[9] Mirza Mohammad Hadi Ruswa, *The Courtesan of Lucknow*.
[10] *Biba Jan* v. *Kalb Hussain*, *All*, XXXI, 136, 145.
[11] Najiban herself claimed to be a *Sunni*; see also *ibid.* and *OC*, w. 51 of 1915, for similar examples.
[12] Lelyveld, *Aligarh*, 51–52.
[13] *Mazhar Husain Khan* v. *Abdul Hadi Khan*, *All*, XXXIII, 400ff.

rect, because the courtyards and roofs were places where interaction between the family and outside world occurred. For the males, during the day the courtyard was the focus of life. Friends, relatives, servants and others constantly arrived and departed. The rooftops were the preserve of the women. By moving along the housetops, they were able to visit other women in neighbouring dwellings.[4] Thus, despite appearances, each household was connected physically and socially with its neighbourhood (*muhallah*). *Muhallahs* often grew up around the dwellings of a single kin group or the house of a nobleman. So long as vacant land was available, the neighbourhood expanded to make room for new arrivals or to allow families to separate. Even if extra space was not available, a residence could be divided by putting up a wall or by adding another set of rooms in another storey.

These sprawling residences often contained places of worship. Muslims did not have to pray in a mosque. *Masjid*, from which the English word "mosque" derived, meant literally "a place of prostration". Therefore, any room or structure could be set aside as a *masjid*, provided it was kept free of defiling substances, had water for ritual ablution nearby and was open to any Muslim wishing to offer his prayers. A mosque in a home was not a private chapel, it was open to the rest of the *muhallah*'s residents. The character of neighbourhoods, however, meant that some bond of kinship or acquaintance usually existed between the founders and those who used their mosques. Shaikh Ahsanullah's family supported two mosques of that sort. One was located in the family compound in Chittagong, another in the village near Chittagong where they held property.[5] Even when *waqfnamahs* did not describe mosques as located in the home, they noted the location as "near the house" or "in the *muhallah*".

Endowments offered cash to mosques to provide oil for their lamps, or to pay for prayer callers, prayer leaders and reciters or teachers of the Holy *Quran*. The sums dedicated varied with the wealth of the donor. Shaikh Hajji Abd al-Khansaman of Calcutta left RS. 300 per month for the upkeep of a mosque located in his residence.[6] Qamr ud-din gave Rs. 50 per month to buy lamp oil and pay for a *Quran*-reciter for the mosque of Qasbah Uran, the market town near Bombay where he lived.[7]

Imambarahs frequently received funds. Like mosques, they were often located in the founder's dwelling. Mirza Ali Busrawi, a *Shiah*, owned three valuable plots along Canning Road in Calcutta. During his

---
[4] Lelyveld, *Aligarh*, 35–38.
[5] *Shaikh Mahomed Ahsanulla Chowdhry v. Amarchand Kundu (and others)*, Cal, XVII, 496–504.
[6] OC, w. 43 of 1909.
[7] *Nizam Ghulam (and others) v. Abdul Gafur (and others)*, LI, vol. 367, 751.

| Rs. | 40 | To provide a feast on the Prophet's birthday. |
| Rs. | 60 | For food during the commemoration of the martyrdom of the Imam Husain during the month of Muharram. |

In addition, a small, unspecified sum went to support someone to teach *Quran* in the neighbourhood mosque in Serai Kheta.[3] In any given endowment, the amounts set aside for these activities depended on the prosperity of the individual or family which founded it. Usually, as in Qaim Ali's *waqf*, the larger portion of the income went to members of the founder's own family. The deeds themselves gave no evidence that the donors had any reservations about the appropriateness of this unequal division.

As with the temporal arrangements of endowments, donations for spiritual activities began with the family group and moved outward to embrace more individuals who were less intimately connected to the donors. The endowments clearly focused on the community of faith formed by the neighbourhood or town in which the founders lived. In this tendency, endowments reflected the most common organizational pattern of the Islamic faith: a series of local congregations not usually connected by formal, hierarchical structures. They seemed to show that the unity of the Muslim world was something which existed primarily in the minds and hearts of Muslims. So far as everyday life was concerned, the connection between individual Muslims and the world-wide community seemed less important than ties which bound them to institutions closer to home. Endowments did support ceremonies connected with the "Great Tradition of Islam": the birth of the Prophet or the Karbala tragedy. But they gave almost equal prominence to local ceremonies and to the "*shādī-o ghammī*": the joyous and sorrowful events which marked the life of the founders' families.

The founders' homes and mosques, *imambarahs* and schools

A strong personal bond existed between *waqifs* and the sacred places and practices which they financed. Founders of endowments lived in cities or towns. They were not country squires with houses located on their estates. Their urban dwellings, like those of most Indians who possessed substantial wealth, consisted of rooms or buildings clustered around a central courtyard. Wealthier households had larger courtyards and more rooms or buildings. In more congested towns, houses had several storeys. Because their compounds were walled and had gates, houses appeared to be self-contained and isolated. That impression was incor-

[3] *Muhammad Munawar Ali* v. *Rasulan Bibi*, *All*, XXI, 335–337.

3

Endowments and the faith

Most contemporary studies of Islam define a *waqf* as a "charitable trust" or "pious foundation".[1] The previous two chapters expanded on that notion by concentrating on the familial and temporal dimensions present in many endowments. The institution did not lend itself to facile distinctions between "private" and "pious" interests. An individual who was childless and without close relatives might have created a *waqf* which sustained only religious and charitable activities.[2] However, most endowments were not devoted purely to one purpose or the other. They were mixed. As noted later (chapters 5 and 6), the tendency to distinguish sharply between the apparently selfish and the seemingly altruistic was in large measure the result of the examination and criticism of the institution in colonial legal and political contexts. Deeds of endowment themselves simply mentioned the sums of money given to family members and dependants alongside of those which supported more public activities. This can be seen in the *waqf* created by the *wakil* Qaim Ali who lived in the town of Serai Kheta in Janpur district. The total income from the properties placed in the endowment was Rs. 9,000 per year. After paying the government's revenue and meeting the costs of managing the property, the remaining income was supposed to be spent in the following ways:

Rs.	2,400	To the six children of the founders and their descendants. Also, the custodian received his salary from this amount. The custodian had the power to add or exclude beneficiaries.
Rs.	600	For a hospital in Serai Kheta.
Rs.	20	To bring water from the *zamzam* well at Mecca.
Rs.	36	For recitation of the *Quran* for the benefit of the souls of the founders.
Rs.	150	To be distributed as doles for the poor. The founders distributed a similar amount during their lifetimes.
Rs.	50	For repair of the local mosque. Again, this was a donation made by the founders while they lived.
Rs.	24	For repair of the founders' tombs.

[1] Hardy, *Muslims of British India*, 283, and Robinson, *Separatism*, 39.
[2] *Wasiq Ali Khan* v. *The Government*, SDA, VI, 130ff; *Muhammad Ahsan (and others)* v. *Umar Daraz (and others)*, *All*, XXVIII, 633ff.

ties as "charity", but seemed to assume that they went along with being a *rais* or *nawab*. Also most of those who founded endowments had servants working for them on a full- or part-time basis. The richest families had the most servants. Endowments often provided stipends to support old retainers.[63] Also, by custom, retired servants continued to eat at their employer's expense. They received, in addition, special gifts of clothing or money on festivals and holy days.

This chapter focused on Muslim endowments from the perspective of the people who established them. Their aim was usually to pass their wealth on to the next generation, while ensuring that only a few individuals controlled their estates. The problems they faced were similar to those met by individuals the world over. The methods they used to deal with problems created by death, taxes and heirs were not all that different from those employed in England.[64] Yet, as noted later in this study, when these endowments eventually came under the scrutiny of India's colonial courts and government, that similarity, that human dimension, somehow did not enter the discussion. For colonial judges, the simple prudence of the founders of *awqaf* began to take on the sinister cast of legal subterfuge. This was especially evident in the courts' discussion of the "public" and "private" roles of *waqifs*. For them, the patronage and leadership they exercised within their own families blended easily with patronage and leadership exercised in the wider social networks in which their families lived. For the purpose of description, this study separated the more intimate concerns of founders from those dealing with larger social connections. But the founders themselves recognized no clear boundary. The support they offered indigent relatives or retired servants merged with that given in broader social frameworks, in societies in which most of them occupied, or claimed to occupy, a commanding place.

---

[63] Shahzadi Begam's *waqf*, *OC*, w. 51 of 1915.
[64] Cooper, "Patterns of Inheritance", 192–226.

date of marriage became *mutawalli*. At the death of the last wife, the eldest daughter took responsibility. At that point, Sayyid Mehrban Ali's deed, like most *waqfnamahs* of this type, restored control to a male. If any of the daughters had sons, then control of the estate went to them.[56]

As managers, women were hampered by the common practice of restricting the movements of respectable females. They seldom left the women's quarters of the home where only a few select males could enter. A female *mutawalli* had to depend on close male relatives or, more rarely, upon some intimate friend of the family. The very closeness of the personal ties between women and their representatives may have helped to ensure the honesty of go-betweens. Still, agents sometimes abused their trust and used endowments for their own benefit.[57] Despite the obvious limitations, some women did act as effective managers. Some, apparently, even left their homes to press lawsuits in the courts. Judging from the frequency with which women's names appeared on civil court reports, they were tenacious litigants.

Adoption of a stranger or relative was contrary to the traditions of the faith and this option was never used. More distant relatives stepped forward to claim control of property only when the direct line of descendants completely failed. For example, when all four of Qamr ud-din's daughters died childless, his distant cousins, descended from his paternal great-uncle, took over that *waqf*.[58]

Beyond the inner circle of the family, endowments took notice of distant relations, dependants or servants. Most modestly affluent homes had a shifting population of poor but respectable guests. Most often they were women, widows or spinsters, sometimes kin and sometimes not. They stayed for months, sometimes years. When they left to become someone else's guests, other women in similar straits invariably took their places.[59] Deeds of endowment sometimes remembered individuals by name and gave them small monthly allowances.[60] Most deeds, however, just set aside money for "feeding of guests and visitors".[61] The amount spent in that way depended on the wealth of the founder. Sayyid Mehrban Ali, who was a very rich man, spent Rs. 348 per year in direct payments to indigents. Part of the yearly "*zenanah* expenses" of Rs. 393 went to pay the cost of feeding "travellers".[62] Hospitality of this sort was part of being socially prominent. The deeds did not describe such activi-

[56] Mujibunnissa's case, *LI*, vol. 441, 610.
[57] For example, *Mazhar Husain Khan* v. *Abdul Hadi Khan*, *AA* (1911).
[58] Nizam Ghulam's case, *LI*, vol. 367, 735.
[59] Malihabadi, *Yādōn*, 30.
[60] Shahzadi Begam's *waqf*, *OC*, w. 51 of 1915.
[61] Mujibunnissa's case, *LI*, vol. 367, 701.
[62] *Ibid*.

time to pass on an estate. Sometimes they were merely simpletons. Begum Kanizak Fatima, the daughter of the Muhammad Ali mentioned above, faced that problem when she established her endowment. Though she professed love for her son, she did not think him capable of managing her property. Therefore, she gave her daughter and son-in-law charge of the endowment. In addition to their salaries, they each got a four *anna* share of any profits. The son had an income, but no control over the holding.[53]

One of the great advantages of a *waqf* was that it allowed a settlor more choices when deciding how to dispose of property. The *shariah*, taken in its strictest sense, prescribed heirs and the shares they received.[54] Also, in its apportionment of shares, the letter of the *shariah* distinctly favoured male kin.[55] When a man left only daughters, the percentage of the estate which they got did not significantly increase; uncles and male cousins took most of what would be a son's share. But the testamentary freedom which endowments offered allowed founders to exclude more distant kinsmen in favour of their own daughters. Therefore, women often figured prominently in the terms of *awqaf*. Though excluded when there were sons, women had clear preference in the absence of sons. For instance, Begum Kanizak, the woman with the incompetent son, got control of her father's estate by means of a *waqf*. In her turn, she used a *waqf* to bypass her son in favour of her daughter and son-in-law.

When wives and daughters were favoured in endowments, the same constraints operated. How many wives and daughters had to be supported? Who received the custodianship? Polygamy was allowed, but among the founders of endowments monogamy was more common. When a founder had more than one wife, it appeared to be related to an absence of sons. Being untroubled by knowledge of the relationship between a male's X and Y chromosomes and the sex of offspring, husbands assumed that producing sons was a woman's responsibility. Thus, Qamr ud-din had two wives and four daughters. The slightly daft Sayyid Mehrban Ali left three widows and four daughters. His deathbed *waqfnamah* even added a plaintive note that any son born after the document's promulgation would eventually gain control of the whole estate. In the absence of sons, founders made the same sorts of choices about who should control and how much they should receive. Some put all wives and daughters equally in charge. Others, like Sayyid Mehrban, named the senior wife custodian. At her death, the next in seniority by

[53] Agha Ali Khan's case, *AII*, XIV, 435–436.
[54] S. Vesey-Fitzgerald, *Muhammadan Law*, 121ff.
[55] N. J. Coulson, *Succession in the Muslim Family*, 33–42.

Hajji Bikani Mian, put brothers equally in charge. Others placed the eldest son in control. Shaikh Ahsan-ullah Chaudhri followed that course. He placed his eldest son in control as *mutawalli* and allowed him a salary of Rs. 100 per month. The next in age became the deputy (*naib mutawalli*) and got Rs. 90. The youngest had the longest title, "deputy to the deputy *mutawalli*" (*naib'al manaib mutawalli*) and the smallest salary, Rs. 80. The only daughter received Rs. 30 per month. Shaikh Ahsan-ullah's own wife and the wives of his sons got small amounts as pin money.[49] Only the eldest had the power to collect the rents and pay the bills. When he retired or died, the next in age assumed the office.

Shaikh Ahsan-ullah's deed limited the income of the women of his family. If one of the sons died, his widow continued to be supported, but only so long as she remained unmarried. His granddaughters were restricted in similar fashion. They were entitled to a stipend only until they married.[50] Some deeds of endowment specifically prohibited the women of a family's control of the estate.[51] That kind of restraint was prompted, in part, by the expectation that a woman would marry and leave the family home. Also, these provisions prevented a daughter's husband from obtaining a share of the holding. Once again, founders enforced a very narrow conception of who was included in the family and had some right to its resources.

In the real world, however, sons were not always a blessing. A man named Basharat Ali used his *waqfnamah* as a vehicle for expressing his disgust at the behaviour of one of his sons, Mehdi Husain. In his father's eyes, Mehdi Husain was a "pleasure-seeker", a spendthrift, a constant source of woe. Though disgusted with Mehdi Husain, Basharat Ali was pleased with his other son, Qurban Ali. Qurban Ali seemed a model child. He had assumed the burden of pursuing litigation in the courts to help preserve his father's estate. Not surprisingly, Qurban Ali, not his thoughtless brother, became the custodian of his father's *waqf* with sole control of the property. The wastrel Mehdi Husain got only a small monthly allotment.[52] According to a strict interpretation of the rules of inheritance, a person could make no distinction between heirs who were dissolute and those who were models of probity. But the terms of an endowment gave people the power to exclude individuals the *shariah* recognized as inheritors.

Sons did not have to be scoundrels to present problems when it came

---

[49] *Shaikh Mahomed Ahsanulla Chowdhry* v. *Amarachand Kundu (and others)*, *Cal*, XVII, 501; *LI*, vol. 340, 128–129.
[50] *LI*, vol. 340, 125.
[51] Murtazai Bibi's case, *All*, XII, 265.
[52] *Ibid*.

The most effective method of preventing division was to limit the number of those who controlled and benefited from an endowment. Taking this step tended to contradict a fundamental element of the European perception of Indian inheritance practices. As noted above, some British officials lamented the increasing fragmentation of agricultural holdings. They often blamed it on Muslim and Hindu attachment to "traditional" legal systems which recognized a plurality of heirs. In this instance, some Muslims understood the problem and took steps to avoid excessive subdivision. They found the legal mechanism to achieve that end in their own legal "tradition" which was much more flexible than British officials admitted. However, the Anglo-Indian courts remained dedicated to a textbook understanding of Muslim inheritance practices and they ultimately forbade the use of *awqaf* to settle substantial property on selected heirs. Thus, the British understanding of Muslim law actually contributed to the break-up of estates.

With regard to the definition of "family", a common view of both Muslims and Hindus was that they lived in "extended" or "joint" families. This implied that a family included much more than the basic reproductive unit. Parents' parents, parents' siblings, nieces, nephews and others supposedly shared all of the family's wealth. Likewise, households were commonly described as "extended" or "joint" enterprises. People dwelt with large numbers of kin and dependants.[48]

The deeds of endowment studied here narrowly defined the family. So far as the control and transmission of property were concerned, the family consisted of the reproductive unit: fathers, mothers and their offspring. Founders gave clear preference to sons. In the usual course of events, if they had sons, they became the custodians and received the largest shares of the income. If they had no competent sons, then daughters got those benefits. Only if founders were childless did more distant relatives receive control and substantial stipends. Apparently most *waqifs* did live in homes well stocked with kin and servants. However, the joint household exercised only minimal influence on the disposition of property. Retired servants or poor relations (sometimes referred to as "*rishtahdār*": "connections") received small cash allotments only when the endowment generated sufficient funds.

Preceding paragraphs outlined some of the general constraints operating on the distribution of wealth through endowments. The paragraphs which follow describe the terms of a number of individual endowments to show how individuals operated within those limits. If a *waqif* had more than one son, the choice was between having them share equally in the management of the property and its income. Some, like

[48] A. M. Shah, *The Household Dimension of the Family in India*, 122–159.

founder's concern: "that my sons and daughters and their descendants may be decently maintained out of the income of those properties, and the properties may not suffer in consequence of disputes among my sons and daughters ... or their descendants".[43] The size of the shares distributed in any given endowment depended on how many sons, daughters, relatives, friends or servants had to be provided for. The number of individuals needing support and the size of the income were the basic constraints on any endowment. The larger a *waqf*'s income, the more persons it could support. In the face of limited resources, a founder faced critical decisions about how to allocate the proceeds of an endowment. Another important issue was the appointing of a custodian (*mutawalli*).

Hajji Bikani Mian had a large family, but his *waqf* generated a small income. His endowment provided for his wife, his two sons and four daughters. The sons were supposed to act jointly as custodians. Their first duty, according to the deed, was to pay the government's revenue and meet the expenses of managing the property. After meeting these responsibilities, each son received Rs. 100 per year, while their mother and sisters got Rs. 50.[44] Only the income was divided; the property itself remained intact.

The problem of how much or how little to give heirs was not uniquely "Muslim" or "Indian". European historians have described the methods employed in that area to settle questions of inheritance. The basic choice was between keeping property intact and passing it on to one individual or dividing it among all possible heirs.[45] In Europe, the option exercised depended on the customs and economic conditions prevailing in a given region. Even within the borders of a single, small nation, England, considerable variation existed in patterns of inheritance.[46] Muslims who created endowments faced similar options. On the one hand, they could follow the letter of the Quranic law and divide their property among a number of heirs. On the other hand, by employing a *waqf* they could restrict heirs' access to their estates and prevent partition. Thus, repeated again and again in *waqfnamahs* were sentiments such as "that the management ... should remain forever in the hands of one person, whereby our name and memory and the pomp and dignity of the estate [*riasat*] may continue".[47]

[43] *Ibid.*
[44] *Ibid.*
[45] H. J. Habakkuk, "Family Structure and Economic Change in Nineteenth Century Europe", 1–12.
[46] J. P. Cooper, "Patterns of Inheritance and Settlement by Great Landowners from the 15th to the 18th Centuries", in *Family and Inheritance*, 192–226.
[47] Muhammad Munawar Ali's case, *All*, XXI, 331.

major undertaking. After all, Joseph Conrad's description of the fate of the pilgrim ship *Patna* was based on a real incident.[39] It showed that even in the age of steam ships the trip to Mecca involved considerable risk. Moreover, in those days before the Bedouin knew of petrodollars, the Holy City offered pilgrims rough and ready accommodation. Cholera, typhoid and dysentery often ensured that pilgrims were blessed by being able to depart this life while engaged in a sacred duty of the faith. In view of the rigours of the journey and taking into account his own advanced age, Bikani Mian thought it wise to settle his earthly affairs before embarking on a path leading, perhaps, to his heavenly abode. So in 1874 he dictated a deed of *waqf* which included provisions for his children. Bikani Mian's intimations of mortality proved unfounded. He returned safe from Mecca and added the title "*Hājjī*" to his name. He lived for many more years, long enough to find himself embroiled in a series of lawsuits which overturned all the arrangements he had made so carefully.[40] No one recorded whether or not Bikani Mian came to regret his rugged constitution.

Whether death was close at hand or merely a spectre lurking in the future, a *waqif*'s thoughts were usually focused as much on this world as on the hereafter. Sayyid Qaim Ali, the *wakil* of Jaunpur, showed how easily both realms blended when he wrote in his deed of *waqf*, "It is absolutely necessary in order to secure the love of each individual among friends in this world and to earn merit in the next world that sufficient provision be made for the thorough management of the entire property."[41] According to Qaim Ali, settling one's own earthly affairs brought spiritual merit.

Most deeds of endowment also expressed the founders' desire to leave behind some record of their existence and achievements. As Hajji Bikani Mian, a man who enjoyed rude good health, expressed it, "Whereby my name [i.e. reputation] and memory may be perpetuated forever...".[42] Obviously, the task of preserving an individual's memory fell to his or her heirs. Therefore, most *waqf*-deeds paid close attention to the specific terms under which the dedicated property was supposed to be managed, who managed it and how its income was distributed.

Endowments and the family

Those who created endowments usually provided for those who were near and dear to them. Once again, Hajji Bikani Mian described well a

---
[39] J. Conrad, *Lord Jim*, ed. T. Moser, 309–343.
[40] *Bikani Mia* v. *Shuk Lal Poddar (and another)*, *Cal*, XX, 116ff.
[41] Muhammad Munawar Ali's case, *All*, XXI, 331.
[42] Bikani Mian's case, *Cal*, XX, 119.

for those heirs a leading place in society. All of them knew that certain obstacles stood in the way of attaining those things. Mortality was the first among them.

Endowments and the life cycle

The creation of many endowments was prompted by the founder's desire to set his or her financial affairs in order before death. Sometimes, as in the case of Muhammad Ali of Kanpur, the period between deeding and dying was short. On 3 November 1863, Muhammad Ali composed a *waqf* setting aside the income from four villages and two houses to support an *imambarah*, the ceremonies held in it and the charity distributed through it. On 14 November of the same year, he dictated another deed of endowment giving the income of one village to maintain his dead son's widow. On 23 November, he had another document written which set aside the rest of the property for his only daughter, Begum Kanizak Fatima. On 27 November he drafted another deed confirming the previous three. He died on 11 December.[35]

Sayyid Mehrban Ali, the successful government servant mentioned above, suffered for several years from a mental disorder described in the precise psychiatric jargon of the day as "softening of the brain".[36] Whatever the root of his dementia, many signs of it were recorded. On one occasion he slapped a servant in the presence of a noted guest, the Deobandi scholar Muhammad Qasim Nanotawi. Even though Sayyid Mehrban was a major contributor to the school at Deoband, Muhammad Qasim walked out of the room and a permanent break between the two men occurred.[37] In October of 1889, Sayyid Mehrban claimed that he had recovered his wits and he secured a certificate of sanity from a local doctor. On 16 October, a deed of *waqf* in his name was presented to the district registrar. The registrar refused to accept it on the ground that the property covered by the deed was not fully described. Sayyid Mehrban died on 4 November, before the deed was corrected.[38] Sayyid Mehrban's case illustrated a problem which arose when a founder's death followed closely the establishment of a *waqf*. A disgruntled heir had an excellent legal reason to challenge an endowment by claiming that the founder was *non compos* when he or she wrote the deed.

Sometimes the thought of death was enough to prompt the founding of a *waqf*. For example, in 1874 a citizen of Dacca named Shaikh Bikani Mian decided to make the pilgrimage to Mecca. He knew that this was a

---

[35] *Agha Ali Khan (and another)* v. *Altaf Hasan Khan (and another)*, *All*, XIV, 430ff.
[36] Mujibunnissa's case, *LI*, vol. 441, 610–611.
[37] B. D. Metcalf, *Islamic Revival in British India*, 169.
[38] Mujibunnissa's case, *LI*, vol. 441, 610–611.

raj. He was an honorary magistrate and a Companion of the Indian Empire.[31]

Muhammad Idris Khan of Sylhet in Assam was another prosperous bureaucrat. He had served as a district revenue officer (*sadr amīn*) in Bengal Province. He invested his salary in land in his home district, Sylhet. Muhammad Idris also did well in marriage. His wife was a member of the family of the Nawabs of Dacca.[32]

British legal and administrative systems also opened up new professions. The practice of any one of a number of legal trades was lucrative. Some of those who made a career in the law bought land. For instance, Sayyid Qaim Ali, a *wakil* living in Janpur, was able to purchase an estate which brought him an income of Rs. 9,000 per year.[33]

Many of those who created endowments came from the families of self-made men, people whose ancestors did not belong to the Mughal aristocracy. Perhaps founding a *waqf* was part of an attempt to secure higher social status. The origin of their claim to the *rais*' place may have been of fairly recent origin, but the public dimensions of a *waqf*, its support of a mosque for instance, allowed these parvenus to proclaim their eminence. On the practical side, an endowment helped them make sure that their gains could be turned over to their descendants.

Alongside the men who established *awqaf* were the women who created them. Women usually gained control of property by inheriting it from their fathers or husbands. A few women gained possession of their husbands' estates by successfully asserting a claim for the payment of the bridal gifts (*mehr*). Though there were plenty of widows and childless couples, an unmarried man or woman rarely possessed substantial property. Among the founders of *awqaf*, a woman named Najiban stood out. She was a truly independent woman: a courtesan. During her active years as a dancing girl and prostitute, she accumulated enough money to purchase a *zamindari* and build a fine house in the town of Bareilly. When she died, at the age of ninety, her property was worth over Rs. 40,000.[34]

As the preceding paragraphs showed, founders of endowments came from a wide variety of regional and occupational backgrounds. Though they acquired their property by different means, they all shared an interest in keeping that wealth intact and passing it on to their heirs. All of them seemed to believe that keeping their estates whole would preserve

---

[31] Mujibunnissa's case, *LI*, vol. 441, 616–617.
[32] *Abdul Fata Mahomed Ishak (and others)* v. *Russomoy Dhur Chowdhry*, *LI*, vol. 382, 607ff.
[33] Muhammad Munawar Ali's case, *All*, XXI, 331ff.
[34] *Biba Jan* v. *Kalb Husain (and others)*, *All*, XXXI, 136ff.

only to increase their prosperity. Leaders of the family did not begin to invest in land until after the establishment of the Permanent Settlement in 1793.[28]

Among founders of *awqaf*, the connection between commerce and landowning was strongest near centres of trade like Dacca or Bombay. Profits derived from agriculture were invested in commercial activity: an indigo factory or a sugar cane mill. At other times, perhaps more frequently, wealth gained in trade bought land. Also, city-dwellers had the chance to buy lots or houses and then live off the rent. For example, Fatima Bibi controlled houses worth over Rs. 300,000 on Bombay Island.[29]

In the United Provinces of northern India, land had more value than commercial wealth. There, founders of endowments acquired estates in a number of ways. In Mughal times, government employment provided the material foundation for the leading status of many of that region's prominent families. When the Mughals declined, many Muslims found employment in the bureaucracy of the British empire. Some of them also found wealth in British service. As many complaints indicated, officials sometimes used their government posts to get money and land through coercion and fraud.[30] Despite that, government employment was financially rewarding even for officials who were scrupulously honest. Their salaries were secure and comparatively high. By 1880, for example, a subordinate district judge earned as much as Rs. 1,000 per month, far more than a peasant earned in a year. Government servants also invested in land, adding thereby to whatever their families already possessed. A number of endowments indicated that the founders combined government service and landowning. While some members of the family worked in the bureaucracy, others remained at home and managed the land. Sayyid Mehrban Ali of the town of Gulaothi in the U.P.'s Bulandshahr district was an example of a successful government servant. He was the former chief secretary (*mīr munshī*) in the office of the British political agent attached to the "native state" of Bharatpur. He greatly increased a modest family holding by buying land, houses, two indigo factories and shops in the town, all worth about Rs. 400,000. His government service and wealth brought him recognition from the

---

[28] *Khajeh Solehman Quadir* v. *Nawab Salimullah Bahadur*, IA, XLIX, 153ff; B. C. Allen, *Dacca*, 181.
[29] *Fatima Bibi* v. *The Advocate General of Bombay and Shaik Hassan Rogay*, Bom, VI, 42ff; also, *Shaikh Mahammed Ahsanullah Chowdhry* v. *Amarachand Kundu*, LI, vol. 340, 64ff.
[30] P. Khan, *Revelations of an Orderly*, 1–30.

ish were creating. The deeds of endowment they wrote were couched in the terminology of the older world, but their specific property arrangements showed that the founders were acutely aware of the demands of the newer one.

The individuals who created endowments acquired control of their property in a number of ways. Some of them belonged to families which had once ruled large kingdoms. For example, the relatives and descendants of the Nawabs of Avadh controlled a great deal of wealth and they created many endowments, both in Lucknow, where many lived, and in Calcutta, the city to which the British sent the last of the Nawabs.[25] The British also exiled the family of the sultans of Mysore in Calcutta, where they created many *awqaf*.[26]

When the British legal and revenue systems turned less exalted leaders, a *rais* or *malik*, into landlords, their holdings were often founded on grants from the Mughal or other states. The descendants of a man known as Khwajah Mubin, who came to India in the days of Sultan Muhammad bin Tughluq (*c*. A.D. 1350), provided an example of how that process worked. Khwajah Mubin and his brother came from the Hijaz. They were apparently religious scholars and the sultan appointed them *qazis* in the Muhammadabad *parganah* of Ghazipur district. Throughout the years that followed, the eldest male descendant of one or the other of the brothers always held the *qazi*'s post. All the succeeding sultans and emperors renewed the appointment and continued the revenue grants which supported the family. When the British arrived, they converted what were originally grants of the state into *zamindari* holdings.[27] However, very few families seemed to have had that kind of long running success. Invasions, changes of dynasty and mortality made truly old families rare.

The history of the Nawabs of Dacca showed how many changes in fortune one family might experience. The title "Nawab" may have conjured up images of an old Mughal aristocratic family, established for centuries and having an ancient claim to their lands. That image was only partly correct. The family did claim descent from a Nawab: Khwajah Abd al-Hakim, the governor of Kashmir in the reign of the emperor Muhammad Shah. Khwajah Hakim fled to Dacca during Nadir Shah's invasion in 1742. His family acquired wealth in that city as traders in hides and gold dust, not as landlords. The arrival of the British seemed

---

[25] For a *waqf* established by Hajji Begum, the daughter of Muhammad Ali Shah, *Baqar Ali Khan* v. *Anjuman Ara Begum*, *All*, XXV, 236ff; for one founded by Nawab Sultan Jahan Mahal, one of Wajid Ali Shah's wives, *Izzat un-nissa Begum* v. *Mussamat Kaniz Fatima Begum*, *OLJ*, III, 677ff.

[26] *OC*, w. 51 of 1915.

[27] Irvine, *Report*, 48–50.

ings, *raises* or *zamindars* employed regal terminology. The *rais* sat upon a throne (*masnad* or *gaddī*). *Ra'īyats*, whom the British preferred to call "tenants" or "cultivators" were, literally, "subjects". When a *rais* met with his *raiyats* he described himself as holding court (*darbār*). The money which a *raiyat* paid his lord was tribute, not rent. The place where he paid the tribute was called a "*kacahrī*", just as government revenue offices. The clerks who collected the tribute and kept the *rais'* accounts bore the same titles once used by the officials of the Mughal emperor's treasury. Even the toughs employed by a *rais* to make sure that the tribute kept coming were known as "*sipāhīs*", the term for a horse-trooper, not a landlord's bully.[22]

Even in the homes of the modestly affluent, Mughal courtly style influenced terms of address, forms of polite conversation, hobbies, dress and household organization. Any family asserting its own noble (*sharif*) status followed imperial usage as closely as possible.[23] The cook was known as the "*Khānsāmān*", the title of the court chamberlain; no respectable family used the common Hindustani word for cook: "*bāwarcī*". Even the lowly sweeper received a high sounding title: "*jama'dār*", which the Mughals used for the officer in charge of the royal wardrobe. The household servants, the wet-nurses, nursemaids, gatekeepers and butlers all bore honorifics once employed in Mughal palaces. This heritage continued to be the model long after the Mughals lost their power.

The cultural values surrounding the *rais* were shaped by the royal tradition. Perhaps that accounted for the friction which sometimes existed between courtly behaviour and that of pious Muslims. An epigram in Josh Milihabadi's memoir of his own *zamindari* family summed up the tension between the ideals of the faith and those of the Mughal court. Josh described the highly emotional loyalty which his father, grandfather and uncles professed for Islam, but none of them kept the *Ramazan* fast. 'When it came to acting on their convictions", wrote Josh, "they were more *rais* than *Mussalman*."[24]

British legal theory, as this was applied in India, gave scant attention to the cultural values associated with titles passed on by defunct empires. The courts primarily considered sets of contractual and economic relationships. The legal system concentrated on the formal rights of landlords and tenants: the value of the land or the apportionment of the government's revenue. The people who created *awqaf* were caught between the values of the Mughal world and those of the world the Brit-

[22] T. R. Metcalf, *Land*, 237–280, and Musgrave, "Landlords", 265–270.
[23] Lelyveld, *Aligarh*, 28–30.
[24] J. Malihabadi, *Yādōn ki Barāt*, 73, 30.

Endowments and the temporal order

Why did the founders of *awqaf* emphasize the necessity of maintaining a unified holding? To discover the basis for that concern, one must look to pre-British notions of the ways in which individuals were connected to the land. The *waqfnamah* of Basharat Ali of Gorakhpur expressed in typical fashion the reasons for a founder's interest in keeping an estate intact.

Let it be known that this property, together with its income, has been assigned to my heir for maintenance and for protection and perpetuation of *riāsat* and not for any sort of transfer ... without division of any land, for by division power will be diminished and the *riasat* will be reduced to small parts. Then there will be neither the perpetuation of *riasat* nor the perpetuation of honour and then the distinction of the family will be lost.[14]

British court reporters consistently translated "*riasat*" with the English word "estate". However, the etymology and colloquial usage of *riasat* were more suggestive of "state" than they were of "estate". To have *riasat* was to have dominion, to exercise command, to resemble a king, not a landlord.[15] Persian and Urdu dictionaries defined *riasat* with terms such as "*sarkārī*" or "*sardārī*", which also conveyed the meaning of "state".[16] The other words used to describe agricultural holdings – *milk*, *taalluqah* and *'illāqah* – had overtones of the kind of possession or interest which a ruler had in his domain. A *riasat* was not a "little kingdom" in the sense that it was territorially contiguous.[17] Its holdings were too scattered to constitute that kind of state. But the notions of a kingdom expressed by the Mughals and other rulers of India did not require formal boundaries.[18] A state existed in the personal bonds between rulers and subjects.[19] A *riasat* was a little kingdom because it had a little king.

In deeds of endowment, the founders most often used the word "*rais*" to describe themselves and the position which they held in society.[20] Though the word meant "chief" or "leader",[21] legal documents used the words "landlord" or "landowner". Similar terms, such as *malik* or *zamindar*, also appeared as "landlord", even though these titles implied that the individual who bore them was more ruler than proprietor. When describing almost any aspect of the management of their hold-

---

[14] *Murtazai Bibi* v. *Jumna Bibi (and others)*, *All*, XII, 264–265.
[15] J. T. Platts, *Dictionary of Urdū, Classical Hindī and English*, 610.
[16] *Farhang-i Asifiyyah*, II, 394.
[17] P. J. Musgrave, "Landlords and Lords of the Land", 262–264.
[18] S. P. Blake, "The Patrimonial–Bureaucratic Empire of the Mughals", 77–94.
[19] Lelyveld, *Aligarh's First Generation*, 23–26.
[20] For example, *Mujibunnissa (and others)* v. *Abdul Rahim and Abdul Aziz*, LI, vol. 441, 661ff.
[21] Platts, *Dictionary*, 613.

Description of property	Hasan Ali's share	Est. value of share
One share of three in a brick (*pakka*) house, used by the males (*mardanah*) of Hasan Ali's family.	Rs.	20.0.0
One share of three in another brick *mardanah* with veranda.	Rs.	20.0.0
One share of a house known as "Kathwari".	Rs.	20.0.0
One share in a cattle shed.	Rs.	7.0.0
One share in an unused indigo warehouse and vats.	Rs.	50.0.0
Vats, boilers and equipment for unused indigo factory.	Rs.	34.0.0
One share in a sugar cane mill.	Rs.	10.0.0

If Quranic rules of inheritance were followed in Hasan Ali's case, at his death the property would be further parcelled out among his heirs. At the end of the nineteenth century, some officials of the revenue administration began to express their concern over the increasing fragmentation of agricultural holdings.[11] Settlement officers and others involved in revenue collection put the blame for excessive subdivision on the systems of inheritance used by both Muslims and Hindus. Both of them, according to British officials, recognized a plurality of heirs which reduced estates to collections of unprofitable morsels of land.[12] Government critics apparently ignored the impact of their own legal and revenue regulations in contributing to the break-up of holdings. By making land something worth owning, by measuring it, describing it in minute detail on revenue rolls, and by enforcing "native" legal texts to the letter, the administration itself helped to guarantee the division of estates.

The authorities also tended to ignore the efforts which Indians made to prevent the excessive division of their property. Sayyid Hasan Ali listed his possessions so carefully because he wanted to prevent them from being carved up by his heirs. Endowments were a way of keeping an estate intact. In deeds of endowment, statements like "so that the property itself and the principal wealth of the estate may always be preserved from all manner of partition, division, transfer, and succession ..." were almost always included.[13]

[11] For example, note by P. P. Hutchins dated 24 April 1892 in (NAI) *HJP A* (May 1893), nos. 47–55.
[12] W. Irvine, *Report on the Revision of Records and Settlement Operations in Ghazipur District, 1880–1885*, 61ff.
[13] For example, *Muhammad Munawar Ali v. Rasulan Bibi*, *All*, XXI, 331.

Even the British officials who administered the settlement and collection of revenue found it confusing.[9] The Indians who had to arrange their lives around such minutiae probably found it even more troublesome. They confronted "estates" composed of bits of land scattered here and there, often in more than one revenue division (*parganah*) or district. Since revenue resettlements occurred at long intervals, the names of the plots' owners were often those of individuals who had died years before. When individuals created *awqaf*, they had to take account of these complications. For example, Sayyid Hasan Ali of Jaunpur, who created an endowment in August of 1886, described his holding as follows:[10]

Description of property	Hasan Ali's share	Est. value of share
"Ancestral property" in *mauzah* (village) Kalanpur, together with groves, scattered houses and trees used by cultivators.	4 *gandas*	Rs. 200.0.0
Part of the above, known as "Mir Jokhu's share".	2 *annas*	Rs. 1,400.0.0
As above, known as "Mir Mohsin Ali's share".	8 *gandas*	Rs. 250.0.0
As above, "Sakina Bibi's share".	6 *gandas*	Rs. 200.0.0
Mortgage right, purchased by Hasan Ali in "Shaikh Qadir's share".	10 *gandas*	Rs. 300.0.0
Part of a *zamindari* known as "Kalsum Bibi's share", purchased by Hasan Ali.	6 *gandas*	Rs. 200.0.0
A full *zamindari* located in *mauzah* Hamzapur (otherwise known as Usargaon) in Ungli *parganah* of Jaunpur district, purchased by Hasan Ali.	16 *annas*	Rs. 4,000.0.0
Zamindari located in *mauzahs* Katwalia and Khanwai, Ungli *parganah*, Jaunpur, held under mortgage by Hasan Ali.	5 *annas* 4 *pice*	Rs. 600.0.0
One share of three in house used by the females (*zenanah*) of the family of Hasan Ali's nephew, Awlad Husain.		Rs. 20.0.0

[9] *Ibid.*, 128.
[10] Based on tables in *Syeda Bibi (and another)* v. *Mughal Jan (and others)*, *AA* (1902). Appellate papers have no consistent pagination and a more specific reference cannot be supplied. These files are stored in the record room according to the title of the case and date of decision.

used in Marathi to refer to "Hindu" legal texts.[5] The tendency for local usage to influence the vocabulary and concepts of Muslims appeared strong. In Calcutta, many of the deeds were written in Bengali. Although copyists and lawyers using that language might explain that, Muslims usually signed their names in the Bengali script. One Muslim woman even allowed her deed to begin with an invocation to the goddess Durga.[6] The *waqf* coming from Madras was written in Tamil. All the technical terms used in it were taken from the Sanskritic vocabulary common in that language. For instance, the custodian did not bear the title *mutawalli*, derived from Arabic, and was instead called the "*dharmakarta*".[7] Some of the *waqfnamahs* from Bombay and Calcutta were composed in English, reflecting the considerable British influence in those cities.

By intention, though not always in practice, the law of property introduced by the British was the same for everybody. It cut across regional or cultural divisions. It forced individuals from many different backgrounds to confront a similar set of problems.

Likewise, the British revenue system, for all of its many regional variations, had some consistency because it concentrated on the land itself. Pre-British revenue arrangements were much more interested in the value of the land's produce. Despite the new regime, revenue registers preserved older forms in the way they described an individual's "share" in an estate. The registers still noted the monetary value of each portion. In the currency of the raj each *rupee* was divided into sixteen *annas*, each *anna* into twenty *pice*. However, local traditions employed different and more exacting terms than the officially sanctioned system. In North India, for example, the *rupee* was divided into 320 *gandas*, the *pice* into twenty *kirant*, the *kirant* into nine *jao* and each *jao* into twelve *tond*.[8] Individuals' portions were expressed in terms of the number of *annas*, *jao* or *tond* which they were supposed to receive out of every *rupee* the land generated. But the British administration measured and divided land, not income. At the time the revenue demand was fixed, each monetary share became identified with a particular plot of land.

After the establishment of a land-based revenue system, if a family grew in size, the land, not the income, had to be further divided. Thus, the vocabulary of real estate became as complicated as that of cash. The *bigha*, which in North India measured about 3,025 sq yards, was divided into twenty *biswas*, each *biswa* into twenty parts known as *biswansis*.

---

[5] *Nizam Ghulam (and others)* v. *Abdul Gafur (and others)*, Bom, XIII, 618ff, and *LI*, vol. 367, 732ff.
[6] *OC*, w. 43 of 1909 and w. 38 of 1907.
[7] *Mutu Ramandan Chettia* v. *Vava Lavai Markayar*, Mad, XXXIV, 12ff.
[8] B. H. Baden-Powell, *The Land-Systems of British India*, II, 126–127.

Region	Number of instances
Bihar	
Patna	1
United Provinces by district	
Gorakhpur	1
Ghazipur	1
Kanpur	2
Janpur	2
Meerut	1
Bulandshahr	1
Allahabad	1
Farukhabad	1
Lucknow	3
Shahjahanpur	1
Bareilly	1
Moradabad	1
Madras	
Madras City	1

Locating a *waqf* in a particular district was slightly misleading because holdings were often dispersed over a wide area. An individual's property was not always located in the place where she or he had a residence. Someone living in Calcutta might own land in one of the upcountry districts, or a person living in Kanpur might have fields in a neighbouring district. Deeds of endowment showed that their founders lived in cities and towns. This reflected the heavier concentrations of Muslims in urban centres. For instance, in the United Provinces in the late nineteenth century, Muslims constituted only one-eighth of the province's population, yet they accounted for two-fifths of the population of the cities and towns.[4] The deeds also pointed to the large Muslim populations of Calcutta and Bombay.

The deeds of endowment themselves indicated some of the important ways in which regional differences influenced the lives of individual Muslims. A difference in locality often meant a difference in language and culture. Qamr ud-din, who lived in the market town of Uran near Bombay, composed his deed in Marathi and signed his name to it in the Marathi script. Linguistic and cultural differences also seem to have influenced the way Muslims looked at their faith. This same Qamr ud-din claimed adherence to the "school" of *shariah* associated with Imam Shafii. Later, during a court action on the endowment, a man who identified himself as an "*'alim*", someone learned in the doctrines of that school, constantly referred to Shafiite texts as "*sástras*", a Sanskrit term

---

[4] Robinson, *Separatism*, 13.

Decade	Number of instances
1820–1830	3
1831–1840	2
1841–1850	3
1851–1860	3
1861–1870	2
1871–1880	6
1881–1890	5
1891–1900	12
1901–1910	4

These endowments came from most of the regions of British India with two major exceptions. The first was the Panjab. Perhaps because that region's inheritance customs limited the division of land among heirs, *awqaf* found there did not usually include provisions for settlor's families.[2] Also, the Panjab government was especially concerned with the maintenance of the *status quo* among landholders. This limited to some degree the impact of the property laws and the number of inheritance related court cases. "Native states", where British rule was indirect, were the second major exception. Perhaps those states, ruled by Muslim or other indigenous princes, permitted the use of endowments to settle estates.[3] More importantly, such states did not radically change their patterns of land tenure, making the use of *awqaf* for that purpose unnecessary. In any event, sources did not report that endowments were an issue in princely states. With those two exceptions, a rough geographical distribution of our *awqaf* was as follows:

Region	Number of instances
Bombay City	6
Bombay Province, Thana district	1
Calcutta City	9
East Bengal and Assam by district	
Dinajpur	1
Chittagong	1
Dacca	2
Faridpur	1
Sylhet	1

---

[2] Opinions of A. Kensington, Judge of the Panjab Chief Court, and H. A. Rose, District Judge of Ludhiana, and others in (10) L/P+J/1079 (1911) and D. Gilmartin, "Kinship, Women and Politics in Twentieth Century Panjab", in *The Extended Family*, 151–173.

[3] *PGGC*, vol. 51 (1912–1913), 219–220.

2

Muslim endowments and the temporal order in British India

Until the 1920s, no one made a serious attempt to count the number of Muslim endowments in India. Between 1920 and the present several provincial and all-India laws came on the statute books which required custodians of *awqaf* to register their institutions with government supported agencies. Such legislation generally fails to command full compliance of the individuals concerned and even today no one seems to have a precise idea of the number of endowments in the subcontinent. Likewise, the number in operation during the British period remains uncertain. At present, about 100,000 are registered with the Indian government.[1] If reports from officials, custodians and founders are correct, the effect of those laws passed over the past fifty years is to discourage the creation of *awqaf*. Therefore, many of those currently existing date from the British period. Though exceedingly vague, a safe guess is that several tens of thousands of endowments were founded during the British period.

For this study we selected a total of forty endowments. Availability of information in legal archives was the primary reason for selection. Another twenty-five lawsuits dealing with allied questions of inheritance, debt and family relations supplemented material drawn from them. Obviously, forty was too small a sample to develop statistical arguments about India's Muslims as a whole. Even so, each endowment had a story to tell about the people who founded it and whose lives were affected by its existence. The material collected from them was suggestive rather than statistically conclusive. They spoke of the way in which their founders thought of themselves, of the values they professed and the problems they faced. The British system of law, land tenure and administration created some of those difficulties. All forty of these endowments were created in the ninety years between 1820 and 1910. During that period the British completed the conquest of India and began perfecting the machinery of their government. The foundation dates of the forty *awqaf* are as follows by decade:

---

[1] S. K. Rashid, *Wakf Administration*, 25–58; in private conversation, many officials and custodians will acknowledge that registration laws are ignored.

threatened to attack the investigators. In the end, the British had to compromise. They resumed some *lakhiraj* and added thereby some Rs. 3,250,000 million rupees to the annual revenue, but at least as much wealth remained under the tax-free control of the landholders.

Large public endowments and those based on tax-exempt land drew government attention because of the large sums of money involved. Officials did not, apparently, notice that smaller owners were beginning to convert their estates into endowments. The chapters which follow will discuss these Muslim endowments in more detail. As they describe these *awqaf*, the reader will note how the desire to maintain a family's fortune mixed with desire to continue the public patronage which was a mark of elite status. However, the need to create endowments which were in part family settlements seemed to develop only after the imposition of British rule. If wealthy individuals created endowments bearing the names "*waqf-e awlad*" or "*waqf-e khandan*" in pre-British times, no record of them has appeared to date.[72] This doubtless reflected the influence of the changes in the law of property which the British made. Such an endowment would have been useless in the days of the sultans and emperors, because their policy worked to prevent permanent attachments between nobles and the land. Muslims received control of land only as some form of royal grant or by right of conquest. For most notables, a place in court was the best patrimony which could be left to one's children.[73] The British, by contrast, made the land itself worth owning. Moreover, the British courts enforced the laws strictly. In the field of inheritance, the Anglo-Indian courts tended to take a rather "orthodox" view of Quranic regulations. They adhered to them to the letter, something pre-British, Muslim governments did not always do. The court's literal approach to inheritance encouraged those Muslims who sought some legal way of hanging on to their holdings to create *awqaf*.

---

[72] Habib, *Agrarian System*, 312–313. During conversations held in Aligarh in July 1979, Professor Habib confirmed that his extensive researches in Mughal documents have yet to uncover such endowments.
[73] M. A. Ali, *The Mughal Nobility under Aurangzeb*, 11–12.

on an *imambarah* located at his residence. At his death, a friend took charge. In time, British officials became convinced that he was appropriating the endowment's funds for his own use. A government regulation, Number XIX of 1810, gave officials the power to guarantee the good management of any "trust" of a "public nature". Invoking this rule, local authorities appointed a visitor, Akbar Ali Khan, who was supposed to make the custodian behave in line with the government's standards for honest trusteeship. When the *mutawalli* refused to cooperate, the government appointed Akbar Ali in his place. After that officials gradually made many changes in the way in which the endowment's funds were used. They helped convert the Shiite shrine into the Hooghli College, an institution of learning serving both Muslims and non-Muslims.[69]

Another instance of government involvement with endowments touched more closely on the issues discussed in the following chapters. When the Permanent Settlement failed to provide all the money necessary to support the government administration, officials turned their gaze on a class of revenue free grants called "*lakhiraj*", literally "without tax", a broad category which apparently included some *awqaf* established by *zamindars*. Bengali landowners made use of *lakhiraj* to maintain temples, mosques and schools. Scholars and priests also received support. However, some of the *zamindars* gave money to their relatives, especially poorer members of the family. The Maharaja of Nadia, for example, gave the income from 20,000 *bighas* of *lakhiraj* land to his youngest wife, his son and mother.[70] Looking at this use, revenue officials decided that this was a tax dodge.

The government set up special commissions to look into the matter of spurious endowments. They had the power to revoke any which they considered suspicious. Since they set out to find irregularities, it was hardly surprising that they were soon retracting the tax-free status of a large number of these endowments. The use of those funds to support members of the family aroused particular criticism. The *zamindars* united to oppose the work of the commissions. They appealed to the government, arguing that the establishment of such endowments was an integral part of a ruler's duties, and that revoking them damaged their status.[71] When this protest failed, they destroyed their records and even

[69] K. Zakariah, *History of Hooghly College*, 1–10, and *Wasiq Ali Khan* v. *The Government*, SDA, VI, 130ff.
[70] C. Palit, *Tensions in Bengal Rural Society*, 29ff; the word is local pronunciation of the Arabic "*La Kharaj*": "without tax".
[71] (Beng) *Territorial Department of the Revenue Department, Original Consultations* (May 1829), 5, a petition of Syyud Kaduin and others; I am grateful to Professor Paul Greenough for providing a typescript of this document.

Texts of *shariah* were another possible source of information, for those who had access to them. The texts described two uses for a *waqf*. The first was known as a *"waqf alā 'al 'ām"*, "a *waqf* for the public". The second was called a *"waqf alā 'al-awlād"*, "a *waqf* for one's progeny". The Persian forms of these terms, *"waqf-e 'ām"* and *"waqf-e awlād"*, or *"waqf-e khāndān"*, were better known, since only a few scholars knew Arabic and understood the texts of *shariah*.

Persian literature, especially poetry, contained references to endowments and these served to inform the majority of Muslims who knew little of the sacred texts. Both Hafiz and Sadi mentioned *awqaf*, not always in a favourable fashion. Lesser known poets also employed the terminology. A Persian dictionary, the *Bahar-i 'Ajām*, composed in the 1740s by Tek Chand Bahar, quoted a number of verses which mentioned *"waqf-e awlad"*. Of course, the poets did not use the term with reference to property, but applied it within the conventions of the *ghazal* love lyric. One couplet quoted by Bahar described the world as God's *waqf-e awlad*. In another, a disappointed love declared that pain was the *waqf* he left his children.[67] Thus, many well-to-do Muslims would have known that an endowment had potential as a safe method of disposing of their property in a way which would benefit their children.

Until the 1870s British officials seemed only dimly aware of endowments. Those which they took notice of were those connected with large shrines. For instance, when a disagreement arose over the distribution of the *waqf* income of the shrine of Khwajah Muin ud-din Chishti, officials stepped in and forced a compromise.[68]

The "Hooghli Imambarah" in Calcutta was another institution which received close government attention in the 1830s. One Muhammad Mohsin founded the *Imambarah* in 1806. The property which provided the endowment's income was a tract of land in the Jessor *parganah*. Alamgir I had awarded it as a *jagir* to a man married to Muhammad Mohsin's mother. When he died, the mother acquired control of the *jagir* and later married Muhammad Mohsin's father. An older half-sister of Muhammad was the next to control the land. By the time she died, the British had installed the Permanent Settlement and the *jagir* was converted into a *zamindari*. Muhammad Mohsin gained control of the holding, but he was an unworldly man. He had never married and was childless, having spent most of his life on pilgrimages to Mecca, Medina and Karbala. When he acquired the estate, he spent most of its income

---

[67] The section on *"waqf"* in *Lughātnāmah* seems to have picked up some of the verses noted in the *Bahar-i Ajam*. I am grateful to Professor I. Habib for pointing out these verses. On Tek Chand, see *Tārīkh-i Adabīyat-i Mussalmānān-i Pakistān-o Hind*, IV, 395.
[68] S. K. Rashid, *Wakf Administration*, 112–113.

haphazard work. They were often forced to bend their orders to conform to local conditions not considered in the regulations.[64]

India's gradual incorporation into a global economy dominated by Britain was a further source of uncertainty. India's place in that international market-place was primarily as a supplier of one or another agricultural commodity: cotton, indigo, grain. As such, it was particularly susceptible to boom and bust cycles. When demand for indigo was high, thousands of peasants planted that crop. Wealthier individuals provided them with advances and began to set up factories to handle the initial processing of the indigo to prepare it for shipment to Europe as dye. When cloth manufacturers were glutted with the stuff, the price fell, investors lost capital and the cultivators lost a cash crop. Cotton and grain were subject to similar fluctuations. Despite that kind of uncertainty, the affluent had little choice but to invest in agriculture. Basic industries like cloth and steel did not appear until the twentieth century and British capitalists financed the major development projects of the nineteenth century: railroads and irrigation canals.[65] Any Indian with capital had to look to the land, commodities trading and money lending.

Britain's aim in ruling India was to ensure peace and security of property. Yet the character of the laws of property may have created a new problem. A British official writing in the 1870s summed it up: "The greatest wrong which we did to the Mussalman aristocracy was in defining their rights. Up to that period their title had not been permanent, but neither had it been fixed ... we gave them their tenures in perpetuity; but in doing so, we rendered them inelastic."[66]

The first portion of this chapter described some of the ways in which Muslims tried to use endowments to smooth a transition into a new economic, social and political situation. In the early years of the nineteenth century, a number of India's Muslims began to convert their property into *awqaf*. Though they probably did not know in detail the history of the institution outside India, they did have a number of ways close at hand of learning about the advantages which it offered. They probably noted how the families connected with sufi shrines managed to support themselves for generations, even in troubled times, on the proceeds of *awqaf*. That kind of stability must have been attractive to people casting about for a way to protect their family's fortune and the social prominence which accompanied it.

[64] N. Rabitoy, "System vs. Expediency: The Reality of Land Revenue Administration", 529–546.
[65] B. Chandra, "Reinterpretation of Nineteenth Century Indian Economic History", in *Indian Economy in the Nineteenth Century*, 35–76.
[66] W. W. Hunter, *The Indian Musalmans*, 139.

In Bengal and in other provinces big "landlords" were at the top of a pyramid of subordinate leaseholders. Some of these individuals, who were nominally tenants, were wealthy and influential in their own right. Even if a big *zamindar* fell, they managed to hold on to their economic and social position.[59] A legal change of title did not always lead to the eviction of defaulters. Even though the government altered their official status, calling them tenants rather than owners, their place in society was secure.[60] The individuals who were the prime source of endowments for Muslims, Hindus and others were able to maintain their position.

In other regions of British India, a different set of circumstances obtained. In the United Provinces of Agra and Avadh, the largest landholders, the *taalluqdars*, received special protection from the government. At the opposite economic pole, cultivators were essential and therefore immune from the full rigour of British legal–administrative innovations. Middling landholders, without the *taalluqdar*'s resources and lacking the peasants' indispensability, were gradually squeezed out.[61] They were pressed more closely than the affluent or the indigent. In the Panjab, the provincial administration favoured cultivators over those urban, mercantile groups who were in the best position to acquire ownership of agricultural property. In the south, the government often tried to give property rights to the cultivators; even so superior landholders managed to enlarge their estates.[62] New laws and courts did not instantly remake the social and economic landscape. Indians experienced their impact in an uneven fashion, at different rates in different places, but in itself that irregularity may have been a source of uncertainty and anxiety.

Especially during the early years of British rule, the character of the administration contributed to a lack of consistency. British officials were usually ignorant of all the complexities of the situation, literally, on the ground. They had to depend on local agents who did not always meet their standards of honesty or efficiency. In the Guntur district of Madras Presidency, for example, a group of clerks related by kinship and patronage managed for years to put large amounts of the government's revenue into their own purses.[63] Even British officers found it difficult to apply the rules strictly. The immensity of the task before them led to

[59] R. and R. Ray, "Zamindars and Jotedars", 81–102.
[60] B. Cohn, "Structural Change in Indian Rural Society", in *Land Control and Social Structure in Indian History*, 53–121.
[61] E. Stokes, *The Peasant and the Raj*, 205–227.
[62] D. Kumar, *Land and Caste in South India*, 9–12.
[63] R. E. Frykenburg, *Guntur District*, 1–28.

tenants", "tenants at will" or "cultivators", depending on which administrative jargon was in fashion. The government had the power of creating categories and then developing policies which took those new definitions seriously. Were Indians affected by that process? Did social realities alter to conform with administrative designations? To some extent Indians did reorder their self interpretations, but as the history of particular regions showed, they did so in ways which were not in complete conformity with the government's categorizations.

Soon after the establishment of the Permanent Settlement, British officials noticed that *zamindars* fell into arrears on their tax payments. Also, *zamindars* seemed to be making a habit of borrowing money with their estates as collateral and then defaulting on the payments. In both instances, the only remedy under the law was to dun the landlords, to imprison them and, eventually, to sell their lands to satisfy the revenue demand or personal debt. Thus, the government calculated that during the first ten years of the Permanent Settlement's operation about 68 per cent of the land in Bengal changed hands.[58]

Sales of *zamindari* estates, however, implied much more than met the official eye. The Raja of Burdwan, for example, was something of a fiscal chameleon. The government of Bengal classed him as an ancient aristocrat. That was stretching the point a bit because his rajadom had been set up in 1696 by the Mughals. His ancestors were of the *khatri* caste with their origins in the Panjab, but they were loyal to the Mughals and owed their place to that fidelity. When the Permanent Settlement arrived, the Burdwan Raja found himself among the fifteen largest *zamindars* who between them paid 60 per cent of the Bengal Province's revenue. According to official estimates, he was hard hit by the seizures and sales which came in the wake of the creation of property rights. However, the Raja apparently defaulted on loans and tax payments intentionally. When the government put his lands on the auction block, the Raja had his agents buy them in his mother's name. When her turn came, the dowager Rani played the same game: defaulting and waiting for government sponsored sales.

Despite his apparent losses, the Raja of Burdwan was prosperous enough to buy out other *zamindars* like the Raja of Bishnapur. Similar feats of financial skulduggery followed that purchase. Others apparently followed Burdwan's example. Many transfers were fictitious and land usually remained in the hands of its original holders. Thus, local gentry were able to manipulate the new system of law to their own advantage.

---

[58] The discussion of the Burdwan Raja's affairs follows R. Ray "Land Transfer and Social Change under the Permanent Settlement", 1–45.

others believed that the Mughals, like all oriental rulers, claimed possession of all lands in their kingdoms. Mill urged India's British rulers to take advantage of that ancient prerogative to remove oppressive, useless overlords like the *zamindars*. The state should settle the revenue directly with the cultivators and eliminate all intermediaries.[54]

Utilitarian critics had some influence on the formulation of another type of revenue arrangement. In the Madras Presidency, officials developed a system which, in theory, made the cultivator (*ryot*) responsible for payment of the land tax. Supposedly, the cultivator enjoyed the same ownership rights which the Bengal province granted the *zamindar*. Although superior forms of tenure were not eliminated, official policy awarded possession to the farmers.

In 1801–1802, British rule spread north and west into the territory between the Ganges and Jumna rivers when the Nawabs of Avadh were forced to cede some of their domain. At first, officials thought of applying the Permanent Settlement, but they compromised by allowing for periodic readjustments of the revenue demand.[55] Despite such compromises and the excoriations of the Utilitarians, the idea of fixing ownership with the gentry never lost its appeal for some in the Government of India. For example, after the Revolt of 1857, officials in Avadh made a special arrangement with the local magnates known as *taalluqdars*.[56] Although they were not really landlords, but a mixed group of Nawabi courtiers, tax farmers, clan chiefs and successful *condottieri*, the government recognized their property rights over any land claimed as part of their estates.

As British rule moved further into north-west India yet another form of revenue settlement came into vogue. It was based on the idea that each village was an independent, isolated "republic". Each village had a "proprietary brotherhood" which owned the land in common.[57] The new policy, pursued in the region around Delhi and extended to the Panjab, assumed that since a village commune controlled the land, it should pay the state's revenue.

The result of this process was that no matter which system they employed, or how inconsistently they applied it, British administrators created and imposed a social and economic lexicon. Old, indigenous terms like *zamindar*, *rais* and *ra'iyat* entered the language of government in translation. Groups whose relationship to the land and each other was complex assumed new titles. They became "landlords", "occupancy

---

[54] E. Stokes, *The English Utilitarians and India*, 87–89.
[55] I. Husain, *Land Revenue Policy in North India*, 6off.
[56] T. R. Metcalf, *Land*, 200–236.
[57] L. Dumont, *Religion, Politics and History in India*, 112–132.

tunity and forced the ambitious to find new tasks, different ambitions.

Endowments were dependent on the individuals who controlled wealth derived from agriculture. So far as endowments were concerned, the most important influence which the British exerted was in the realm of landholding. The British began to define land tenure, to establish norms for deciding who did or who should *own* land. In this way, they created new opportunities at the same time that they closed others.

The first British attempt to settle the question of land ownership occurred in the Bengal province. An experiment with tax farming proved disastrous, so in 1793 the British government set up what was known as the "Permanent Settlement". Inspired partly by the theories of the French physiocrats and partly by the Whiggish views of the Governor General, Lord Cornwallis, officials decided to make a few individuals responsible for the payment of revenue. To make sure that they met their obligation, those *zamindārs* (literally "one who holds land") were given permanent legal title to the lands forming their "estates". The government fixed the amount of the revenue demand in perpetuity in the hope that this security would help create a rural "gentry" interested in improving its holdings. Officials did not agonize over whether the *zamindars* had owned their land before the settlement. They were much more interested in turning a profit for the directors of the East India Company. Lord Cornwallis himself summed up their view: "It is immaterial to government what individual possesses the land, provided he cultivates it, protects the *ryot* [cultivator] and pays public revenue."[52]

By establishing private property rights in land, the settlement of 1793 made land something worth owning. Thereafter, land might be used as security for a loan. In the event of default, a creditor could seize and sell it. It could also be traded or inherited. At the same time, the British created an administrative apparatus, the courts, to enforce these rights. Revenue collectors, the courts and the police power of the state stood ready to enforce the law that land was private property. Though the influence of these institutions was slowly felt,[53] the emphasis of the British government was very different from that of the Mughals or other indigenous systems which had focused on the produce of the land rather than on the land itself.

In time, the terms of the Permanent Settlement drew criticism from self-styled progressive thinkers in Britain. Known today as Utilitarians, James Mill and his mentor Jeremy Bentham argued that *zamindars* and their ilk were a class of drones who never did own the land. Mill and the

---

[52] R. Guha, *A Rule of Property for Bengal*, 8, 5–17.
[53] D. A. Washbrook, "Law, State and Agrarian Society in Colonial India", 649–721.

was so troubled by the urgent need to compose suitable encomiums that even his prayers were disturbed. A physician (ḥakīm) not only had to cure, he had to prevent disease. When his patron sneezed, a hakim trembled. A religious scholar could find work only if he had a good voice and could recite elegies at his employer's religious gatherings. A teacher had to endure his pupils' boyish pranks all day and then sit up late at night keeping the master's accounts.[49] Life had lost its sweetness. Wealth and honour were lost. Old standards were forgotten and the future was uncertain. Curiously, Mir Sawda and other poets said little or nothing about a new force which appeared at the time. The British, barbarians in Mughal eyes, began to acquire for themselves a paramount role in shaping new standards, new definitions of honour and even of wealth.

Endowments and the new empire

In political terms, the British saw themselves as India's saviours. They brought order into a world consuming itself in internal conflict. They did come to power during a period of tumult and for that reason no one could have predicted what kind of polity might have emerged from the conflicts of the eighteenth century had the British not been there. But chaos and order were, in the context, relative terms.[50] The British eventually developed fairly definite notions about the order they wished to impose and they were inclined to view anything else as anarchy. From a different perspective, the eighteenth century was an age of opportunity. Mir Taqi complained that, in his day, "ten soldiers make a kingdom", but the chance to become kings drew the energies of many men of talent and courage. Official history subsequently consigned them to a dustbin marked "adventurer", a victor's categorization if ever there was one.

During the interregnum, even those who did not succeed in founding new empires managed to gain – for instance, the "mushroom taʻalluq-dārs" of the kingdom of Avadh. Though nominally officials of the Nawabs, they took advantage of the Nawabs' comparative weakness to enlarge their own domains.[51] Elsewhere in India, individuals and clans were able to extend the territory under their control, to found petty states and live in a more regal style. As the British slowly extended their rule, they put a stop to this form of expansion. They restricted oppor-

---

[49] Naqsh-i Dilpaẓīr, *An Anthology of Classical Urdu Poetry*, ed. M. A. R. Barker et al., I, 107–109, 113–114, 139–140, and R. Russell and K. Islam, *Three Mughal Poets*, 37–68.
[50] T. R. Metcalf, *Land, Landlords and the British Raj*, 36–37.
[51] Ibid., 29.

of a way of life fast approaching extinction. They are also reminders of one of the major dangers facing a *waqf*: the possibility that changing economic conditions will devalue its income.

The pensions provided to dependants pointed to the ways in which an endowment was not simply a "public" institution. It served the needs of its founder *and* the faithful. Thus, the Husainabad *waqf* also paid for the commemoration of the founder's death anniversary as well as that of his mother.

Kings and princes usually considered themselves essential props of society. They ensured order in a chaotic world. The wealth that came to them, they believed, was a well-deserved reward for the role they played. However, having wealth did not by itself confer superior status. Only spending it did that. Conspicuous expenditure on religious buildings and ceremonies was an assertion of high rank. It reminded contemporaries and later generations of the prince's place at the centre of life. It also brought the patrons the esteem of the populace.[48]

The court of the Nawabs provided only a temporary refuge for those who had known the splendours of the Mughals. The social order which they had created was disappearing. Poets like Mir Sawda and Mir Taqi seemed to capture best the sense of desolation felt by those for whom the Mughal decline was a personal tragedy rather than a historical abstraction. Mir Sawda employed a poetic form known as the *Shahrāshūb*, a "lament for the city". In his poems Delhi appeared as the dwelling of jackals and bandits. They portrayed many scenes of misery and ill fortune which probably reflected the poet's experiences. One described the fate of a well-born lady, used to the security of the harem, who was forced to go out of her home in search of alms. Too proud to beg, she tried to sell a rosary made from the sacred clay of Karbala. The attempt to preserve her dignity failed when a male of the *Sunni* sect approached and started a theological wrangle which forced her back indoors to starve in silence behind the veil.

Calamity touched all sections of society. In another of his laments, Sawda listed all the professions once thought honourable, but which were no longer secure. A mounted soldier no longer found a respectable commander. He worked for upstarts or became a robber. Any trooper lucky enough to have a sword was forced to pawn his shield. His horse, if he had one, was just another source of trouble because it had to be fed. Only poets who excelled at writing flattering verses (*qaṣīdah*) could find a patron, generally some boorish *nouveau riche*. The poor poet's mind

---

[48] J. Calmard, "Le Patronage des *Ta'ziyeh*: Elements pour une Etude Gobale", in *Ta'ziyeh: Ritual and Drama in Iran*, 121–130, and Mrs M. H. Ali, *Observations on the Mussulmauns of India*, I, 66.

month of Muharram. *Ruzahkhwani* contained flashbacks to the time of the Prophet, which acted to bolster *Shii* theological views. Authors also took the opportunity to comment on current events, drawing analogies to events at Karbala. Along with the *ruzahkhwani*, poets read elegies (*marsiyah*) which described the same episodes and individuals but added the emotive element of verse. Though originally written in Persian, *marsiyah* and *ruzahkhwani* became a popular genre in many of India's vernaculars.[47] Lucknow became especially famous for Urdu *marsiyah* and a number of poets grew wealthy by composing them. Finally dramatic presentations (*taziyah*) portrayed the tragedy of Husain in graphic and heart-wrenching terms. Though Muharram was the usual occasion for a *majlis*, a pious sponsor sometimes held one to commemorate some family event: a wedding or funeral.

Two different types of procession took place during Muharram. The first imitated Imam Husain's march towards Karbala. These had a distinctly military aura featuring armed men, drummers and trumpeters with some marchers carrying banners or martial insignia. This procession served to remind onlookers of Husain's courage and prowess. The second type of procession recreated the burial of Husain and his followers. During this phase of the ritual, replicas of their tombs, also called *taziyah*, were carried through the streets and taken to a field outside the city. The participants took the *taziyah* to a field, called "Karbala", in imitation of the original site, and buried the ones specially built for the occasion (more elaborate models were saved for constant use). Both the processions and the *majalis* provoked intense emotions. People wept copiously, beat their breasts and even wounded themselves with knives or chains. The rites of Muharram marked one of the most memorable seasons of the year.

During the Muharram rituals, but also at other times of the year such as *Ramazan*, the poor received clothing, blankets and food. Every *majlis* was followed by a distribution of sweets. Apart from gifts intended for the poor, the endowment provided for annual cash gifts to relatives and retainers of the Nawabs. Since the Nawabs supported upwards of 70,000 people, the list of pensioners was long. The payment of those stipends (*wasiqah*) has continued to the present day. Due to the proliferation of beneficiaries and the rupee's decline in value the amount distributed is very small. Still, every month men and women appear to collect their two or three rupees. They are usually old and bent, dressed in shabby coats or torn veils, but quick to remind the questioner that they are the descendants of noble families. We are "*nawabzadah*", "born of Nawabs", they say as they hobble off, the last living reminders

[47] C. Shackle, "The Multānī *Marṣīya*", 281–311.

and then converted into East India Company stock. The endowment provided a focus for the devotions of Lucknow's citizens, but it also supplied many other needs, as shown by the distribution of its income.[46]

1	Pensions for former servants of the Nawabs	Rs. 18,000
2	Repair of the road in front of the *Imambarah*	Rs. 6,000
3	For the celebration of *Muharram*	Rs. 25,000
4	For the salaries of the *Imambarah*'s servants	Rs. 25,135
5	To pay for the singers of *marsīyah* and the readers of *rūzahkhwānī* (see below)	Rs. 5,771
6	Grain for cattle used for work animals	Rs. 800
7	Commemoration of the anniversary of Muhammad Ali Shah's death	Rs. 10,000
8	Commemoration of his mother's death anniversary	Rs. 7,500
9	For repair of the buildings	Rs. 21,000
10	Miscellaneous charity	Rs. 17,000
11	Remittance to the shrine at Karbala	Rs. 15,320
12	For the blind	Rs. 6,000

The Husainabad endowment was exceptionally wealthy. However, it differed from smaller *awqaf* only in the amount of money at its disposal. Endowments established by less affluent individuals supported similar activities with smaller sums. Those created by *Sunni* Muslims sponsored a somewhat different set of ceremonies, but in most other ways were the same. Since we will encounter the same kinds of expenditures in the following pages, we should pause here to describe them and what they imply.

A significant portion of any endowment's funds went to maintain the buildings in which religious rituals were held. India's monsoon rains often damaged stucco buildings, necessitating yearly repairs; only stone buildings escaped harm. The salaries for an endowment's staff were another major expenditure. Religious functionaries were not the only employees; sweepers, watchmen and gardeners were also attached to *awqaf*. Hundreds of individuals worked full-time for the Husainabad. Smaller establishments made do with fewer people and offered only part-time salaries.

Pious gatherings, *majalis*, were a feature of Muharram rituals. At the gathering professional readers declaimed from prose works, *ruzahkhwani*, which described Husain or other personalities involved at Karbala, their momentary triumphs on the field of battle, their torments and deaths. They recounted in detail each episode of the first ten days of the

---

[46] Based on (NAI) *FDP A* (September 1868), nos. 33–46; I am grateful to Dr Veena Talwar Oldenburg for providing a microfilm of this and other documents related to the Husainabad.

Prophet's daughter Fatima and their children Hasan and Husain. They asserted that Ali, Hasan and Husain were by right of descent the leaders, *Imams*, of the Muslim community. An assassin removed Ali. Hasan was forced to abdicate and died under circumstances which some found suspicious. However, much of the twelver's piety focused on the tragic fate of Husain. In A.D. 680 he made a doomed attempt to claim leadership of the community. In the Arab month of Muharram he began a journey to Iraq accompanied by a small band of relatives and supporters. Yazid, the man he meant to replace, sent an army which intercepted Husain at a place called Karbala. After suffering from hunger and thirst, he fought one last skirmish on the tenth day (*'Āshūrā*) of Muharram. He and most of his followers died at the hands of their attackers.

The recounting of these events formed the focus for the ceremonies and institutions which the *Shii* supported through endowments. *Imambarahs* were the buildings in which pious meetings (*majālis*) were held to commemorate the martyrdom of Husain. Also, plays (*ta'zīyah*) recounting these events were presented. Richer members of the sect, like the Nawabs, built elaborate halls for the purpose. Poorer devotees constructed more modest centres or simply used a room of their own homes.

In Lucknow, the Nawabs built and supported many *imambarahs*, but two of them came to be particularly associated with the city. The first was built by Nawab Asaf ud-daulah (d. A.D. 1797) in the 1780s and commonly referred to as the "Big (*Baṛā*) Imambarah". It was (and is) an imposing structure featuring walls so thick that a labyrinth ran inside them. Three large rooms made it possible to hold several ceremonies at once. The second *imambarah* was the Husainabad built by Muhammad Ali Shah a little more than sixty years after the first. In comparison to the first, it was usually called the "Little (*choṭā*) Imambarah". Like the first, it was built of brick and given a white-washed stucco facing. It also had a courtyard reflecting Muhammad Ali Shah's cosmopolitan taste. Gilded statues in imitation of the classical Greek style surrounded a rectangular pool, while on the gate Arabic and Urdu inscriptions mingled with representations of the fish, the royal symbol of the Nawabs. Inside the *Imambarah*, crystal chandeliers and ornate mirrors crowded the walls and ceilings. Other gewgaws and curiosities: an entire *Quran* done in a microscopic hand on a single sheet of paper, a silver replica of Husain's tomb and large, gilt replicas of his tomb used in processions, jumbled together in the hall.

Buildings were only the most obvious portion of the Husainabad endowment. The yearly income it received was Rs. 157,606. Rs. 48,000 of that sum came from an unlikely source, as interest on a loan which the British extracted from Muhammad Ali Shah

the state and local gentry identified wealth with the cash or goods land generated.

The importance of trade in Mughal times reinforced the cultural and political notion that wealth consisted of some form of moveable property. No clear boundary existed between political–military leaders and merchants. Emperors and nobles had no aversion to commerce. The men and women of the imperial household invested in and profited from merchant enterprise. Also, those who derived their wealth from trade were frequently allied to the state and played the same cultural game of aping the emperor.[45]

When the Mughal empire entered its long decline in the first decades of the eighteenth century, most of those striving to become its heirs shared similar attitudes about the nature of property. As noted below, the British were the single exception. As the rivals fought, disruptions occurred in the collection and disbursement of agricultural revenues. The incomes of some endowments were doubtless disturbed in the scramble, but that was an unintended result of the struggle for dominance. As the history of the kingdom of Avadh showed, would-be successors, if left in comparative peace, maintained as much as possible of the Mughal system, including the funding of endowments.

The Nawabs of Avadh were among the most important of the Mughals' heirs. The first of them served for a while as the emperor's chief minister, but having tired of court intrigue, retired to the province of Avadh where he held the post of governor. The Nawabs remained the rulers of this region until its annexation by the British in 1856. Though they controlled considerable wealth, they had less than the Mughals at their height. The Mughals built with red sandstone and white marble; the Nawabs used brick or rubble coated with white-washed stucco. The Mughals counted their followers in the hundreds of thousands; the Nawabs had tens of thousands. Though pressed on the east by the British and beset by rebellious vassals, the Nawabs still managed to collect and spend vast sums of money. Their capitals, first at Faizabad then at Lucknow, were dotted with palaces, gardens, *waqf*-supported mosques, tombs and *imāmbarahs*.

Their attachment to the twelver branch of the *Shiah* sect was a major influence on the endowments which the Nawabs established. The *Shii* revered not only the Prophet, but his cousin and son-in-law, Ali, the

---

[45] M. N. Pearson, "Political Participation in Mughal India", 113–121, and S. Chandra, "Aspects of the Growth of a Money Economy in India during the Seventeenth Century", 321–331.

ority view. Even within the Chishti order, whose traditions were most adamant about refusing *awqaf*, the followers of Khwajah Muin ud-din accepted them.[42]

Since much of the income of endowments came from the dedication of land, any discussion of them must be placed in the context of the systems of landholding developed in the sultanates and the Mughal empire. Most of the kings who preceded the Mughals used assignments of land known as *"iqtahs"* to support the commanders of the troopers which formed the state's army. As with the Seljuk rulers of Iran (see p. 16) the *iqtah*-holders were tempted to convert their holdings into independent seats of power. A refractory noble tried to establish personal ties to the inhabitants of his fief. With their support, he found it easier to defy his sovereign's commands. Under Akbar, the Mughal administration wanted to replace *iqtahs* with cash salaries paid directly to the nobles from the imperial treasury. This attempt failed and imperial officers received instead a grant consisting of state's revenue claim to a given tract of land. Called *"jāgīrs"*, these awards included a significant alteration in the previous system: the treasury periodically shifted a noble's assignment which prevented, in theory, the formation of local attachments.

Both the *iqtah* and *jagir* systems enforced the principle that the ruler alone controlled access to the land and its produce. The latter system proved more effective, but only so long as imperial leadership did not falter. The refusal of *jagir*-holders to accept transfers of their assignments was one sign of the breakdown of Mughal authority. However, the procedures of the state were adaptations to existing, indigenous notions about land and patterns of landholding. These ideas and practices focused not on land, but on its produce and the control of the producers. Control of the "village grain heap" really mattered, land "ownership" was not an issue. A ruler marked his status by the share of the land's yield he claimed and by the number of subjects he commanded, not by the amount of land he "owned".[43] The Mughal's system of land revenue maintained that concern by introducing cash as the medium of tribute. Taking advantage of an influx of silver and of an active economy, by the late sixteenth century the Mughals were able to collect most of the revenue in coin.[44] Thus both servitors of

---

[42] Unfortunately the opinions of sufis on endowments have never been systematically approached. Many of these remarks are based on gleanings from conversations with Professor K. A. Nizami and Dr Warren Fusfeld, Aligarh-Delhi, July 1979.
[43] W. C. Neale, *Economic Change in Rural India*, 5–7, 20–34.
[44] I. Habib, "Potentialities of Capitalistic Development in the Economy of Mughal India", 32–78.

awqaf were favoured as an economic base for institutions because they were supposed to be permanent. In theory, the other grants, *inam*, *madad-i maash*, etc., were revocable by the state, though, in practice, they were passed on to the relatives of the original holder. Even an endowment for a mosque or school had a personal dimension, since the staff obtained their livings from it.

Both Muslims and non-Muslims received grants. Even the most "orthodox" emperors gave them to experts in Sanskritic lore (*pandits*), Hindu priests and monks as well as to their temples or monasteries. In those cases the word *"waqf"* was still used even though referring to a non-Muslim institution.[38] Hindus picked up the terminology and sometimes employed it to describe their own endowments.[39]

Awqaf provided funds for public graveyards, but the affluent also used them to build and maintain their tombs. For instance, when the emperor Shah Jahan built the Taj Mahal in the 1640s, he established several endowments to take care of its upkeep.[40] Based on the income from the revenues supplied by a number of villages as well as on the rents charged to shopkeepers who set up stalls in the tomb's precincts, they supplied salaries for the attendants and for the ceremonies marking Mumtaz Mahal's death anniversary.

Members of the imperial nobility, local gentry and prosperous merchants imitated royal behaviour. They also established endowments to support the kinds of institutions described above. Sufi shrines, mosques, their own tombs benefited from them. Sufi shrines were prominent recipients of the elites' patronage. Some of them, for example the shrine of Khwajah Muin ud-din Chishti, controlled considerable wealth derived from dozens of *awqaf*.[41]

Though many sufis supported themselves, their followers and families through endowments, a few of them displayed a more critical attitude. Nizam ud-din Awliya of Delhi taught that a good sufi must refuse income derived from an endowment. Perhaps he was concerned that the income did not come from an acceptable source. The cloaking of confiscations or evasions through *awqaf* gave rise to the suspicion that their funds were tainted. Nizam ud-din did state his objection to any form of permanent patronage, believing it incompatible with a life of poverty. His *khanqah* accepted only gifts of food, cloth or money. The residents either consumed these presents within a day or gave them away. The Naqshbandi hospice established in Delhi by Mirzah Mazhar Jan-i Janan followed the same practice. However, they seemed to be holding a min-

---

[38] Qureshi, "*Wajh-i-Ma'ash* Grants", 36.
[39] *Sri Thakur Sitaranji* v. *Jadunath Singh (and another)*, *OLJ*, I, 104ff.
[40] I. Habib, *The Agrarian System of Mughal India*, 312–313.
[41] S. K. Rashid, *Wakf Administration*, 111–126.

Sikri procured the patronage of the Emperor Akbar. Akbar believed that Shaikh Salim's intercession was responsible for the birth of his eldest son, Prince Salim, known afterwards as the Emperor Jahangir. Akbar established generous endowments for Shaikh Salim's shrine. Both Akbar and Jahangir gave the Shaikh's sons, grandsons and sons-in-law government posts and places in the imperial nobility. Shaikh Salim's descendants served as governors and army commanders throughout Jahangir's reign.[34]

According to Akbar's theory of government, the *Ā'īn-i Akbārī*, four classes of persons were worthy of receiving some aid from the state:

1 seekers of true knowledge
2 devout persons who had abandoned the world
3 people who were destitute
4 nobles who "out of ignorance" were unable to accept gainful employment.[35]

In addition to endowments, a number of forms of royal patronage were available. Various Persian titles described them: *wajh-i maʿāsh, madad-i maʿāsh, milk, wazīfah* and *inʿām*. Chancery style had more to do with the choice of term than did any real difference in the provisions of the gift.[36] The different types of grant had a tendency to shade off into each other. Also, in practice, the distinction between them and a *waqf* was not always clear.[37] The *wazīfah* was supposed to be a cash allowance paid directly by the imperial treasury. The rest of the terms noted above were some form of revenue assignment. The recipient of one of those grants had a claim to the government's tax/tribute on a tract of land. The grant-holder probably paid more attention to the limitations on the gift than to the title used to describe it. It mattered, for instance, whether the recipient was entitled to all or only part of the revenue demand. Another problem was whether or not the land was already under the plough or, as was often the case, it was "waste" for the cultivation of which the grantees had to make their own arrangements. Grant-holders were also interested in whether or not some service to the state was attached to the grant. Finally, grantees wondered about the duration of the grant. Was it possible to pass it on to one's descendants or was it resumed on the original incumbent's death?

Given that some inconsistency in terminology existed, endowments tended to be reserved for institutions rather than for persons. Perhaps

---

[34] A. Husain, "The Family of Shaikh Salim Chishti during the Reign of Jahangir", *Medieval India*, II, 61–68.
[35] S. Moosvi, "Sūyūrghāl Statistics in the *A'in-i Akbārī*", 284.
[36] I. H. Qureshi, "*Wajh-i-Maʿash* Grants under the Afghan Kings", *Medieval India*, II, 19–20 n. 1.
[37] *Sayyad Mahomed Ali* v. *Sayyad Gobar Ali, Bom*, VI, 88ff; also *Kalb Ali Hosein* v. *Syf Ali, SDA*, II, 139–141, and *Massumat Qadira* v. *Shah Kubueroodeen*, *SDA*, III, 543–549; all these endowments dated from Mughal times.

sufis did not imply a specific dogmatic or ritual stance on the part of patrons.[32]

Sufis in India were affiliated with most of the major "orders" (*ṭarīqāt*) of the Muslim world, including the Qadiri, Chishti and Naqshbandi. Furthermore, each of the orders was subdivided into dozens of branches.[33] Some differences did exist in the spiritual methods of the various orders. However, the significant distinction between them consisted of their different chains (*silsilah*) of teachers and students. The attachment was based on the personal connections between masters (*shaikhs, pīrs, murshids*) and their disciples (*murīds, shāgirds*), whom they initiated and guided on the path to mystical experience. Among them, the reputation of the individual *pir* mattered most. *Pirs* sometimes gained reknown for their spiritual power (*barakat*), a sign of divine favour which enabled them to work miracles such as raising the dead, helping barren women become pregnant and generally procuring the wishes of their followers. With death, a recognized *pir* did not lose the *barakat*. This was passed on to the saint's biological descendants or, barring that, to the descendants of his closest disciples. Also, a *pir*'s tomb continued to be a place where devotees were able to acquire the benefits of the saint's power.

Small cities grew up around the tombs of famous saints. Because being buried in the vicinity of a *pir*'s grave was auspicious, they were partly cities of the dead. However, institutions known as "*khānqahs*" or "*takyahs*" grew up which served the living. A *khanqah* was a combination hostel for disciples as well as a school for would-be mystics. Sometimes, if the saint had been of scholarly bent, the *khanqah* contained a library and disciples transmitted some knowledge of the scriptural traditions of Islam. Most shrines had local importance, but a few became famous throughout India, attracting pilgrims from the entire subcontinent and beyond. The shrines Khwajah Muin ud-din Chishti at Ajmer, or Baba Farid at Pakpattan or Data Ganj Bakhsh at Lahore numbered their devotees in the tens of thousands. They flocked to such places for a number of reasons. A few wished to pursue the path of mystical experience. Most of the others hoped to secure the aid of the saint in overcoming life's difficulties. Also, because most shrines distributed charity in the form of free food and clothing, they attracted the poor.

Almost every ruler had a favourite shrine and these received support in the form of *awqaf*. For instance, Shaikh Salim Chishti of Fatehpur

---
[32] R. M. Eaton, *Sufis of Bijapur*, 45–79, 151–152
[33] *Cambridge History of Islam*, II, 621–622.

their beliefs and whose habits of life differed from their own. Even so, their own diverse backgrounds combined with the non-Muslim environment meant that the ways of the unbelievers shaped the contours of Muslim society, for instance the character of family life. Also, non-Muslims picked up elements of the Muslim cultures which the invaders brought.

The integration of these disparate groups took place in royal courts, market towns (*qaṣbahs*) and popular religious shrines. Market towns were usually centres for local lords and for the agents of larger states. The first Muslim state in India was founded in the Sind in the eighth century A.D., but its influence on the rest of the subcontinent was small. When it came to kingdom building, the Muslims who entered through the passes of the north-west were most successful. They created the many Muslim states which dotted the northern and central portions of the peninsula. The sultanates of Delhi, Janpur, the Deccan and Gujarat were the largest. Successive waves of invasion/migration and the rough and ready atmosphere of the frontier meant that most of these states were politically as well as territorially fluid. Likewise, the distinction between a "king" and a "governor" was not always clear or significant. Individuals who were technically the servants of a greater ruler exercised, in practice, independent power. The Mughal dynasty, which took power in the sixteenth century, brought comparative stability, but of necessity even they left in place a host of local lords.

Muslim rulers, both large and small, created endowments. The earliest recorded *waqf* in the subcontinent dated from the last years of the twelfth century A.D. Muhammad ibn-Sam, one of the Ghurid sultans, set aside the revenue of a single village to support a mosque in the city of Multan.[31] By supporting a mosque in conquered territory, a ruler made a political as well as religious statement. For non-Muslims, the mosque was a constant reminder of Muslim political dominance. Since the name of the sultan was invoked during the Friday prayers, Muslims heard weekly a proclamation of their ruler's piety.

In addition to mosques, religious institutions connected with sufis were frequently supported by the political elite. Although sufis played a crucial role in the conversion of indigenous Indian peoples, individual sufis had widely divergent styles in matters of doctrine and practice. Some preached strict adherence to all the faith's observances: daily prayer, the Meccan pilgrimage, etc. Others ignored or publicly flouted those practices, drank wine, did not fast or pray and dismissed the pious as hypocrites. While some were radical pacifists, others were warriors for the faith. In short, saying that the nobility supported

[31] S. K. Rashid, *Wakf Administration*, 1–2.

piety-minded and confirmed their desire to prevent future encroachments.[28]

Even when the state did not intrude, the management of an endowment could be the subject of bickering among the trustees. Because of the personal benefits which might come to a custodian, charges of corruption were common. According to the textbooks of *shariah*, local judges (*qāzīs*) were supposed to oversee the management of *awqaf* in their jurisdictions, settling any disagreements. Few *qazis* seem to have fulfilled that expectation. When they did intervene, judges often found themselves embroiled in controversies over their own honesty. Moreover, they were open to pressure from the government which appointed them. Even the endowments which supported mosques and religious schools were subject to the plague of conflicting human desires.[29] Doubtless, pious Muslims were scandalized by such squabbling.

Though muted, popular contempt for the institution of *waqf* expressed itself. The verse of the poet Hafiz (d. *c*. A.D. 1389) illustrates the mocking and critical attitude which some took towards endowments. The wrangling of trustees, the use of endowments to evade taxes, cover dubious acquisitions of property and feed personal greed seemed to violate much in the spirit of Islam and gave rise to criticism. Perhaps complaints were rooted in the resentment which the underprivileged felt when they looked at an institution which preserved the property of the rich and perpetuated iniquitous patterns of social dominance.

Muslim endowments in India

For those regions of the Muslim world which lay to the north and west, India was a frontier, a place to move to, settle in and, with luck, grow rich. Muslims came to the subcontinent as merchants, soldiers and administrators. They represented almost every sectarian, regional, ethnic and linguistic grouping which accepted the faith. Both *Sunni* and *Shii* came. Turks, Afghans, Mongols, people from almost every city and province of the Iranian plateau, Arabs and Abyssinians migrated. In addition to the foreign born Muslims, numbers of Indians "converted" to Islam over the course of the centuries.[30] Some converts were peasants, others were artisans, menials and merchants, while a few belonged to high status groups like the Rajputs and Brahmins. In most regions, Muslims remained a minority surrounded by people who did not share

---

[28] C. Petry, *Civilian Elite of Cairo in the Later Middle Ages*, 24–25, 213.
[29] G. Makdisi, *The Rise of Colleges*, 44–45.
[30] P. Hardy, "Modern European and Muslim Explanations of Conversion to Islam in South Asia", 177–208.

proved impossible to enforce and Muhammad Ali violated it himself by creating a number of endowments in favour of his family.[25]

A similar increase in the number of *awqaf* occurred in Ottoman Anatolia.[26] Government officials criticized this trend and made some attempt to halt it. As in Egypt, the struggle to limit endowments, especially when they were really estate-settlements or tax dodges, had little success. Only in the middle years of the twentieth century did states manage to control effectively or eliminate entirely endowments. The governments of Turkey, Egypt and Iran all tried to reduce the amount of land included in *awqaf*, while increasing the amount of government control over them.[27] Sometimes, as in the case of the Pahlavi dynasty of Iran, their actions served only to alienate the religious scholars whose income came from the endowments.

The tendency to discuss the history of peoples who happen to be Muslims solely in terms of some abstract notion of their faith contributes to a skewed perception of the ways in which endowments fit in particular historical contexts. The above discussion indicates that a *waqf* can fill a great many needs. The pious condemned some of the ways people used them. Because individuals created them, endowments affect the donors and their connections as well as a wider circle of believers. The distinction between public and private, pious and personal, is misleading. A desire to gain spiritual merit is not the founders' only aspiration. The place and time in which they live influence their other concerns. The social, political and economic conditions of the moment always shape the provisions of an endowment. That seems equally true of endowments which support mosques or other religious and charitable foundations.

In the preceding section we saw that endowments were sometimes created in an attempt to safeguard an individual's property from confiscation by the state. In a similar fashion, *awqaf* often seemed a way of protecting religious institutions from state domination. Rapacious rulers did not hesitate about stealing from religious institutions. Moreover, frequent tension between the pious and their rulers sharpened the former's desire to limit the latter's influence on schools and mosques. The management of endowments was a common source of conflict. While the state sought to make its loyalists trustees, the pious, most often the *ulama*, tried to retain their hold on those institutions. A strong ruler who succeeded in asserting his dominance only embittered the

---

[25] G. Baer, *A History of Land Ownership in Modern Egypt*, 150, 163–165.
[26] "Waqf", *Encyclopedia of Islam* (1934), IV, 1096.
[27] J. N. D. Anderson, "Recent Developments in *Shari'a* Law IX", 257–261.

In Egypt, the Ottoman administration lowered the tax on agricultural lands included in endowments. That advantage encouraged many members of the noble and scholarly classes to turn their estates into endowments. Also, tax farmers used the creation of endowments as a device to gain control of their revenue assignments. Not surprisingly, the amount of agricultural land tied up in that fashion steadily increased. By 1800, endowments contained something over one-fifth of Egypt's arable territory.

The scholars' membership in and leadership of sufi brotherhoods was another source of wealth and influence. The brotherhoods were popular organizations, attracting both the nobility and general citizenry. As elsewhere in the Muslim world, the brotherhoods' organization was usually based on the tomb of a famous saint. The hope of gaining the saint's intercession with God, combined with the teaching of mystical lore, drew thousands of devotees to such shrines. They also attracted both large and small contributions. Religious scholars had a significant economic resource in the control which they exercised over donations of land and money. Their influence over the brotherhoods' membership enhanced their political power and social prestige.

When arranging their own economic affairs, the *ulama* could not ignore the advantages which endowments offered. Shaikh Abu l Anwar, the nephew and heir of the Shaikh Muhammad Anwar us-Sadat mentioned above, received his uncle's posts as co-manager of more than fifty-two *awqaf*. When he settled his own estate, he did so by creating twenty-five endowments. Through those he distributed his income to his children, wives and other relatives. He also contributed to the support of several mosques and paid for the lavish celebration of feasts such as the commemoration of the Prophet's birthday.

Throughout the 1830s and 1840s the amount of land going into endowments increased. Though at the time British and French influence was indirect, the European powers did stabilize Egypt's borders by preventing expansion into the Upper Nile. That containment affected the upsurge in the number of endowments by forcing the landholding nobility to turn its attention to the resources it already possessed. With the opportunity for the expansion of their domains eliminated, nobles faced increasing pressure to divide their estates among all their heirs. However, with division came the risk that power, prestige and wealth would be fragmented and diminished. Since an endowment was immune from partition by inheritance, the establishment of one seemed to counter that danger. Also, as endowments enjoyed a lower rate of taxation, the Egyptian government experienced a steady decline in its revenues. In 1846, Muhammad Ali, the Khedive, issued an order forbidding the creation of new *awqaf*. His regulation

dependants. The endowments' funds were also lent out to provide another source of income. These loans carried interest charges. Neither the founders, nor the religious scholars who examined them, tried to conceal the taking of interest. The scholars approved of the practice since they did not criticize it by mentioning the Quranic prohibition of usury.[22]

As the endowments of Kayseri showed, the standards of behaviour of seventeenth century Anatolians were not necessarily those of contemporary upholders of orthodoxy. Their practices pointed to the possibility (examined more fully in chapter 5) that some of the rigidity commonly associated with Islamic law arose at a later date. The *shariah* was probably much more fluid than in more recent times. Also, the investment and lending of endowments' funds challenged the notion that "Islam" was anti-capitalist, averse to the acquisition of those monetary resources. In this instance, and in others noted below, *awqaf* served as institutions for the accumulation of capital.[23]

Endowments sometimes played a role in establishing religious scholars ('*ulamā*') as a political and economic force. For instance, in eighteenth century Egypt, the influence of religious scholars was founded on their control of endowments created by the nobility as well as on the profits of *awqaf* of their own. At that time the political importance of the *ulama* grew from their place as intermediaries between Egypt's Turkish overlords and the indigenous, non-Turkish population. The scholars were often native Egyptians. They came from smaller towns and villages, especially from the Delta, but made their careers in Cairo. The ruling elite employed them as mediators between themselves and the people. Religious scholars' increased prosperity was founded in part on the nobility's trust in them and partly on their own financial acumen.[24]

When one of the nobility founded a *waqf*, he or she usually chose one or more of the religious scholars to serve as its custodians. The more prominent the scholar, the greater the number of the endowments he helped to manage. For example, Shaikh Muhammad Abul Anwar us-Sadat was custodian for over fifty-two separate endowments. As trustees, the *ulama* received generous salaries. At the donor's death, the scholar's independence and power over the endowment increased. By investing their salaries in the purchase of coffee shops or bath houses, the *ulama* entered the world of commerce. They also began to purchase land.

[22] R. G. Jennings, "Loans and Credit in Early Seventeenth Century Ottoman Judicial Records", 174–179.
[23] Inalcik, "Capital Formation", 109, 129–134.
[24] The following discussion follows A. L. al-Sayyid Marsot, "The Political and Economic Functions of the '*ulamā*' in the Eighteenth Century", 130–154.

another incentive for those who wanted to protect their wealth through the creation of an endowment.[19]

The nobles of Egypt in the fourteenth century found another way to use a *waqf* to maintain their dominant place. They established endowments in favour of the slaves (*mamlūks*) who served their households as soldiers and managers. This arrangement guaranteed the loyalty of the *mamluks* by guaranteeing their incomes.[20]

In the sixteenth century in Iran, the establishment of the Safavi dynasty led to the confiscation and creation of many *awqaf*. Before the Safavi ascendancy, Iran's Seljuk and Ilkhan rulers favoured the *Sunni* branch of Islam. Endowments created by them supported *Sunni* mosques and schools. As ardent supporters of Imami Shiism, the Safavi seized *Sunni awqaf* and established new ones in favour of the tombs of the *Shii* Imams and other institutions of that sect. In addition, the creation of new endowments often served Safavi kings as a way of keeping land under their personal control. When Shah Abbas came to the throne, he seized the estates of some of the nobles. He converted these into *awqaf* in his own favour. In this way, he tried to secure an otherwise dubious title to confiscated property.[21]

The examples provided above demonstrate two aspects of the history of endowments. That endowments were not always dedicated to the service of the public or for religious purposes was the first. Individuals made use of them for a variety of more personal objectives. The second point was that endowments became favoured instruments for dealing with property, especially land, because they offered the promise of stability, immunity from this world's uncertainties. Despite their poor record in actually achieving that end, people of all sorts constantly resorted to them. Perhaps people easily forgot the failures. Perhaps no other institution offered even the promise of durability.

Warriors and servants of the state were not the only groups to place their wealth in endowments. In the city of Kayseri in Anatolia, the records of the city's courts mentioned dozens of *awqaf* created by merchants. In the seventeenth century, Kayseri was a busy mercantile city with many prosperous traders in residence. The endowments which they created were based on cash, not land. That wealth was invested in business ventures. The profits of those went to support mosques, religious ceremonies and to give allowances to the donors' families or

---

[19] H. A. R. Gibb and H. Bowen, *Islamic Society and the West*, 1, Part 2, 169.
[20] A. N. Poliak, *Feudalism in Egypt, Syria, Palestine and Lebanon*, 37–38.
[21] Lambton, *Landlord*, 106–112.

chief minister to Iran's Mongol ruler, Ghazan Khan. With it he founded an endowment of colossal dimensions. He built an entire city which had houses for artisans, scribes and scholars as well as public baths and markets. Its centre was a mosque with a library open to all students. The scribes and artisans were supposed to make copies of his many compositions, using the best paper and most elegant bindings. The books were then despatched to the great cities of the world. Following Rashid uddin's disgrace and death, the ruler confiscated his endowment and destroyed the mosque-library. Rashid ud-din was not able even to rest peacefully in the tomb built as part of the endowment. Some hundred years after his death, Timur's son demolished the tomb, exhumed the body and buried it in the Jewish cemetery.[17] Kings, princes and notables often created large endowments like Rashid ud-din's. Most fared no better than his.

Awqaf were sometimes connected with an attempt to secure or preserve wealth and power. Just before the Mongol invasions, when Seljuk Turks ruled Iran, the nobility of their states was composed of individuals who commanded bands of mounted troopers. These captains received the revenue from a tract of land known as an "*iqtah*" which was supposed to supply an income for themselves, their soldiers and their dependants. The *iqtah* was not the commander's personal property. The sultans claimed the right to revoke these assignments. Nevertheless, incumbents usually tried to convert the *iqtah* into a permanent holding. *Iqtah*-holders created *awqaf* in the hope of gaining full control over their assignments. The success of their manoeuvre depended on the strength of the sultan. In periods when a king was weak, his nobles converted their *iqtahs* into endowments and built independent power on them. When the ruler was strong, he generally moved against his erstwhile servants. An endowment's religious character did not deter the sultan's reclaiming of the grant. Once repossessed, the *waqf* was classified once again as *iqtah*, distributed to more trustworthy retainers and the cycle began anew.[18]

From the Ottoman empire came other examples of influential persons using *awqaf* in an attempt to safeguard property to which the state laid claim. Ottoman nobles also held grants in lieu of salaries. No less than their Seljuk predecessors, they were eager to convert these grants into personal holdings. Also, the Ottoman government practice of appropriating the property of officials who died or fell from favour provided

---

[17] E. G. Browne, *A Literary History of Persia*, III, 77–80.
[18] Lambton, *Landlord*, 67–69.

"family" a eunuch might possess, it is likely that Faiq had in mind retainers or relatives he wished to provide for.

Faiq wanted his endowment to last forever. He emphasized in the dedication that no one had a right to tamper with the provisions of his endowment. He reinforced the ban on interference with several curses directed at anyone who made the attempt. A threat of misery in this life and hell fire in the next made little impact on those who posed the chief threat to the continuation of Faiq's enterprise. In Faiq's lifetime, Palestine was in a chaotic state. Bedouins and bands of sectarian rebels constantly raided the area. He probably created his *waqf* and composed a set of fearsome execrations with an eye to that danger.

The deed of endowment which Faiq created expressed the hope that somehow the act of dedication worked to protect wealth in times of trouble. Invoking the name of God seemed to secure permanence in the midst of turmoil. All that remains of Faiq's *waqf* is the heap of rubble from which the inscription was recovered.

A gap between reality and the aspirations of their founders made endowments a troublesome institution from their inception. Contrary to the opinions of religious scholars and the hopes of those who made them, they were seldom immune to the influence of changing circumstance. As the temporal distance between a *waqf*'s foundation and the present increased, the temptation grew stronger to seize such property and use it to satisfy some immediate pressing need. The comparatively long lived *waqf* of Sawad, created in the days of the Caliph Umar, was exhausted by successive encroachments. The Buwayhids, a family of Iranian not Arab origin, had a hand in dismembering that endowment. For over a hundred years (A.D. 945–1055) the Buwayhids had a monopoly of the ministerial management of the Abbasid caliphate. They appointed the inspectors and accountants who administered the assets of Sawad. They also had charge of the distribution of the income. By appointing overseers loyal to themselves, the Buwayhids succeeded in appropriating the income of the endowment, turning it to their own use. At first, they gave all beneficiaries a fixed sum instead of a percentage of the gross proceeds. Since the Buwayhids were sympathetic to the *Shiah* cause, most of the profits went to support the shrines of the leading figures of that sect.[16]

Nobles like the Buwayhids gained prominence through control of the apparatus of a state. They often created endowments with the wealth they received from office. However, changes in political fortune usually wrecked the arrangements they made. The famous scholar, Rashid uddin (executed A.D. 1318) acquired considerable wealth while acting as

[16] A. K. S. Lambton, *Landlord and Peasant in Persia*, 27–29.

puberty: the age of majority for Muslims. Donors had to be sane and the creation of the endowment must not defraud creditors. Finally, the income had to go to a "good purpose". Only a few activities were clearly not acceptable. An endowment for a Christian church was not "good", but one for a hospital which served both Muslims and Christians was. A *waqf* to build a tavern was not, but the income from a vineyard might support a mosque. Limitations on the way in which income was assigned or managed were few.[13]

Texts on *fiqh* were in some ways of limited value in understanding the ways in which endowments operated. Scholars were interested, after all, in establishing standards by which Muslims ought to live. They did not record much about the way in which Muslims actually did live. When the scholars noticed the behaviour of the mass of believers, they usually berated them for not following the *shariah*. The questions which the scholars addressed were often hypothetical and abstract, the views expounded impractical. For instance, in theory, judges had to rely only upon the oral testimony of trustworthy witnesses. Documentary evidence had no weight.[14] Yet Muslims made extensive use of deeds, bills of sale, contracts and other written material. The active commercial life of the Muslim world would have been impossible without such engagements. With regard to endowments, the scholars asserted that the use of the word *"waqf"* was unnecessary and that the dedication need not be written. In practice, it would have been impossible for endowments to remain in existence. After a generation or two, who would have known about it? Muslims did write their deeds of endowment. Unfortunately not many of them survived. The few that did gave indication of the wide range of uses to which endowments were put.

The earliest written record of a *waqf* so far discovered comes from the city of Ramlah in Palestine.[15] It consists of a stone tablet setting out the basic terms of an endowment founded in A.D 912 by a man named Fa'iq al-Hadim ("the Eunuch") ibn-Abd-allah al-Siqilli ("the Sicilian"). The property involved was a caravanserai, a rest house for merchants and travellers. The first thing expressed in the inscription was Faiq's desire "to obtain the regard of Allah, hoping for his forgiveness and seeking to draw close to him". The income which the hostel produced was assigned to the *"ahl"*. *Ahl* has a wide range of potential meanings. It can refer to one's own family or it can be applied to a larger aggregate, as in *"ahl 'al Islam"*: "the people of Islam". Though one wonders what sort of

---

[13] J. N. D. Anderson, "The Religious Elements in *Waqf* Endowments", 292–299.

[14] *The Function of Documents in Islamic Law*, 4–10, and A. L. Udovitch, *Partnership and Profit in Medieval Islam*, 3–39.

[15] The following discussion follows M. Sharon, "A *Waqf* Inscription from Ramlah", 77–84.

ditions influenced the views of the recognized masters of *fiqh*. At that time most Muslims lived in cities, towns or the camp-cities of the army such as Kufah. Most of them lived by trade, administration or soldiering. Only a few converts were peasants or members of the landed gentry who had a direct connection with agriculture. Specialists in the application of *shariah* were residents of cities. They usually came from mercantile families. Like the Prophet, their personal experience taught them to think of wealth in terms of moveable property.[10] In questions of inheritance, these habits of thought were significant. An estate, they knew, had to be divided among a prescribed list of heirs. When wealth consisted of cash or similarly portable goods, such a minute division was easier to accomplish. The problems posed by the inheritance of land were potentially much greater. Land was not readily weighed or assigned a cash value. In this murky area of the inheritance of land, endowments found a niche.[11] They provided a way of passing on control of land without actually carving it up among a pack of heirs. Though *awqaf* based on cash did exist, lands or houses formed the basis of many, if not most endowments.

Scholars of *shariah* did disagree about whether a *waqf* was a proper way for a Muslim to dispose of property. According to some reports, Imam Abu Hanifah (d. A.D. 767), the eponym of the *Hanafi* school, completely disapproved of the institution. However, *shariah* application was so fluid that his view did not become a hard and fast rule. An opinion (*fatwā*) given in response to one problem did not always suit other cases. Abu Hanifah himself, despite his statement that all *awqaf* were bad, supplied judgments on other occasions when queries were made about endowments already in existence. For example, he held that a *waqf* need not be permanent, but could be revoked at a later date. His decisions did not bind other scholars. Thus Abu Hanifah's own students, Abu Yusuf and Ibn-Muhammad, disagreed with him. They did consider endowments a valid way of disposing of property. They also expressed the conviction that they had to be irreversible. Once established, they could not be withdrawn or modified.[12]

On the whole, scholars did not spend much time discussing *awqaf*. Most texts on the *shariah* gave them only brief mention. Most references concerned the conditions necessary to attain spiritual merit from the creating of a *waqf*. Those conditions were fairly modest. The settlor had to possess the property dedicated. She or he had to be past the age of

[10] Goitein, *Studies*, 219–229, 231–232; also, H. J. Cohen, "The Economic Background and Secular Occupation of Muslim Jurisprudents", 16–61, and Halil Inalcik, "Capital Formation in the Ottoman Empire", 97–140.
[11] J. Schacht, *An Introduction to Islamic Law*, 19–142.
[12] Burhan al-din al-Marghinani, *Al-Hidayah*, trans. C. Hamilton, 231–340.

immense amount of land. The army and the community of the faithful were large, larger than in the Prophet's time, which made it difficult to parcel out the land as booty. Moreover, the farmers who already occupied it had to be dealt with. Umar's solution was to turn the entire province into a *waqf*. The cultivators continued to plant, harvest and pay a tax/rent, but most of the surplus went to those enrolled in the army, while a portion was sent to the believers in the Holy Cities.[9]

Sawad was administered as an endowment for the benefit of the community for many years. As late as the time of al-Ghazzali (*c.* A.D. 1100) some of its income was still distributed to the faithful. However, military and political leaders gradually appropriated the territory's income. Such encroachment on endowments was by no means rare. Though *awqaf* aimed at permanence, few attained it.

In the second and third centuries of the Islamic era, the ninth and tenth of the Christian, the organization of the faith received close and systematic attention. The attempt to give order to its beliefs and practices influenced the development of Quranic commentary, *hadis* study and dialectical theology. Gradually all of these subjects were transformed into intellectual disciplines with sophisticated methodologies and the institutional apparatus to transmit them to succeeding generations.

Most influential on the character of endowments were developments in the branch of learning known as *fiqh*: the systematic application of the Muslim moral path (*shariah*). *Shariah*'s literal meaning of "the clear path" indicated that in its earliest form it was simply "the way" in which Muslims should live. But the increasing complexities facing believers led to the formulation of tests by which any act could be judged by categories such as "approved (*ḥalāl*)", "forbidden (*ḥarām*)" or "disapproved but not forbidden (*makrūh*)". The Divine revelation of the *Quran*, the practice of the Prophet (*sunnah*), the consensus of the faithful (*ijmāʿ*) and the application of individual judgment or analogy provided the raw material for a construction of guidelines for the behaviour of the faithful. Their elaboration was especially associated with a number of pivotal thinkers, later known as "*Imāms*", who lived in the eighth and ninth centuries of the Christian era. Gradually their different approaches to the subject became identified with four "schools", each of which concerned itself with every aspect of life. All of them addressed questions regarding the disposition of property, including the matter of endowments.

When it came to issues involving wealth, social and economic con-

[9] P. G. Foran, "The Status of the Land and Inhabitants of the Sawad during the First Two Centuries of Islam", 25–37.

The spiritual dimension of the story of Umar's *waqf* arose over his concern to find a morally correct use of property. Muslims were trying to discover ways of using wealth which would be pleasing to God. This was a dilemma not limited to the first generation of believers. The Islamic faith, like many other religious systems, had an ambivalent attitude towards riches.[3] On the one hand, the *Quran* was full of dire warnings about the torment which awaited the acquisitive: "And let not those who hoard up that which Allah hath bestowed upon them from his bounty think that it is better for them. Nay, it is worse for them. That which they hoard will be their collar on the Day of Resurrection" (III, 180).[4] Scriptural commands to support widows and orphans or to be honest in trade displayed a desire to use property in a moral way. Also, many of the *hadis* portrayed the Prophet as a model of simplicity and indifference to wealth. Statements like "No one has ever eaten better food than what he eats as a result of the labor of his hands"[5] indicated some suspicion of propertied luxury. The counsels of the faith maintained a strong egalitarian bent, a fear of the hierarchies which came with wealth.[6] On the other hand, even *hadis* did not speak with one voice. Alongside of the praise of humble work and moderation stood such phrases as "To leave your heirs rich is better than to leave them poor,"[7] which seemed to condone the acquisition of property.

A persistent tension between those who praised and those who condemned wealth was part of Islam's history. In each generation some sought to establish a more equitable division of material goods, while others saw nothing wrong with a few having much more than most.[8] Some of the sufis, for instance, pronounced their contempt for affluence and for the affluent. At the same time, some of their brethren freely associated with the well-to-do and derived their livelihoods from them. In a sense, whether people were comfortable or conscience stricken by opulence mattered little. Islam's continued expansion and the commercial opportunities which that made possible brought more wealth into Muslim hands. New problems, both practical and spiritual, came with it. Endowments played a role in managing them.

References to *awqaf* appeared early in Muslim history. For instance, in the Caliphate of Umar, the conquest of the province of Sawad in Iraq created a major administrative problem. The province contained an

---

[3] V. G. Kiernan, "Private Property in History", in *Family and Inheritance*, 361–398.
[4] Translations of the *Quran* taken from M. M. Pickthall, *The Meaning of the Glorious Koran*.
[5] *Sayings of Muhammad*, 20–21.
[6] M. G. S. Hodgson, *The Venture of Islam*, I, 281, 317–318, 340–344.
[7] *Sahih Muslim*, III, 864.
[8] S. D. Goitein, *Studies in Islamic History and Institutions*, 217–241.

1

Endowments in Muslim history, an overview

> One day a drunken *mullah*
> gave his verdict on the Holy Law.
> "Drinking wine is bad", he said,
> "but having a *waqf* is worse." Hafiz

Endowments outside India

The Holy *Quran* made no mention of *awqaf* or any institution similar to them. When later generations of Muslims sought a sanction for endowments, they turned to the collections of anecdotes (*aḥadīs̱*) which reported the sayings and doings of the Prophet. An incident related by several sources provided the canonical origin of the institution. Umar, the man who became the second caliph, received groves and fields as booty after the conquest of the oasis at Khaibar. Umar wondered about the best use for that property and asked the Prophet's opinion. The Messenger of God told Umar to "tie up" (one of the basic meanings of the verb *waqafa*) the land and gardens and devote any income to the welfare of the faithful.[1]

Endowments, as this narrative showed, had a role in helping Umar deal with a new situation. He, the Prophet, and many of the first Muslims were town-dwelling merchants. Trade goods and cash were the forms of wealth which they knew best. When the community's early triumphs brought moveable wealth as booty, the faithful shared out the newly acquired goods, apparently without difficulty. The same procedure took place with the lands of Khaibar. However, as Umar's concern to do the right thing with his portion demonstrated, believers were somewhat uncertain about how to deal with immoveable property once they received it. Other *hadis* indicated that some of the most prominent of Umar's contemporaries created endowments based on the lands and orchards of Khaibar or on houses located in Mecca and Medina. Moreover, the first reported *awqaf* were not used for mosques, but have a more private dimension.[2]

---

[1] *Sahih Muslim*, III, 867; also, Zia ul-Haque, *Landlord and Peasant in Early Islam*, 53–57.
[2] M. Shibli Numani, "*Waqf-i Awlad*", *Maqālāt-i Shiblī*, I, 81–102; also, Claude Cahen, "*Réflexions sur la waqf ancien*", 37–56.

takes into consideration the reasons for the rapid contraction and the context in which it occurs. Was it a conscious act or the automatic movement of someone afflicted with a nervous twitch? Was it a malicious imitation of a twitcher intended by a burlesque winker to elicit an audience's laughter? Was it only the act of someone practising a burlesque wink? Thick description attempts to lay out all the complexities of inference and implication. Historians too often report the winks without noting the possibility that they may really be twitches or comedic squints.

Another line of anthropological research which proves useful is that which distinguishes between "Great" and "Little" traditions, between the textual embodiments of a "High" culture and the endless variety of local traditions.[10] Thinking in these terms warns historians not to take their documents at face value. Sacred texts do not always inform behaviour. People may proclaim adherence to them while failing to follow strictly what they command or believe everything they assert.[11] Students of Islam seem especially apt to forget that catechisms and law books are not always the best guides to understanding a living faith and the people who profess it.

---

[10] M. Singer, "The Great Tradition of Hinduism in the City of Madras", in *Anthropology of Folk Religion*, 105–166.
[11] To date, students of non-Muslims in India have most fruitfully employed that insight, e.g. C. J. Fuller, "The Attempted Reform of South Indian Temple Hinduism", in *Religious Organization and Religious Experience*, 153–167.

a system of law. By leaving that assumption unquestioned, legal historians ignore the many ways in which *shariah*, before the recent past, does not resemble "law" as that is understood in a European context. Also, legal historians seldom examine law in relation to society. Herbert Butterfield's description of the "Whig" view of history seems an accurate representation of the way in which lawyers, and most legal historians are lawyers, approach their material.[6] Lawyers are trained to know the law as it is. When they look back, they tend to rearrange ideas and events to show how the past creates the present. Whigs and lawyers are far too orderly. This study attempts to place endowments in the messier realm of social history.

Some political historians have taken note of the controversy over endowments. A focus on legislative councils and political associations leads them to discuss the subject as a footnote to the development of a "separatist" Muslim polity in India.[7] Their quest is for the roots of India's partition in 1947. Specifically, they seem to be examining an argument made by Jawaharlal Nehru and other nationalists that Muslim separatism is the product of Britain's imperial policy of "divide and rule".[8] Most contemporary historians seem bent on refuting that notion. They do so by emphasizing the role of religion in Muslim politics. They try to demonstrate that the roots of separatism lay deep in the Muslim community's past, in the character of Islam itself. In the *waqf* question they see an example of how religion comes to dominate politics. Like legal history, this style of political history sees "Islam" in highly abstract, scripturalist terms. It does not consider the complexities which are as much a part of a Muslim's life as they are of any human's existence.

Legal history and political history share a tendency to view society from the top down. The story we tell here begins, if not at the bottom, at a middling rung of the social ladder. In an attempt to shift the perspective commonly employed in historiography on Muslims in India, contemporary anthropologists supplied many useful theories and insights. Clifford Geertz sums up some of those in his stimulating and entertaining essay on "thick description".[9] Taking a cue from philosopher Gilbert Ryle, Geertz points out how a "thin" description of a wink differs from a "thick" description of the same phenomenon. "A rapid contraction of the right eye-lid" suffices as a thin description. A thicker account

---

[6] H. Butterfield, *The Whig Interpretation of History*, 9–25.
[7] F. Robinson, *Separatism among Indian Muslims*, 27, 191–198, and M. Rahman, *From Consultation to Confrontation*, 173ff.
[8] J. Nehru, *The Discovery of India*, 258–270.
[9] C. Geertz, "Thick Description: Toward an Interpretive Theory of Culture", in *The Interpretation of Cultures*, 1–10.

not usually employed in public forums where they were abandoned in favour of an idiom which stressed Muslim unity in purpose and in practice.

The quest for the kind of political solidarity required by imperial politics was begun towards the end of the nineteenth century. In the centuries before British rule, however, the call was for religious unity. In the eighteenth century, for instance, Shah Walli-ullah and his followers warned Muslims to abandon notions and practices influenced by contact with the unbelievers. They favoured a more Arabicized version of the faith, one which paid close attention to the Holy *Quran, Ḥadīs̱, sharī'ah* and the views of religious scholars. Before the nineteenth century, their efforts enjoyed limited success. Likewise, the early politicians made little headway in their attempt to turn India's Muslims into a cohesive political force. By concentrating on the Holy Law, by enforcing the notion that it governed the daily life of a single Muslim community, by supplying a set of sharp and certain categories, the courts inadvertently contributed to the work of the religious and political reformers who have had so much influence on the shape of Muslim history in the twentieth century.

Through a study of endowments from two perspectives, one from the point of view of their founders, the other from that of those officially or politically concerned, we can see the emergence of a split between the public, political *persona* of Muslims and a more varied, internal self-understanding. A confrontation with a potent foreign presence helped produce the public image. Controversy made it sharper. It also made it less comprehensive and less informative about the daily lives, thoughts and feelings of Muslims in the subcontinent.

Because endowments are part of both scripturalist and popular Islam, they have great potential as a source for understanding how the faith is actually practised in different areas of the Muslim world. Studying them gives insight into family relations, attitudes towards property and the ways in which Muslims adapt to changing historical circumstance. To date, however, works on the subject have had a limited scope. Much of the literature consists of law books or legal history.[5] Whether or not they are Muslims, legal historians are primarily interested in the controversy over the theory of *waqf*. In discussing texts and case law, they seek to demonstrate how the British courts misinterpreted or misapplied the "Islamic" or "Muhammadan law". Even in their dissent, legal historians preserve the basic premises of the Anglo-Indian courts. They assume with the courts, for instance, that what Muslims call "*shariah*" is

---

[5] S. A. Ali, *Mahommedan Law*, I, 25–60; for a modern example, S. K. Rashid, *Wakf Administration in India*, 1–50.

defined themselves in the British–Indian context. Because so many politicians were lawyers, the judicial perspective on endowments, and on the people who made them, entered political discourse. The politicians' descriptions usually agreed with those of the judges: Muslims *did* form a distinct community; they *were* fundamentalist in belief and punctilious in matters of ritual or law. The politicians argued that in this particular instance the judges were in error. However, few of them tried to challenge the validity of the basic judicial categories.

Political institutions created by the British required a particular style of leadership. When they introduced "representative" government, aspiring leaders had to find some constituency to represent. Even though the franchise was limited and the leaders almost self-appointed, a premium was placed on a politician's claim to represent a solid group of supporters. The more united the bloc seemed, the greater a politician's importance.

In British India, political identities supplied by government authority did have a way of becoming true.[4] However, as their truth in a juridical or political sense was established, they became less accurate in a broader social sense. Assertions of Muslim orthodoxy and solidarity such as those which accompanied the passage of the Mussalman Wakf Validating Act had meaning in a public context, but they were somewhat detached from the identities which Muslims employed in day to day relationships. The reified language of lawyers and politicians, so useful in courts and councils, conveyed only a limited amount of information about the individual Muslims who had created the endowments in the first place.

Judicial and political discourse did not eliminate the cultural, social, economic, political and religious categories employed in everyday life. "Within" the local societies in which Muslims lived, one set of concepts continued in use, while the "official" terminology came in handy when dealing with those "outside" those social circles. For instance, deeds of endowment indicated that their founders were aware of many internal distinctions which official categorizations missed. Religious differences were significant, not just between *Sunnī* and *Shī'ah*, but between "*Ahl-ī Ḥadīs*", "*Deobandi*" and "*Barelwi*". Regional differences were recognized, not simply between "Punjabis" or "Bengalis", but also between "Lahoris", "Dehlavis" and "Janpuris". Though the *Quran* emphasized the equality of all believers, it still mattered whether one was rich or poor. Cultural differences followed class lines, establishing crucial distinctions between the "respectable" ("*sharīf*") and the "lowly" ("*ajlāf*"). The list of discriminating categories was long, but they were

[4] D. Lelyveld, *Aligarh's First Generation*, 16–20.

argued with parents. Relatives and former friends feuded. Disease and death were always there. But that world, whether tranquil or troubled, was their own and they shaped their endowments to keep it that way.

While chapters 2 to 4 describe the world from the perspective of those who created endowments, chapters 5 and 6 introduce a very different point of view. They deal with the ways in which the Anglo-Indian courts and imperial political institutions interpreted the nature of *awqaf*, their use and the supposed motives of those who used them. The courts of British India were the first government agency to examine endowments from a perspective which was tenuously connected to the world in which their founders lived. In the courts, British judges and Indian judges trained in British law schools discussed endowments in terms of a legal system rooted in the European experience. Beginning in 1879, the High Courts of India handed down a series of decisions which overturned any endowment considered to benefit primarily the settlor's own "family". The Privy Council in London confirmed those judgments and in 1894 issued a definitive ruling on Muslim endowments: they must be "religious" and "charitable", public not private. Courts throughout the empire could no longer sustain an endowment in the interest of the donor's own family, sometimes referred to as "*waqf 'alā 'l-awlād*": literally, "a *waqf* in the interest of the progeny". In those decisions the courts' premise was that Muslims ought to follow their own scripture to the letter. If the *Quran* demanded a partition of estates, Muslims must not evade the rigours of their own legal system. Thus, as judges wrote their opinions, they included within them a series of judgments about who Muslims were and how they ought to behave. They assumed that Muslims were a single community, formally bound by a common faith and "religious law".

In the wake of the courts' decisions, Muslim endowments became a political issue. Both English language and vernacular newspapers began to attack or defend those decrees. The Indian National Congress and the Muslim League considered the question. Local political associations took up the debate. When the extension of "native" participation in government brought Muslim members into the Governor General's Council, they raised the matter of endowments in 1910. The deliberations of that body led to the passage in 1913 of the Mussalman Wakf Validating Act which was supposed to restore a Muslim's right to make a family settlement in the form of *waqf*.

The involvement of official institutions changed the focus on endowments. The local perspective which influenced an endowment's material and spiritual provisions became less important. As a political issue, *awqaf* became mixed up with the larger question of how Muslims

system of social status and responsibility. For instance, they referred to themselves with titles like "*ra'īs*" or "*malik*", honorifics which described the leading roles which individuals had or claimed in the days before there were deeds of ownership and courts of law.

All social privileges exist as part of a complex "grid" of relationships.³ The *rais* and his family expected deference, but their position also carried obligations towards clients and the local community. Patronage of religious institutions and observances was an important duty and an element in any claim to superior status. In providing money for a mosque, a patron reached out to touch the lives of other believers. Such a grant provided not only a place of prayer, but paid the salary of the man who chanted the call to prayer. The donation supported the man who led the prayers, the man who recited the Holy *Quran* and taught it to the children. It even provided a small sum for the man who kept the mosque clean and watched over the worshippers' shoes. A mosque might also be the local welfare establishment, a place where food or alms were given to the poor.

Endowments usually provided sums for the celebrations of several different kinds of religious festivals. Celebrating the Prophet's birthday, sponsoring mourning rites for the *Shī'ī* Imams or providing breakfasts for those who kept the *Ramazān* fast connected the patron with the "Great Traditions" of Islam. At the same time, support for events such as the commemoration of a local saint's death anniversary ('*urs*) placed the patron within the sphere of the "Little Traditions" of Islam in India. Significantly, local feasts were as lavishly celebrated as those hallowed by scripture or the faith's history. Finally, some festivals memorialized events in the donor's own family, for example an ancestor's death anniversary. All commemorations, whether part of the great, little or familial traditions were occasions for the distribution of food, clothing or money, opportunities for the sponsors to assert their claim to patron status.

In their deeds of endowment, donors expressed the desire to preserve the temporal and spiritual worlds they knew best. Both worlds were fairly small, centred on the community formed by close association with relatives, dependants and neighbours. They expressed more interest in the local mosque or shrine than they did in "Islam" as a global phenomenon. Likewise, they did not seem much concerned with "British India" or the great political and economic developments taking place within it. The founders focused on the more intimate universe around them. Of course, that microcosm was not free of trouble. Children

---

³ E. P. Thompson, "The Grid of Inheritance, a Comment", in *Family and Inheritance*, 328–360.

chapter shows, the institutional flexibility created by generations of experience helped some of India's Muslims in their attempt to accommodate the new laws and government organizations introduced by the British.

The British came to India loaded with conceptual baggage about the nature of both property and religion. They brought new rules governing the acquisition, control, loss and transmission of wealth. They had their own ideas about law and its relationship to society. They also established courts which enforced those notions.

Chapters 2 to 4 focus on endowments created during the British period. They describe how endowments were used, who used them and their significance within the context of the legal and economic structures of British India. The deeds of endowment, *waqfnāmahs*, and allied documents examined in these chapters come from four different regions: the area of North India known today as Uttar Pradesh, from Bengal, Bombay and Madras. All of them were founded after the establishment of British rule, most after the Revolt of 1857.

In those deeds of endowment, founders expressed some of their values and fears. All of them seemed to share the worry that their estates would be divided after their deaths. Almost every deed contained two stipulations designed to prevent the fragmentation of holdings. The first of those limited members of the immediate family and other dependants to cash stipends and denied them the right to dispose of the lands or houses which formed the basis of the endowment. The second set of provisions appointed a custodian, set the method of selecting successors to that post and established rules for the management of the endowment. The son, wife or daughter who became *mutawalli* had particular importance. They controlled the *waqf*'s assets and received an extra bonus by getting a salary. Invariably, founders tried to keep control of an undivided estate within the immediate family. Only in the absence of direct descendants did they bestow the office on more distant kin, friends or religious leaders. In part, the character of the system of law which the British enforced in India was responsible for their concern to maintain an estate intact. With the British came the notion that land or houses were owned, that they were "private property". They could be bought, inherited, sold, mortgaged and seized for debt. In addition, the Anglo-Indian courts took literally the *Quran*'s demand that property be divided by inheritance. The courts, with few exceptions, enforced those rules strictly, perhaps more rigidly than Muslims themselves ever had.

When used as family settlements, endowments were a way of coping with the new laws of property. However, the deeds also indicated that many of the founders' values were shaped by the older, pre-British practice, both public and private spheres mixed in any *waqf*; religious and temporal concerns blended together in the minds of its founders.

On the organizational level, the faith of Islam maintains a congregational polity. Mosques, schools, shrines and graveyards are locally funded and controlled. In modern times and in some historical instances, state authorities, for example the Ottoman emperors, attempted to create centralized religious hierarchies to oversee a network of government regulated establishments. But rulers, whether genuinely pious or merely ambitious, seldom fulfilled the role of the faith's paramount supporters and guardians. Indeed, the history of endowments showed that more often they were a way of putting some distance between the state and crucial Islamic institutions. Muslim lords in India did provide some patronage, but the number of institutions which they directly dominated was small. No single authority collected and disbursed funds or commanded the mass of locally sponsored endowments which were a fixture of Islam's daily practice.

Endowments could also provide some continuity in a group or family's material base. When it came time to pass wealth and influence on to one's descendants, a *waqf* offered an alternative to the Quranic method of inheritance. Muslims cannot, according to the Holy Book, choose their heirs; scripture specifies them and the shares which each receives. Large and enduring estates would be hard to create if the Holy Qur'ān were strictly followed. Also, an endowment's supposed immunity from seizure made it a favoured legal instrument in times of political turmoil or when a predatory state threatened the wealth of service elites, merchants and landed gentry. Since status and power accompanied wealth, creation of a *waqf* held the promise of continued social prominence.

Because endowments have served so admirably in both the spiritual and temporal realms, Muslims have set them up in almost every place and time in which they live.[2] A *waqf* meets both a personal and an institutional desire to transmit the religious and secular orders from one generation to the next. The first chapter of this book is not a comprehensive social history of the role of *awqaf* throughout the past of the Muslim world. It does, however, provide a number of examples of how the institution functions in one or another historical frame. We will see that endowments were affected by the rise and fall of dynasties, as well as connected to fluctuations in the fortunes of nobles, gentry, merchants and religious scholars. Especially in times of rapid political or economic change, *awqaf* seemed to offer propertied groups a way of adjusting themselves to a new set of circumstances. As the second portion of the

[2] West Africa seems to be the single major exception.

INTRODUCTION

India was one of the first regions of the Muslim world conquered by a European power. Muslims living in the subcontinent had to adjust not only to a new order of economic and social dominance, but also to the sometimes troubling judgments their colonial masters made about them, their faith and its institutions. This is a study of how that process worked with regard to one old and fundamental Muslim institution known as a "*waqf*".

Waqf and its plural form, *awqāf*, are derived from the Arabic root verb, *waqafa*, which has the basic meaning of "to stop" or "to hold".[1] When the word is employed in a legal sense with regard to a piece of land or a building, it signifies that henceforth that "property" is "stopped". In theory, it can never again change hands by inheritance, sale or seizure. An individual creating a *waqf*, known in Arabic as the "*waqif*", divests him or her self of the formal rights of possession, but retains the power to appoint a custodian: "*mutawallī*" (literally "one who is trusted"), who manages the property dedicated. Founders of *awqaf* also have the power to distribute the income which that property generates for any purpose they wish, provided that the purpose is meritorious by "Islamic" standards.

Awqaf are "endowments" in the general sense that they are gifts made to individuals as well as institutions. Throughout the history of the Islamic world, such settlements provided for many of the spiritual and temporal wants of Muslims. Funds derived from endowments built and sustained places of worship, established schools and hospitals, supported scholars and preachers, provided paupers with graves and supplied weapons to warriors fighting in the cause of the faith. At the same time, founders rarely ignored those near and dear to them. A clause in the deed of endowment could set aside a sum of money for the founders and their dependants. Euro-American legal lexicons do not supply a single technical term which is exactly equivalent to *waqf*. Sometimes a *waqf* serves as a "trust" sustaining some "public" religious or charitable institution. At other times, a *waqf*'s provisions resemble those of a "will" or "entailment" and therefore have a "private" dimension. In

[1] H. Wehr, *A Dictionary of Modern Written Arabic*, 1091–1094.

HJP A	Home Judicial Department Proceedings, A files
HJP B	Home Judicial Department Proceedings, B files
JP Civ	Judicial Department (Civil) Proceedings
L/P+J	Legislative/Public and Judicial (IO)
PEBGD	Proceedings of the Education Branch of the General Department
PGGC	Proceedings of the Legislative Council of the Governor General of India
VPP	*Selections from the Vernacular Press, Panjab*
VPN	*Vernacular Press Reports for the Northwest Provinces*

ABBREVIATIONS

Published Law Reports

All	*Indian Law Reports, Allahabad Series*
ALJR	*Allahabad Law Journal Reporter*
Bom	*Indian Law Reports, Bombay Series*
BLR	*Bombay Law Reporter*
Cal	*Indian Law Reports, Calcutta Series*
IA	*Indian Law Reports, Indian Appeals*
Mad	*Indian Law Reports, Madras Series*
OLJ	*Oudh Law Journal*
SCR B	*Supreme Court Reports, Bombay*
SDA	*Sadr Diwani Adalat Reports, Calcutta*

Unpublished Legal Documents

AA	Papers submitted in support of appeals lodged with the Allahabad High Court, filed by title of case and date of decision in High Court record room.
AC	As above, Calcutta High Court, appellate side record room.
OC	Papers submitted in support of cases heard under the original jurisdiction of the Calcutta High Court, original side record room.
LI	The library of Lincoln's Inn, London, papers submitted with regard to appeals made to the Privy Council, bound in volumes titled *Cases on Appeals to the Privy Council*.

Government archives

(Beng)	West Bengal State Archives, Calcutta
(IO)	India Office Archive and Library, London
(NAI)	National Archives of India, New Delhi
(UP)	Uttar Pradesh State Archives, Lucknow

Government documents

EDP	Education Department Proceedings
FDP A	Foreign Department Proceedings, A files

NOTE ON TRANSLITERATION

Many of the technical terms used in the following study are derived from Arabic. However, the pronunciations of Arabic words common in Persia and India differ from those of classical or dialectical Arabic. For instance, the Arabic letter ذ (*dhāl*) is pronounced as a "z". Though scholars of Arabic will be initially puzzled, I have opted for a system of transliteration which represents the Indo-Persian pronunciations. For the most part, I have used the Library of Congress system with the single exception of using "w" for و (*wāw*) rather than "v". In order to simplify the process of printing the text, full diacriticals, including "*'ayn*" and "*hamzah*", are given only at a word's first occurrence.

Some of the sources for this study employ transliterations currently out of favour. For instance, some use "*wakf*" or "*wukf*" instead of "*waqf*". I have retained them in quotations.

Transliterating names presents an irritating problem. Court records which are a major source for this work feature wildly eccentric representations of Muslim names. The same individual will be recorded as Amir Ali in one source, Ameer Aly in another and Amer Alley in a third. Once again, in the interests of simplicity I have not included diacritical marks in personal names, though I have tried to be as consistent as possible. References to sources, however, will contain older and odder forms of personal names.

Kopf's seminars on the History of India. Throughout the process of gathering material and writing, Professor Kopf was a source of support, encouragement and countless letters of recommendation.

My *"Ustad"*, and friend, David Lelyveld, was an ideal teacher. He gave neither too much nor too little. Indeed, I claim that he is the world's foremost exponent of the "Zen" method of supervising doctoral candidates. By alternating a benevolent smile with occasional, intellectual cuffs on the ear, he made my apprenticeship enjoyable and enlightening.

The Persian word for "nomad" is *"Khānah bah dōsh"* which means, literally, "home on the shoulder". It describes the kind of life a scholar lives. Doris, my wife, Renee, Rebecca and Charlotte (who recently joined the caravan), my daughters, put up with life on the road for my sake. Though the prospect was sometimes bleak, their persistent, if not unfailing, good humour gave much joy.

Finally, Linda Kozlowski and Jean Moran typed various versions of this manuscript. Despite all the "weird words", they were patient and professional.

ACKNOWLEDGMENTS

While researching and writing this work, I acquired many material as well as intellectual debts. I cannot name all those who have supported or inspired me and the few I mention should know that the words of thanks I offer are only tokens of deep gratitude.

Research on this project took me to London and several cities in India and Pakistan. Grants from the American Institute of Indian Studies, the McMillan, Special Dissertation Research and Minneapolis-Andrews Funds, all administered by the University of Minnesota, made those journeys possible. Timely loans from my parents and brothers helped when help was most needed. The College of Liberal Arts and Sciences of DePaul University provided leave from teaching and financial assistance in preparing the typescript.

Dr Peter Hardy of the University of London first suggested that I pursue the study of Muslim endowments in India. He was also kind enough to read several drafts of the work. Drs Gail Minault, Francis Robinson and Chris Fuller read the entire study. They provided valuable suggestions and encouragement. Though a coward's instincts incline me otherwise, tradition dictates that I absolve them, and all the others who reviewed the study, from blame for any errors. Dr S. M. Yunus Jaffrey of Zakir Husain College, Delhi, provided me with his friendship, tutelage and the benefit of his extensive knowledge of Persian literature. He was also the source of countless anecdotes about the history and culture of Old Delhi.

A number of outstanding people were my teachers at the University of Minnesota. Professors Muhammad A. R. Barker, Sajida Alvi and Iraj Bashiri were patient guides in the study of the Urdu and Persian languages. All three possess a wealth of historical, ethnographic and linguistic information which they generously share. Professors Barker and Alvi undertook the burden of reading this in thesis form. I hope I have not disappointed them.

I was similarly blessed by my teachers in the history department. Professor Byron Marshall took the time to read this carefully. His perspective as a historian of Japan was refreshing and heartening. My first essays on the subject of Muslim endowments were presented in David

CONTENTS

Acknowledgments	*page* vi
Note on transliteration	viii
Abbreviations	ix
Introduction	1
1 Endowments in Muslim history, an overview	10
2 Muslim endowments and the temporal order in British India	41
3 Endowments and the faith	60
4 The unsettling of endowments	79
5 Creating a law of Muslim endowments	96
6 Muslim endowments and the politics of religious law	156
Conclusion	192
Bibliography	197
Index	209

Published by the Press Syndicate of the University of Cambridge
The Pitt Building, Trumpington Street, Cambridge CB2 1RP
32 East 57th Street, New York, NY 10022, USA
10 Stamford Road, Oakleigh, Melbourne 3166, Australia

© Cambridge University Press 1985

First published 1985

Printed in Great Britain by
Redwood Burn Limited,
Trowbridge, Wiltshire

Library of Congress catalogue card number: 84-29275

British Library cataloguing in publication data
Kozlowski, Gregory C.
Muslim endowments and society in British India.
– (Cambridge South Asian studies; 35)
1. Charitable uses, trusts, and foundations
(Islamic law) – India
I. Title
345.4065'9 [LAW]
ISBN 0 521 25986 X

Published in India by Orient Longman Ltd.
5-9-41/1 Bashir Bagh, Hyderabad 500 029

Branches at
Kamani Marg, Ballard Estate, Bombay 400 038
17 Chittaranjan Avenue, Calcutta 700 072
160 Anna Salai, Madras 600 002
1/24 Asaf Ali Road, New Delhi 110 002
80/1 Mahatma Gandhi Road, Bangalore 560 001
5-9-41/1 Bashir Bagh, Hyderabad 500 029
S.P. Verma Road, Patna 800 001

© Cambridge University Press 1985

First published 1985

To my parents,
Leonard J. Kozlowski and Margaret E. Krieser Kozlowski

MUSLIM ENDOWMENTS AND SOCIETY IN BRITISH INDIA

GREGORY C. KOZLOWSKI

Published in association with
Orient Longman

BOMBAY   CALCUTTA   MADRAS   NEW DELHI
BANGALORE   HYDERABAD   PATNA

CAMBRIDGE UNIVERSITY PRESS

CAMBRIDGE
LONDON   NEW YORK   NEW ROCHELLE
MELBOURNE   SYDNEY

Library of
Davidson College